DOCE ME STATUTA TUA

BRADFIELD COLLEGE LIBRARY

DAMN YOU, ENGLAND

DAMN YOU, ENGLAND

Collected Prose

John Osborne

faber and faber

LONDON · BOSTON

First published in 1994
by Faber and Faber Ltd
3 Queen Square London WC1N 3AU

Photoset by Parker Typesetting Service, Leicester
Printed in England by Clays Ltd, St Ives plc

John Osborne is hereby identified as author of this work
in accordance with Section 77 of the Copyright, Designs
and Patents Act 1988

A CIP record for this book is available
from the British Library

ISBN 0–571–16921–X

2 4 6 8 10 9 7 5 3 1

Contents

Prologue

Whenever I sit down to write, it is always with dread in my heart. But never more than when I am about to write straightforward prose, because I know then that my failure will be greater and more obvious. There will be no exhilarating skirmishes, no small victories on the way to defeat. When I am writing for the theatre I know these small victories: when the light on my desk is too bright and my back aches, but I go on writing because I am afraid that my pen will lose the words that come into my head; when I watch an actor on an empty stage deliver something that proves to me that my sense of timing has been exact, after all. Timing is an artistic problem, it is the prime theatrical problem. You can learn it, but it cannot be taught. It must be felt. Things like this – composition, sonata form, the line that is unalterable – there are small victories to be won from them, because these are things that seem worth doing for themselves. If you are any good at all at what you set out to do, you know whether it is good and rely on no one to tell you so. You depend on no one.

It is not true to say that a play does not 'come alive' until it is actually in performance. Of course it comes alive – to the man who has written it, just as those three symphonies must have come alive to Mozart during those last six weeks. One is sure to fail, but there are usually enough perks to be picked up on the way to make it bearable. It is the pattern of life itself, and it is acceptable. But whenever I sit down to write in prose about my present feelings and attitudes, my dread is enormous because I know that there will be no perks to pick up, or if there are, that they will be negligible.

For years – ever since I started earning my living in the theatre – I have been having the same dream: I am about to make my entrance on the stage, and behind the flats I can hear the other actors performing a play I know nothing about. My entrance is important, but I don't know when to make it. I stand there, peering through the cracks in the scenery trying to find out what is going on. Eventually, I decide that I have missed my entrance long before, and grab the door handle and push. Everything rattles and I am suddenly in a world where I cannot see anything although the light is so bright. I don't know any of my moves, or even what my first line should be, but I make a great effort to speak, to say something. I open my mouth and drive all the strength I can find into my diaphragm. But I can make no sound. I try to force my eyelids open, and I can't. I can feel the light, but I can't see.

I have dreaded writing this piece. If I were ever capable of doing it, I am not capable of doing it now. Months ago some kind of weakness or vanity made me agree to contribute to this book [*Declaration*, ed. Tom Maschler], but I have procrastinated to the point of downright bad manners until I am now the only writer in this symposium who has not delivered his copy. They are all – apparently – waiting for me. I do not relish having to address myself to what is almost certain to be a self-conscious literary mob, people who write sneering, parochial stuff in the weekend reviews. I can't solve anybody else's problems, least of all these creatures', collecting their literary cocoa-tin lids every week. The people I should like to contact – if I knew how – aren't likely to be reading this book anyway. If they have ever heard of me, it is only as a rather odd-looking 'angry young man'. Surprisingly enough, the posh political weeklies are less scrupulous than even the popular press about digging into the private lives of people like myself. When I say 'people like myself', I mean people who have been over-publicized because of something they have written, and made money out of. Almost always the first question I am asked by press men is, 'How much money have you made?' At least it is not quite so impertinent as 'What are you angry about?'

Part of my job is to try and keep people interested in their seats for about two and a half hours; it is a very difficult thing to do, and I am proud of having been fairly successful at it. *Look Back in Anger* has been playing to large audiences all over the country for months, at a time when touring is all but finished. Provincial audiences (who, on the whole, are far more receptive than West End audiences) don't remember what the posh papers said about plays, even if they read them. They go to the theatre because the guvnor's wife went on Monday night and said it was a jolly good show. I simply want to point out that my job has not been an easy one to learn, merely because I have had what looks like an easy success. I shall go on learning as long as there is a theatre standing in England, but I didn't learn the job from the *Daily Mail* or the *Spectator*.

I want to make people feel, to give them lessons in feeling. They can think afterwards. In some countries this could be a dangerous approach, but there seems little danger of people feeling too much – at least not in England as I am writing. I am an artist – whether or not I am a good one is beside the point now. For the first time in my life I have a chance to get on with my job, and that is what I intend to do. I shall do it in the theatre and, possibly, in films. I shall not try and hand out my gospel version of the Labour Party's next manifesto to prop up any journalist who wants a bit of easy copy or to give some reviewer another smart clue for his weekly written-up crossword game. I shall simply fling down a few statements – you can take your pick. They will be what are often called 'sweeping statements', but I believe we are living at a time when a few 'sweeping statements' may be valuable. It is too late for caution.

from 'They Call it Cricket' in *Declaration*, ed. Tom Maschler (1957)

The Theatre
==

Ensemble Performance

In August 1956 the Berliner Ensemble, founded by Bertolt Brecht and his wife Helene Weigel, performed in Britain for the first time.

Sir – In his remarks last week about the effect of the visit of the Berliner Ensemble upon actors, authors and producers, Mr Kenneth Pearson made the suggestion that a tangible reaction may be found in my next play [*The Entertainer*]. Anticipating the possibility of a 'Yah! Brecht!' or 'So what?' response to my new play, I should like to make my position a little clearer.

The point I was trying to make in discussing my own work and the effect of having seen the Ensemble was simply that, as a playwright, I had been made suddenly aware of the horseless carriage in theatrical technique. One could not fail to be taken aback. It may seem to stink and fume, but it *is* faster, more convenient, and somehow, the inescapable fact is that it *works*. Whether it would work on the treacherous, overgrown roads of Shaftesbury Avenue and Charing Cross Road is another matter.

On the face of it, it seems a dangerous idea to jump on some kind of home-made Brechtian bulldozer and rip the place up, tempting as the idea might have been on coming out of the Palace Theatre the other week. Oh, the jungle certainly needs clearing, and it would be great fun knocking down lots of prosperous, jay-walking pedestrians who would get in the way of any new method. But this infernal machine needs careful handling. Perhaps one shouldn't try tinkering with it at all.

That sturdy old animal the Ibsenite Punch, still slogging patiently for the British dramatist, is looking pretty deadbeat, and the sooner he can be packed off to some happy home in the country where his Auntie Edna can come down and tempt him with lumps of sugar the better. Most people seemed to agree that *Look Back in Anger* was, at least, a slightly younger-looking horse. And a jolly nasty, ill-tempered, unattractive brute too, some would add. But it was still a horse. I have always been aware of this.

I, and others, may be obliged for the time being to carry on as we have done, even though it is slow, wasteful and inefficient. The Brechtian bulldozer may not be *our* answer. We need to invent a machine of our own. What this may be we shall have to find out. But please don't expect to find it necessarily at work in my new play. The horse can look an endearing, reliable old thing when you are sweating blood in the workshop.

John Osborne

Sunday Times, 30 September 1956

The Revolutionary Moment

The English middle classes have always dealt with domestic revolutions in the same way. Possessing little vitality but a great deal of cunning endurance, they throw down their pens and open the barricades with a haste which they themselves would describe as 'a great scuttle' or a 'big climbdown' if the weapons used had been guns instead of ideas.

They disarm revolutions by simply not appearing to fight them. Like a wary old pug they step into the ring, walk into the first haymaker, and immediately lifting their opponent's glove above his head, they sportingly proclaim the new champion before he knows what hasn't hit him.

It is the technique they have perfected in politics and with which they have tried to debilitate every progressive movement in the Arts.

Let us see how this technique has operated recently in the theatre. A legend has been deliberately circulated that a revolution has taken place. The reality is that a revolution has begun to take place. As yet there has been little fighting in the streets, a great deal of whispering behind closed doors, with odd, isolated, blustering outbreaks; but the machinery of government goes on much the same as ever.

Three years ago, the English Stage Company was sneered at for being avant-garde and eccentric. Now it is sneered at for being 'fashionable' – a breathtaking form of belittlement, coming as it does from people who have consistently dedicated themselves to being nothing else but fashionable. This is the whore's scorn for virtue, like the familiar Tory trick of looking amused and civilized and dismissing your opponent as 'old-fashioned.'

How much has changed? What has been achieved? The answer is that much has been done in a very short time to change the outlook of a form of entertainment largely provided by and for a narrow, self-absorbed public, incapable of imagination or excitement. For many years the London theatrical managers slavishly cultivated this boring public. As a result, the theatre came to be regarded as a mild, middle-class pursuit, and its scope, ancient and modern, preserved for ever in the first line of its hymnal, 'Anyone for tennis?'.

'Anyone for theatre?' is now perhaps a slightly more serious question than it was a few years ago. What the theatre managers have always failed to understand is the elementary principle of Art and Commerce: you can create demand but you can't embalm it.

Theatre and cinema audiences are made in much the same way as users of deodorants and detergents. Just as people can become cleaner and less smelly, so the playgoing public can be made intelligent and imaginative. One great advance that has been made, then, is that not only have some plays become less boring, but audiences have become less boring also. Exciting plays have found their way to people capable of excitement.

When I first went to America I was surprised at the casual contempt in which the English theatre was held, outside the culture-vulture circle of Old Vic and Royal Ballet worshippers.

However, the position now is that London has more potential theatrical excitement to offer than any city in the world. The full-time, acting, unpaid intellectuals have even left their old playground of the cinema in alarming numbers, and their shrill voices can be heard constantly from Sloane Square to Angel Lane and even in Shaftesbury Avenue.

Until 1956, the character of the English theatre had been determined by its various professionals: managers, the real-estate men, the critics, and the big drawing stars like John Gielgud and Laurence Olivier. When I first entered the profession, the London theatre was dominated by H. M. Tennent and its subsidiaries. It was the General Motors of British show business, presided over by Mr Hugh 'Binkie' Beaumont.

Binkie, a tough, shrewd professional – in a field where the amateurism of showmanship was almost matched by the amateurism of its business – possesses the charm of an antique dagger and the manners of a diplomat overawed by his own archetype. He had become almost a legend, a grey-flannel eminence, an almost sinister abstraction which finds description somewhere between a well-manicured Henry Ford and the Queen Mother.

For a brilliant decade or so, Binkie exercised a virtual monopoly of taste, backed by his superior acumen, his control over theatres, and his history of first-class personal relations with the starriest talents in the profession, and aided considerably by the mediocrity of his competitors.

With Mr Peter Saunders apparently requisitioning theatres indefinitely for Miss Agatha Christie – thus seeming to prove that if you make the building creatively empty, you could automatically put out the 'House Full' notices for good – with Mr John Clements's well-bred revivals, and with Mr Henry Sherek's grotesque, sporadic courtships with culture in the form of T. S. Eliot, it is unremarkable that Binkie's streamlined 'tasteful' product should have often seemed interesting if not exciting.

The methods of the Tennent assembly line were well-known, well-tried, and deceptively simple, the formula being to find exquisitely oiled and upholstered vehicles to harness to a more or less permanent stud of stars. The Tennent organization was constantly finding innocuous little plays, written by wistful, sweet-tempered gentlemen (and gentlewomen) often living comfortably in remote country towns – plays which gave offence to no one's delicate sensibilities or upset the prejudices of anyone.

Or, rather, the organization was looking more specially for parts rather than plays. Managerial judgements were summed up by remarks like: 'What a wonderful part for Ralph.' Or John, or Larry, or Alec. 'Vivien would be marvellous.' Or so would Edith, or Peggy, or Sybil, or Dorothy and so on. Adding one of several directorial wizards, a brilliant stage designer with a facility for creating theatrical Christmas calendars, a great deal of technical abracadabra, and you were in business.

And highly respectable, professionally adept, and very profitable business it was. Nobody was able to make it quite so magical or appealing or so profitable as Binkie. His imitators never managed to achieve the touch of the master.

How much has the situation changed? Superficially, it may seem to have changed a great deal. For one thing, the activities of the Tennent organization are not so widespread or intense as they were a few years ago.

Some of the effort has been diverted into television, and also some of the Tennent imitators have managed to imitate a little more successfully; and the theatres where one would have once expected to see the H. M. Tennent banner (often in association with the Arts Council) have been replaced by other less glamorous names.

It can hardly be called competition. The Golden Age may have dimmed but its remaining glories are simply shared by more people. A very exclusive club took in more members; the house rules were unchanged.

The West End managers did their business best to ignore the implications of the experiments at the Royal Court and Theatre Workshop. They were patronizing. They even occasionally came visiting like rich uncles to see what the boys were fooling about with. But eventually they were forced to take notice because the boys looked like invading their own sacred frame of reference – the box office.

It was disturbing and it was nasty, but some of the boys looked like making money. They still didn't like what was being done, but if money was being involved, then, in the words of Mrs Willie Loman, 'Attention must be paid.'

Attention has been paid, often reluctantly, but grudging tribute has been paid. Paid, for example, in the form of plays which earlier would never have seen the light of day. Admittedly they were plays like *Flowering Cherry* [by Robert Bolt] and *Five Finger Exercise* [by Peter Shaffer] which seemed to make exciting gestures towards a new theatrical feeling, but which were still carefully tailored to offend or disturb no one. They were, in fact, Rattigan with knobs on.

The English Stage Company and Theatre Workshop took the risks, did the fighting, and Shaftesbury Avenue exploited the results carefully, with their eye, as ever, on their own carefully coddled market and their stable of stars.

In their smooth manipulation of counter-revolution, the West End managers have been constantly encouraged by the majority of the newspaper critics, with the exception of an honourable handful.

No one has done more to encourage the theatrical status quo than most of the professional critics. The frivolity and dedicated conservatism of some of the daily-paper critics – particularly those of the expensive papers – is often unbelievable. It seems that the more you pay for an opinion, the more frivolous it must be.

The pronouncements of *The Times* in this respect, for instance, are as much a joke in the theatrical profession as other statements of that newspaper are elsewhere. The following notice of *West Side Story* is a superb example of *The Times* in the theatre (Mr Anthony Cookham in this case):

> It is this sense of authentic vibrancy which contends during the evening, on the whole successfully, with the difficulty of taking a tragic view of characters who are represented starkly as morons. Only Doc, who serves behind the bar of the boys' gymnasium, and a police sergeant, are of average intelligence. The rest are self-pitying teenagers with hardly any control of their savage instincts who accept it as a glorious destiny to do battle for a piece of street.
>
> The West Side boys produce a Romeo whose Juliet belongs to the rival gang of Puerto Ricans, and it is then only love and disastrous change which bring either of them to a dawning realization that life has more to offer than street scuffles with fists or bricks or bicycle chains or knives.

How lofty, how detached and how meaningless is *The Times* when it reports on each dejected evening sitting in the stalls. *The Times* notices invariably read as if they had been written by a junior Minister blandly blocking a difficult one at Question Time.

The police sergeant whom Mr Cookham admires in the above notice would do well as a police trooper in South Africa. The point that a whole world is concentrated on doing battle for a piece of street is lost on him, which is hardly surprising.

Between them, the theatrical managers and the majority of the critics have resisted every fresh current of life introduced into the theatre. There is nothing to suggest that they will not go on doing so. It is true that they are uneasy; but the fact remains that they are still where they were before, doing very nicely in their twin Easy Streets east and west of the Temple Bar.

If you don't believe it, pick up your newspaper to see who is playing in what and who is presenting them – and what was said about them.

You still want to be a revolutionary? You've plenty of time. The party has scarcely started.

Tribune, 27 March 1959

Schoolmen of the Left

Birds of a feather flock together
And so do pigs and swine
Rats and mice do have their choice
And so do I have mine.

A few weeks ago in New York I was trying to describe to an American journalist the feelings of that minority of British people like myself who are opposed to the American Alliance, believing that blind men are best left helpless rather than dependent on the guidance of a dog who, for all his sweetness and friendliness, shows every sign of recurrent madness. After he had listened for a while, he looked mildly irritated and said: 'You British – all you seem to bring over is your contempt.'

My other companion, also American, shrugged: 'That's what they're selling.'

As Kenneth Tynan pointed out last Sunday, there is an already excellent, domestic compact in contempt available in the work of people like Mort Sahl, Lennie Bruce, Mike Nichols and Elaine May, so I was not displeased.

Apart from a mild sense of gratitude for an unexpected variant on 'anger', it seemed to me to be an advance in response, indicating not so much 'Why persecutest thou me?' but 'If you have to kick against the pricks, must you mention them by name?'

The situation in most fields in Britain is misreported and often deliberately misrepresented abroad to such an extent, especially in America, that one constantly feels that discussions about this country like, for example, the one published on this page two weeks ago under the title 'The Gentlemen of England', cannot possibly be England, *your* England. It may be that we each have our own, private, intensely personal England so that it is always England, *his* England we hear about.

But these are the feelings of one more desperate minority. Most people have given up England like potatoes or Romantic love and feel all the better for it. The condition of being English is one of the last hideouts of guerilla Romanticism. Now that Christians and Gentlemen are assumed to be safely muffled up in the catacombs of Cabinet room and television studio, what is left of Holy Mother Church but the pillars of our derelict Englishness? It is the remaining relic of authority, the last leaky vessel of moral sanction, the rod of Aaron, inevitably a square 'un, the Home and

Colonial ethos, or, as they would say in the literary pages – the Ark of the Covenant *de nos jours*.

(English reviewers seem to be so much happier and wittier in French that one wonders why they haven't abandoned their native tongue entirely, although the way some of them use it suggests they may be simply ashamed of it.)

However, the fact remains that many Americans bring up topics like what the *Observer* still relentlessly calls the Young Angries with the same baffled inflections that they use with 'Of course, you have socialized medicine, haven't you?' (Then, as if they were asking after the cancer in your left ear: 'How do you find it works?')

But from where do they manage to experience the texture of life in these islands? Possibly from watching John Mills staring at them through Admiralty-issue binoculars, *New Yorker* advertisements, *Carry on Nurse!*, *Time Magazine*, Mark Saber, Mr Cronin ('they fired him for buying Brand X'), Supermac, the British Travel Association, the Royal Ballet and Maurice Evans. Then there is Mr David Susskind's television discussion programme, *Open End*. This is often admirable enough, but occasionally seems like a cheap-rate Anglophile's bargain counter and forcing-house of English reaction.

Apparently, there are also odd vagrant academics like Mr Martin Green on this page the other week who seeks to explain life in England through an examination of some of the novels written during the past forty years. In this case the pay-off is nostalgic approval of the 'Anti-Gentlemen', none other than our old A.C. and D.C. friends That Certain Critic and his favourite author, unhappily no longer with us. Of the other two, one is dead, one is living at the last count, and if you don't know the answer you've picked up the wrong Sunday newspaper by mistake.

There is nothing harmful in selecting any of these writers if you feel compelled to flog life into some very flyblown theoretical horsemeat. What is odd is that anyone should fail to notice that their influence has long been assimilated all over the literary place.

But then the solemn assumption that you can analyse the sterility and artificiality of English life through a discussion of a dozen or so novels is only orthodox penclubmanship. Nevertheless, it's like discussing a country's economy 'particularly as revealed in its egg production'. There is no reason to minimize the importance of The Novel, but since Mr Green went into exile there has been a certain amount of significant activity and energy in other fields. Energy especially, and this is rare enough in Britain to be remarkable for itself.

But whatever may be its ultimate value, the face of this country now emerges most often, most clearly and most vigorously from television, cinema and theatre. To recognize this is not to disregard or despise those private voices that speak only to themselves, but simply to remind those who play incessantly at games-about-writers that England lives outside hard covers, too. Or to put it another way: the popular arts have become The Novel *de nos jours*.

All of which could lead to the foregone conclusion that the greatest enemies of the English language and character, as well as its artists, are rich men, Government agencies and working intellectuals.

I still feel that contempt is good, and with the whores off the streets, policemen indoors reading our books, and the current price of betrayal at thirty pieces of fruit and nut, whole new areas for conformity may be opening up for development and every new cliché should be gratefully received.

> Oh what a deal of scorn looks beautiful
> In the contempt and anger of his lip.
> *Twelfth Night*

Contempt *is* more accurate, more apt because it contains the element which the Gentlemen of England usually ignored or failed to recognize when the fixtures with Lawrence and Orwell were more or less over, and they were confronted instead with a scratch but regular bunch of Players. It contained ridicule, and even if it didn't achieve very much, it served as an antidote to the belief that working-class or non-Gentlemen writers wrote principally out of resentment at not being able to get into Literary Society and/or become Gentlemen. Eventually the message did seep through that the complaint had never been that it wasn't possible to get in, but that it had never been worth getting into in the first place.

> Strontium and US Air Force zones may break my bones
> But words will hurt me never.
> Marching song

What was expressed in the words was contempt, but they were smart enough to call it something else. 'Anger insignificantly fierce.' Camus called it passionate disbelief, or something like it, and it has been found very difficult indeed for anyone to believe that such feelings could be elevated into a principle, that the only way to deal with tablets of stone might be to deface them; that this might be the mood of men intent on not being deceived, least of all by themselves, prepared but not resigned to doing *their* little bit of writing on tombstones. Like every outgoing generation, they couldn't understand or forgive the inability to make grateful noises.

However, rebels without a pause were to be encouraged and asked to take out their ovaries and show them around that they might be seen to be as barren as those loafing about on the periphery. They were slipped twenty guineas to write about the Role of the Writer in Society, and romanced into long statements about the Socialist Responsibility to the New Techniques of Mass Communication.

And all to be written whenever possible in the schoolteachers' prig prose that helps to give Left magazines their special odour of intellectual carbolic and sanctity; and to exploit education as a substitute for imagination. The most apparent influence of Marx on British Socialists has been to persuade them to write English in such a way as to give the impression that their native tongue was German.

It is by insisting on an impossible standard of perfection that the sceptic makes himself secure.

A. J. Ayer.

The prose style of such magazines may seem scarcely worth the trouble of fixing into anyone's sights, but, unfortunately, the style does proclaim the men, although 'proclaim' does suggest robustness. They are the Schoolmen of the Left, and with their unending, sterile exegesis, they'll fasten their German–English on to the merest rustle of activity, like Lady Chatterley's husband training binoculars on the gamekeeper. They certainly make their special contribution to a context in which any concrete endeavour often becomes too depressing to contemplate.

This always seems particularly so whenever one returns from America. There is something uniquely dispiriting about the climate surrounding most of the arts in Britain, generated principally by the linesmen who hardly ever consent to take part in the game, but manage to make the existing one as difficult and joyless as possible.

A good example of all this can be seen from the history of Theatre Workshop. Our only formally left-wing theatre could scarcely have bought tea and sandwiches for the stage management from what it earned over the years from the support of left intellectuals.

In the same way, brutal duels will be fought for months on end, years even, in film magazines over matters of critical honour like form *v.* content. Blood might even get spilled over the seats at the National Film Theatre, but there is very little likelihood that anyone engaged in this kind of war would ever consent to involving themselves in actually trying to make a special film. Of all the difficult film projects already made in this country, and those presently being attempted, I cannot think of one that has been initiated in any way by such people.

The reason for this is that they are exclusively concerned with their individual substitutes for creativity. This is not simply a case of every man wanting to be a critic. Every man is, or should be, a critic. After all, Resnais and Truffaut are both critics who have learned the use of their limbs quite successfully. What is disturbing is the danger that the arts are following a familiar pattern of turning every man into a spectator, and often a professional spectator who wants to be the referee, and change the rules to suit his idea of fun. The time may come when there are no players left, no spectators, only referees. And no game.

Oh show us the way to the next little dollar.
Oh, don't ask why – oh, don't ask why!
For we must find the next little dollar.
For if we don't find the next little dollar
I tell you we must die – I tell you we must die.
I tell you – I tell you – I tell you we must die.

In America, the atmosphere in the popular arts at least is entirely different. For one thing, the air is not charged with the resigned, listless envy that often makes breathing alone difficult in British Show Biz. On Broadway, for instance, an attitude of expectancy seems so obligatory that it is possible to feel hepped up to such an extent that it might be ages before you realize that nothing very significant, nothing outside the prescribed Broadway formulae, is likely to turn up.

All the same, it does mean that nearly everyone is constantly trying out their reach, making an Englishman realize that he's been living in a world without wonder, and quite a few degrees under. The climate of simple effort is bracing in itself, even if the grasp does belong to the real-estate men, ticket-scalpers, union men or any of the other people who have converted New York Theatre into something between a lottery and a big-time racket.

This month a show opened called 'An Evening with Mike Nichols and

Elaine May'. Nichols and May are two highly successful cabaret artists who are known in this country only from a long-playing record, which gives a fair impression of their wit, bottled in ice and improvisation.

No one else appears on stage during the evening, which consists entirely of a succession of sketches. This production, which could be comfortably presented in the sitting-room of a semi-detached, cost $80,000 to produce at the John Golden Theatre. For this sum it is still possible to present about six one-set, six-character straight plays in the West End.

In order to put these two people on the stage with enough props and changes to allow a moderately competent ASM time to knit several pairs of socks in the prompt corner every week, union restrictions also make it necessary to employ no fewer than sixteen stage-hands. Now what sixteen grown men are doing for two hours every evening is difficult for anyone watching the show to imagine. However, anyone who has ever worked in an American theatre will safely assume that they are playing gin, smoking cigars, and complaining about the actors making so much noise that they can't hear the World Series. Thus the sacred cow of free enterprise ends up being milked to death.

With the Broadway Season's winners more or less selected without right of appeal by the critics of the *New York Times* and *Herald Tribune* ('You may be able to fight one, but you can't fight 'em both' is what any producer will tell you) the operation resembles less good old capitalist horse-trading than horse racing; with rake-offs for nearly everyone except the runners.

For instance, there is the established system of 'ice'. This is the money from the sale of hot tickets at what we could call black-market prices, and enables people like box-office clerks to buy themselves Cadillacs and houses by the beach out of long runs.

Fortunately the system hasn't yet been introduced to this country, which may be why one often has to wait for the privilege of buying a ticket, staring nervously at the top of someone's head, whose attention appears to be riveted on something in that mysterious space below the box-office window and out of one's sight. Anyway, their attitude usually marks them down as mere activity-haters, abstraction queens and certainly sworn enemies of the theatre employing them. What are they doing behind there? Polishing up their German–English perhaps, and preparing another thousand words. As Sainte-Beuve says somewhere:

Don't care was made to care
Don't care was hung
Don't care was put in a pot
And boiled till he was done.

Observer, 30 October 1960

All Words and No Performance

The trouble with books written about the theatre in England is that they are almost always written by default. No doubt this is because no one takes the subject very seriously. It is probably because nobody else has bothered to take up the subject that Professor Allardyce Nicoll has become what is lazily known as an authority. The simple fact is that nobody more distinguished or imaginative could bring themselves to the task or thought it worthy of them. The glum result is that we have Nicoll on Theatre as if he were as authoritative as Jackson on Divorce. (The same applies to Eric Bentley. How anyone who is responsible for such lamentable versions of Brecht, to say nothing of his limping theatrical theory, could be thought worth even an American reprint is puzzling.) The people who are paid to write about the English Theatre are a sad bunch.

What is occasionally alarming to those of us who devote our time and vitality to the exercise of this art is that such writers, by force of sheer pushiness and lack of shame, should gather any attention or respect at all. Can it be because the subject is an esoteric publishing enterprise which anyone vain or hardy enough can undertake? Like angling? I say this because almost any journal or publication from *The Encyclopaedia Britannica* to the stewed gentilities of the British Drama League, attracts the same kind of contributor. As for the British Council, they are probably still pushing Charles Morgan, and not merely to appease the French but from simple inclination.

Look for a moment – don't buy it – at the *Oxford Companion to the Theatre*. Oxford and Companion, academic distinction and a chum to lead you through. But, as Harold Hobson has said, as a work of reference, it is useless; as a Bedside Book still more so because of its deadpan power to keep you awake with laughter. It is just these publications, scratchy and undistinguished, that have currency among innocent students and seekers after the bare approximate. They look to these botched, arrogant, ignorant volumes for information. Unfortunately, they are unaware of the special nature of modern critical neurosis with its presumptions, its fearfulness and bullying guessing games.

How to protect the sixth-former from Sunderland, the graduate from Karachi? I wish I knew. The lack of responsible information is almost total, and the harm done repeated and perpetuated. For example, in the *Penguin Dictionary of the Theatre* suspect opinions are represented to the unwitting as facts, and productions are actually listed as 'successful' like a *Variety* rating. It is also full of know-all shots in the dark as when it says I drew 'unsuccessfully' on Brecht for *The Entertainer* at a time when Brecht was little more than a name to me. I had, however, been going to the music hall before the compiler was born.

There was a time when I used to have the odd drink at the pub next door to the Royal Court Theatre in Sloane Square but it became the occasional haunt of aggressive, fawning critics and their followers. Those of us who had worked in the building next door for some ten years had to go elsewhere or be put off our beer. But long before this sad time I had been driven away by Israeli playwrights and Pakistani Ph.D.s clobbering me with misinformation and speculation wrenched from the drab pages of a few books on recent British Theatrical History.

All of which brings me, as the reviewers say, to *The Rise and Fall of the Well-made Play* by John Russell Taylor, double first and film critic of *The Times*; and *Theatre at Work* edited by Charles Marowitz and Simon Trussler, a collection of reprinted pieces from the mercifully defunct theatrical magazine *Encore*. To anyone who never read that publication, it must be impossible to convey the sanctimony, the aridity and humour-lessness of it. True, it was more readable than *The Tulane Drama Review*; but less funny. *Theatre at Work* has an introduction by the drama critic of this newspaper, which is fitting enough.

In this introduction, Irving Wardle suggests that one of those reviewers' inventions, The Theatre of Cruelty, has 'been scrapped as an outmoded fashion'. What a misreading of the creative process, and how predictable and understandable. I am quite certain that if anyone ever dropped The Theatre of Cruelty or any other cant-monger's pet pussy down the well it was because the subject had lost its interest for them, not because it bored the press or public. He also makes the statement that there is 'no longer a place in London for a small theatre specializing in new British work. There is ample new British work about.' About where?

Mr Wardle says there is no point in assembling talented writers under the same roof, principally because they have little in common with one another. (None of us at the Royal Court ever had anything in common, thank God.) He goes on to suggest that the National Theatre has usurped the function of an organization like the English Stage Company.

This is not so. Writers may be 'about', but the West End theatre managements will not give them fourpence or even a polite acknowledgement of their expensively typed manuscripts. The Royal Court will at least cheer you up with a beer and a sandwich even if they won't go to a fully mounted production. As for the National Theatre, its constitution dictates that it should present the World Classics and its endorsement of new work is inevitably limited by this clear policy. Apart from this, how many playwrights can afford to write a full-length play for a couple of performances a week in one season? As Kenneth Tynan, the Literary Manager of the theatre, has himself said, it is the in-built flaw of the building. Commentators seem to be so giddy with the glories of that institutionalized palace that they seem unaware that all the practitioners mentioned in this book – Arden, Bolt, Wesker, Pinter, Littlewood, Brook, Peter Hall – have made their reputation elsewhere and continue to do so. Most interviewers are uninterested in their subjects, and in this book one can't help feeling that the editors are longing for the writers and directors to shut up and let *them* get on with it.

Mr Russell Taylor's book takes us trippingly through the Landseer school of dramatists, from Scribe through Pinero to Rattigan, with the pleasing proposition that there is still a place for the well-made play. I wouldn't care to argue about this, much less go to the excess of writing a book about it. There is still a place for the bicycle and I wouldn't deny anyone a book on the subject. However, Mr Russell Taylor has written one, and as he is in the commentating and thesis business, I suppose he succumbed to an overwhelming urge.

The case seems to be that there is a deprived audience gasping for well-made plays, if only some reliable firm of solid craftsmen will turn them out. You deliver the goods and we'll take care of the rest. Well, there it is. If any of you want to pay off your mortgage and gain an adoring and grateful public, write a few well-made plays. That is the answer, and a sweetly obvious one as explained by the author. After all, people still paint representational pictures. They even ride bicycles. I do myself. The yearning contention here is that in the days when a decent dramatist gave you a damn good yarn, the honest professional had to keep his audience 'interested' just as a popular newspaper editor has to give his readers a wink and a promise every five minutes.

These are the crafty fairground tactics of the old bourgeoisie where every picture-frame tells a story according to ancient and classical theories of balance and proportion. It is the Keep 'Em Bareminded and Pregnant School of Drama. Or, as I am dallying with commentators' coinage, 'The Theatre of Sucking Up'. 'Cut that line, they don't know what you're talking about. . . . They start to get restless round about here, can't you slip in a joke about nationalized railways?' It is a world inherited from bouquets or poison sent to the wrong lover, mistaken identities, half-masks, dropped blooms, misplaced necklaces, and unopened or incorrectly delivered letters. Formula writing, as Mr Taylor admits, for how could anyone write, as did Scribe himself, 500 plays in only forty-five years? Such a formula was dependent on a closed social system, itself ritualized outwardly in everyday life in ideas of property, the inviolable marriage contract, cuckoldry, masters and servants, and concepts of revenge, honour and romantic passion. All of this is still splendid when worked up by a popular genius like Verdi, but it's hard to believe that anyone would seriously like the National Theatre to mount five acts of what-will-old-Scribe-pull-out-of-his-bag-of-tricks-next. Even Uncle Pinero makes most of the kiddies yawn nowadays. Yeah, so then what happened, Ma?

The direct descendant of the 'well-made' play (that is to say, where you can point out the joins) is the Hugh and Margaret Williams play. True, it is a pretty sucked-on fag end to have to pick out of the West End gutter but there are two running presently and doing very nicely no doubt. Why should Mr Taylor complain?

Landseer, OK: *si*. But Bacon *si*, Picasso *si* also. We live in a society of such lurching flexibility that it is no longer possible to construct a dramatic method based on a shared social or ethical system. The inexorable process of fragmentation is inimical to all public assumptions or indeed ultimately to anything shared at all. A theatre audience is no longer linked by anything but the climate of disassociation in which it tries to live out its baffled lives. A dramatist can no longer expect to draw many common references, be they social, sexual or emotional. He can't generalize in the old way. He must be specific to himself and his own particular, concrete experience.

The Williams well-maders work in so far as they succour and flatter a bewildered, disinherited middle-class audience bawling after a decadent and dummy tradition. One day I expect Mr Williams will be on stage opening a jar from Fortnums and snarling some forced banter about au-pair girls or Pol Roger, and he will suddenly find himself in the midst of an Ionesco nightmare. The entire audience will rise out of their seats, invade the proscenium arch and demand that they be allowed to *live* there. With Hugh Williams. I think they would deserve squatters' rights.

The Times, 14 October 1967

Backward Glances

Suddenly everyone is pointing to decades as if each might reveal the secret-whatever-it-is. With less sense of Self, everyone is oddly self-conscious. However, it's just another game to play.

As for the Theatre Game, it has been what is known as a period of consolidation rather than innovation. You can't have revolutions all the time.

There was some effort to import the Theatre of Participation (US mostly), in which audience and actors grapple and strive in a democratic transport of BO, squalor and self-fixing bafflement.

The Labour Party discovered the Theatre too late for its own or anybody else's good. However, they did give away a little money – about the same amount spent on military bands and that sort of thing.

An institution called the National Theatre opened its doors to general moos of self-approval and very little of any import has happened there since.

A great many fine actors have emerged from all over the place and scarcely any actresses, who continue strangely to complain that parts are not written for them.

The Lord Chamberlain's office was abolished after sixty years of agitation, to the relief of most actors (now being allowed to mouth vile words like 'crumpet') and the dismay of Emile Littler and Peter Saunders.

Mr Littler is a well-known horse fancier and play-doctor, according to his own description, and Mr Saunders is the producer of 'The Mouse-trap', which entered into its eighteenth something-boggling year. I have yet to meet anyone who has seen it but there are something like 2 million of them around, which means that I am either a hermit or just permanently out of touch with good old public taste.

The main fruit of this flush of simple freedom was a musical called

Hair. This, a rather smug, simple-minded, slightly poovy boulevard piece, was about Young People being generally pleased with themselves and their own mind-boggling thing. They preferred peace to war, exposing their private parts in public places, not caring – indeed not knowing – which were the girls or the boys in any old band.

Princess Anne saw it and reportedly enjoyed it. Decent old folks in their thirties went and were reassured by its odour of energy and gentleness.

All over the country, glass-box theatres sprang up or old working men's institutes were refurbished.

Coventry, Guildford, Leatherhead, Nottingham, Stoke, Exeter. They were opening like supermarkets.

The older repertory companies, like Bristol, served as testing grounds for cautious West End managers who find reading scripts difficult but newspaper notices easier going for them.

In this way, a trickle of new plays came in on a tide of managerial timidity to London, to what was once called the West End.

The audience for this was largely inherited by the Royal Shakespeare Company and the National. The Royal Court Theatre still contrived by a combination of reputation, arrogance and subsidy to have no regular audience at all.

Critics invented all kinds of cults for want of better things to do – Theatre of Cruelty, the Absurd, Mind-Boggling, you name it. And people invented the Critics.

Mostly unheeded, derided or ignored by profession and public, these gloomy men were astounded to find themselves attacked on all sides by those they had reviled and patronized in print for years. They affected to be the offended upholders of freedom, the Public Interest and all manner of priggish newspaper cant. They sounded very wounded, but no one got really hurt and a good time was had by nearly all.

Television didn't affect the Theatre after all. A lot of people yearned aggressively for what they call A Good Evening's Entertainment and presumably got it seeing Dame Anna Neagle kick her way through *Charley Girl*.

The Theatre simply went on dying, as it has done for centuries. Like everything else.

Daily Mirror, 31 December 1969

Piled Stones

I find the *Evening Standard*'s endorsement of the Barbican Arts scheme puzzling. It is well-meaning, but I also think it is wrong-headed and the other case should be made out.

And there is another case. By this, I don't mean that of the City, which is clearly and predictably philistine, unimaginative and grasping. No, the case against the scheme is quite different and not reactionary but a creative and realistic one. It is this:

A glib mythology has been created over the years by people who really do wish the theatre well but misinterpret the very nature of the creative process. This legend is centred on the existence of the two main London-based subsidized theatres, the National Theatre and the Royal Shakespeare. An opposite view is widely held within the profession but it is felt impolite, immodest or disloyal to express it publicly.

I should like to do so now.

Take the National Theatre first. Since its creation its record has been poor to disastrous. It opened with a lamentable *Hamlet*. In fact, its record of productions of the classics, for which it is supposed to exist, is appalling. This includes a black-and-white-minstrel *Othello*, a dismal undercast *Three Sisters*, a one-shot intellectual reading of *The Merchant of Venice*, and a *Hedda Gabler* which must have made poor old Ibsen turn in his Northern lights.

As for new plays, hardly anything significant has emerged with the exception of the deservedly prize-winning *National Health*, and Peter Nichols was already a writer of established reputation. No risks there, my friends.

Sir Laurence Olivier is possibly the greatest actor of the century and has a genius for interpreting this nation to itself. As an administrator, he is hesitant and headstrong.

As for his assistant, Kenneth Tynan, he seems to attempt to be the archetypal Oxford clever dick and ringmaster. And the theatre's use of glum gimmicks like plant-hire machinery and golden genitals are to him a joke.

Policy has allowed waves of distinguished actors to be recruited, used and quickly discarded, then a telly personality or two in order to court a popular cultural image. In short, the organization has dwindled into what one always feared, a factious institution with all the pressures of the commercial theatre and an indecisive, uneasy policy.

As for the Royal Shakespeare, the less said the better, for it has done little that is memorable, let alone remarkable. It has to some extent lived on the immoral earnings of Shakespeare, the Arts Council, gullible tourists and schoolchildren. True, it has produced the plays of Harold Pinter, but not as efficiently as he could have well done himself.

My point is this. The fallacy in the pro-Barbican Arts lobby is simply that buildings, facilities and money in themselves lead to art and achievement. They manifestly do not.

To talk, as Trevor Nunn does, of there being a creative emigration is ludicrous. Look at New York. All it can boast is Mike Nichols, Neil Simon and the Lincoln Center, which is like watching theatre in an airport, and there are no grounds, as far as I can see, for suggesting the Barbican would be very different.

The two buildings which have contributed most to the English theatre are the Victoria Theatre Royal, Stratford ('Theatre Workhouse') and the Royal Court, which is an old Nonconformist chapel where even the one backstage lavatory doesn't work properly.

In other words, forget buildings and so-called amenities. Concentrate on originating talent and give the actors more money instead. They should be gypsies not computer clerks.

Evening Standard, 19 March 1971

Anniversary Parade

It is difficult to write a piece which may read like an obituary for something which is still very much as alive, consistent and changing as a living organism. Which is what, fifteen strange years after its opening at the Royal Court in April 1956, I believe the English Stage Company still to be.

It is hard to resist the temptation of going down Memory Lane and I don't intend to resist it. I remember the year before we ever moved into the Royal Court, when we thought we were going to take over the old, bombed Kingsway Theatre. However, it turned out to be Sloane Square. There were months, long before we opened, when we auditioned hundreds of actors, including myself. During this time, I was taking home dozens of new plays to read for the company, including one by Robert Bolt, to which I gave a schoolmasterly recommendation, and innumerable plays about Mary Queen of Scots and the destruction of the world by the H-bomb – most of which seemed to be written by schoolteachers and clergymen's wives.

Memory Lane again: I think of all the actors I worked with and watched. Nobody could deny that it is a pretty remarkable list. Kenneth Haigh, Alan Bates, Mary Ure, Keith Michell, Joan Greenwood, Joan Plowright, Nigel Davenport, Laurence Olivier, George Relph, Brenda de Banzie, Richard Pasco, Vivien Leigh, Alec Guinness, Gwen Ffrangçon-Davies, Ralph Richardson, John Gielgud, Nicol Williamson, Jill Bennett, Alan Dobie, Michael Gwynn, Paul Scofield, Albert Finney. One could go on endlessly.

Time becomes history so quickly nowadays, and people constantly ask me what the beginnings of the Court were like and what we were setting out to do. The truth of it is that I simply don't know. For one thing, I don't remember clearly and I also know that there was never at any time any sense of a laid-down constitution. We were very English, factious, what they call 'empirical' and totally unclear about what the future might hold for any of us.

I do believe that there were some vague leanings towards creating something of a 'poetic' theatrical climate, rather along the lines of the old Mercury Theatre. This initial objective got lost somehow in the accident of history and something entirely different took place. What that may be is for everyone to judge. But I don't think by any standards it could be described as anything but half bad.

Apart from the actors, the mere list of productions and writers is fairly remarkable. Having gone through a list of actors, I won't do the same with the productions, but it might not be a bad idea to remind people of some of the names of the people who have worked at the Royal Court. Just at random: Arnold Wesker, Harold Pinter, N. F. Simpson, Lindsay Anderson, Tony Richardson, John Dexter, Edward Bond, William Gaskill, Peter Gill, Ann Jellicoe, Ionesco, Beckett, Donald Howarth, Jocelyn Herbert – and so on.

One doesn't want to be sanctimonious about someone who is dead and who was also a true friend. However, I think it would be hard for anyone to contest that the unique historical function of the English Stage Company was very largely due to the administrative genius of its first artistic director, George Devine. He almost changed character with the job. Changed shape. He was able, by some strange, hard-won alchemy, to unite the inevitable warring and bitchy factions within the building without ever losing his own authenticity. No one has replaced him and probably no one ever will for it is a very special kind of talent. Certainly, no other theatre has since found anyone to match him. He protected us from the sin of competition, and helped us find fun and sheer enjoyment in what we did.

Observer, 18 April 1971

Devine and Fall

Richard Findlater, *At the Royal Court*

Richard Findlater's account of the first twenty-five years of that unique institution, the Royal Court, is masterly.

From a disorderly house of information, verifiable as well as disputed history, faded faction and quiescent conspiracies, he has produced a document which is not only fascinating reading for those who know their Ayckbourn from their Ubu, but a succinct, sharp record of social history.

Of course the book should have been titled, *The Rise and Fall of the Royal Court*. To turn from the first fifteen years of the Court to the present day is to lurch from the Rome of Augustus to that of Justinian, from the Republic of George and Tony to those barbarous, rapacious mercenaries, Ron and Les.

A few months ago I visited the Court with a heavy but unclosed heart to watch a dull, presumptuous play, *Not Quite Jerusalem*. In the programme there appeared a self-righteous, overweening footnote: 'The theatre is subsidized by the workers of this theatre, many of whom receive less than the national average of £119 a week.'

Running counter to this prevailing cupidity of the day is the theme which emerges from the contributors [myself among them] to Mr Findlater's book. We never considered that we were being ill-used, least of all that we were being 'exploited' by a capitalist society that had its values wrong.

We knew that *they* were wrong because *we* belonged to an ancient and honourable company of gypsies that did not whine for justice from a society we naturally condemned. This is why I describe the book as social history, wherein the Court's decline foreshadows our common fall in the flood tide of national avarice and the reign of banality.

I protested about this programme, pointing out that when I was on the payroll of the Royal Court I was paid £2 a week, that Tony Richardson was receiving £14 a week and George Devine a little over £30; that the Arts Council's initial grant of £2,000 never rose above £100,000 until the early seventies, when it soared to the present absurd figure of £450,000. 'I'm afraid', said the chairman dolefully, 'that sort of idealism doesn't exist any more.' Neither, alas, does the talent.

What was the Court *about*, apart from the shop-soiled dictums of being a writer's theatre and the 'right to fail' – a favourite this with pushy Ron and Les, out to bring down a corrupt society at no cost to themselves. I will give you one lone example which embodied its human values: John Arden.

This playwright, abhorred by many and revered by some, would have had neither career nor reputation if he had not had the benefit of the Court's special and particular care. 'Not another *Arden*,' Chairman Blond would say to George. His alarm was understandable. All Arden's plays were box office disasters: *Live Like Pigs* (25 per cent box office capacity), *Sergeant Musgrave's Dance* (21 per cent), *The Happy Haven* (12 per cent).

With such figures before him, Trevor Nunn would scarcely give Arden a cup of tea let alone another production. David Mercer in a letter to me some time ago wrote: '*Cousin Vladimir* is limping along at about 50 per cent houses. Already Trevor Nunn has cold feet about doing my next play, which is at present gathering dust on his secretary's desk.'

Peter Hall to me in 1976: 'I'm afraid the play will have to come off, John. It's playing to less than 90 per cent and we have to do better than that in this theatre.'

'Oh George,' I thought, 'up there on your pipe-smoking cloud, if only you would look down upon the dismal plains of Colditz and, like the good bird in the book of Tobit, squeeze out a black juicy sludge of dottle and drop a large mess of it in his eye.'

There is a magnificent selection of photographs, and the contributions are mostly illuminating. Wesker is open and sweet-natured about his excitement and bafflement at his rough treatment. Lindsay Anderson is schoolmasterly but shrewd: 'Not the theatre as a "vehicle" for ideas, which is itself a form of philistinism . . . visions of society untouched by the crudity of propaganda.'

Edward Bond, owlish and purblind, 'explains' Devine's initial failure of doctrinal vision which, surprisingly, brought him fame and righteous reputation. Bill Gaskill's summing-up: 'He [Devine] had grave doubts about his own talent and a corresponding belief in other directors, particularly young directors. He was the ideal master to be apprenticed to.'

New Standard, 7 April 1981

Something Concrete

Peter Lewis, *The National: A Dream Made Concrete*

Thirty years ago I insensitively compared the creation of a National Theatre with the Albert Memorial, a structure of devout, tasteless charms. Predictably, I added, 'If it is built I only hope someone sets fire to it.' It was no more than an opinionated squib, tossed away with the playful object of smoking out the closet prigs and 'culture' pushers before they became today's battalions.

Now, like one of those wartime pillboxes glimpsed from a train, the monstrous concrete piety of the National Theatre broods, a monument to prevailing madness fixed on a fantasy future in which present chaos will give way to a world of orderly richness for everyone's children and, worse, grandchildren. One doesn't have to be childless to be repelled by the spectacle of such fanatics hurling themselves Into Europe as if it were as tangible as the River Jordan. Carry me over into sceptical, camp ground rather than that benighted certainty called the Twenty-First Century. I must say, I'd like to be around to pick up the pieces when somebody breaks the kiddies' hearts.

So it is with the National Theatre. Who's going to tell them it was only a dumb dream? I am chided by Peter Lewis in his account of the theatrical future that did not work for my ingrate opposition to subsidy. But when I was taken up by the Royal Court its allowance from the Arts Council amounted to £2,000, which exactly covered George Devine's salary. Like Brendan Behan, Shelagh Delaney and Harold Pinter, my career was launched not by public patronage but by private faith.

'Raise tempers, goad and lacerate. Raise whirlwinds,' read the battle pennant inscribed over Kenneth Tynan's desk in his front-line HQ in Aquinas Street. Olivier's cynical appointment of the self-proposed Tynan as *Dramaturg* was his first and probably most disastrous strategic mistake. He disliked him unwaveringly, seeing him as an irredeemable alien, though not perhaps with the intensity he reserved for the insider, Peter Hall, whose succession was insidiously forced upon him. Only an unworldly reviewer could have failed to comprehend Olivier's transparently foxy ruse to truss him up in a high-sounding subordinate role where he could be effectively contained. Passing the letter of application from his prospective Duke of Clarence to his wife, he rasped, 'How shall we slaughter the little bastard?'

Whatever havoc Clarence Peacock Tynan might have caused as a visiting gourmet inspector, let loose in the kitchen, he created panic among the distinguished nonentities on the board. His confrontational method of promoting dubious one-sex productions of Shakespeare, worthless offerings of agit-prop like *Soldiers* [by Rolf Hochhuth] or *Tyger* [by Adrian Mitchell and Mike Westbrook], or his foreign obsessions and flights of fancy with fork-lifts and phalluses, was a model of radical crassness and ineptitude.

One Sunday evening, he telephoned to engage my support for the Hochhuth play, suggesting that I should inform the Board forthwith of my intention to withhold the rights of any of my own works if they persisted in their opposition to *Soldiers*. I replied that this was unacceptable on the grounds that (a) I had not read the play and this might be a negligible weapon to launch a risky offensive of artistic principle, and (b) such a threat on my part, far from intimidating them, would gladden their hearts and enforce their opposition. Tynan was mystified. He could only see the whole managerial process in gladiatorial terms, publicly conducted, not grasping the fact that the public cared little for the contest or not at all. Guile and deceit behind closed doors, as practised by Devine at the Court, he dismissed as 'gradualism'.

But it was this manipulative, tactical patience which George, at the admitted cost of health, sanity and life, deployed so intelligently that it enabled him to outflank opposition with a minimum of adversarial histrionics. He bridged divisions from within and without by stealth and a devotion to the voracious demands of his followers which engaged loyalties to a realistic corner-shop tradition, a home and a retreat rather than the corporate anonymity of a cultural supermarket.

Neither Tynan nor Olivier was endowed with a great gift for friendship (virtually none in Tynan's case, who was emotionally impotent without the close stimulus of stardom), and their relationship dwindled into that of plagued sorcerer and prankish apprentice. Oppressed by financial anxiety, cancer of the prostate, and thrombosis, and cautious of his own generation, Olivier was no more fortunate in his selection of younger associates.

John Dexter, perhaps the most talented and versatile of them all, was a valuable but prickly NCO and unpredictable as officer material. The eclecticism necessary to a national institution was opposed to Bill Gaskill's taste for Marx and Masks which required a more indulgent home, like the Court to which he sensibly returned. As for Jonathan Miller, in Olivier's historical perception of English Drama the Hampstead Nanny's polymath prodigy was surely the theatrical equivalent of Macmillan's Armenian carpet-seller. For the rest, Olivier's looming presence was possibly too awesome and inimical to the tyrannical pietism of democracy.

What cherished memories remain of the National Theatre — *The Recruiting Officer, Trelawny of the Wells, The Master Builder, Dance of Death, Uncle Vanya, Three Sisters, Love for Love* — are confined to the Old Vic, its little grey home away from the West. Whatever its technical inadequacies, the Vic was scaled to human affection for its performers and audience and palpably *worked*. But Olivier had warned that these good days would not last: 'They never do'. With the game afoot to move the pleasure steamer to the land-locked Titanic across the road, and with the departure of the very visible Captain (whose advice was always 'Go for the laughs') and the imminence of glum Commodore Hall, it was downhill all the way.

If you are the kind of archivist who collects bits of the Berlin Wall, you may care to ponder Lewis's cool account of the South Bank's Groundnuts Scheme for The Arts. It's all here, the productions that would have been more appropriately and profitably mounted in the West End: all the Ayckbourn plays, the admirable Ben Travers, *Guys and Dolls*; the ones that should never have seen the console light at all — *Jean Seberg, The Romans, The Women*; the 'unproduced masterpieces' presented to ensure employment and consolation to those reviewers weary of their thirty-third *As You Like It*. As for the New Writers, one might have thought most would feel happier with Hanif Kureishi's tame yobberies, Max Stafford Clark and Ms Churchill at the Royal Court, which, in spite of its pitiful descent, is a decent building even in which to produce acts of sponsored indecency.

Persevering with *A Dream Made Concrete* is like thumbing through Uncle Sidney's scrapbook before he got caught and took off to chokey. The grim images return for the unfunded visionaries to contemplate: the

Castle of Doom itself must be fed £2 million a year before it may open its unwelcoming doors; the striking unionists, whose wildcat enthusiasms for 'the arts' was as intense as their concern for dying hospital patients in those pre-Thatcher days of libertarian conscience. The cheerless dressing rooms, the Kafkaesque (yes, critics have been there, too) corridors, the 4 per cent transfer pay-off; the secure warren for freeloaders and carpet-baggers, secretaries' assistants' secretaries, wig-makers, carpenters, *three* full-time armourers, caterers, enough to serve the 7th Armoured Brigade.

Perhaps, as usual, instinct was superior to reason, and a torch *should* be put to this morbid reminder of the sanctimony, avarice and personal ambition that engendered such loveless days and joyless nights.

Spectator, 5 January 1991

Dear Diary . . .

I NEVER THOUGHT I would live to miss Binkie. 'Who?' readers may ask. Hugh 'Binkie' Beaumont, General Manager of H. M. Tennent, was the Scargill of the iron-lilac Stage Establishment for almost thirty years. Feared and fawned upon by gonged actors, famous playwrights and even the Arts Council, of which he later became a member, Binkie dominated theatrical fashion as long as I could remember. Dealing with one of the subsidized managements last week made me remember almost fondly his formidable and poisonous efficiency.

I dined at his renowned house in Lord North Street early in 1957. A dutiful crone of a housekeeper was serving me disapprovingly when he turned to her and said: '*Now*, Mrs Crocker [pre-Pinter pause], Mr Brendan Bracken has just died and his house is up for sale. *Don't* you think Mr Osborne should buy it?' She looked down at me and, after a gimlet glance, replied very emphatically: 'No!' Binkie's lizard lips fluttered beneath the folds of perennial sunlamp tan. 'Really? But why on earth *not*, Mrs Crocker?' '*Because*', she explained huffily, ''e's not *ready* for it *yet*.' Game and set to Binkie.

Shortly before his death, I spent an evening with him *à trois*, as the other guest, Noël Coward, might have said. Binkie berated and accused me professionally and personally throughout the evening, ending up on his knees, drunk, his face in the fireplace of his most elegant drawing-room, smoking-jacket awry and monogrammed slippers discarded, his behind in the air. Coward watched him irritably but, I thought, with some satisfaction. He had himself been an unadmitted victim of that silken Judas. 'Oh dear,' he clipped over his cigarette holder. 'What a thoroughly *dis*agreeable evening!' It was my last glimpse of either of them.

ON HOLY SATURDAY, Channel 4 showed a film called *God Rot Tunbridge Wells!* It was certainly a 'flawed work' as they say. (I often wonder what is deemed to be 'unflawed'. Orson Welles has been hobbled by his 'flawed' genius all his life.) It was, if nothing else, a reverent, almost devotional, testimony to George Frideric Handel, produced and directed by Tony Palmer, with Trevor Howard as Handel and written by myself. The result, if a bit over-energetic and robust for some maidenly tastes, patently displayed our shared admiration for a God-given, devout and joyful worshipper of life itself. The reviews were almost uniformly dismissive if not hostile. The Old Buck still seemed hedged in by Victorian pieties from undevout journalists. Predictable enough, and by Easter mid-Monday I had almost forgotten an unremarkable incident. Within hours I was swiftly despatched in a state of coma to an intensive-care unit.

A few weeks after this event, I watched a programme about the same subject so banal and lifeless that it could have been intended for the Open University on one of its Social Science courses masquerading as English History or possibly Baroque Music and the Working-Class Movement. A critic on an Arts Game show compared it most favourably to the 'Palmer–Osborne *outrage*'. Par for the course again, and no surprise to anyone. However, my critical shock had already visited me three days after Easter when I regained consciousness. I looked up to a young, pretty nurse astride my chest screaming, 'Do you know *where* you are?' 'New York', I suggested 'No', she yelled, beating me alive with her fists. 'No?' 'You're *in* – Tunbridge Wells!' Perhaps that's what critics mean by a Kafkaesque experience.

In my screenplay I had GFH saying: 'Mediocrity is a great comforter.' It had never occurred to me that God might support mediocrity's devotees so ferociously, almost in the manner of York Minster, and strike me down thus. How, I pondered, did the citizens of that opinionated spa and a bunch of hireling scribblers command such a divinity unto themselves? Moreover, a lifelong, paltry pleasure in the erotic properties of nurses has, like other careless delights, begun reluctantly to fail. As a haggling madame in Mexico once said to a friend and myself: 'If I was a man, my balls would ache.'

RACE RELATIONS of yesteryear. Talking of these things, as people seemed constrained to do, I once took my mother, the maligned Nellie Beatrice, to supper with Paul Robeson. Perhaps fortunately she did not wear what she called her nigger-brown and coral 'rig-out'. This consisted of a 'costume', with matching hat and shoes in the same fashionable shade of nigger, 'accessoried', as BBC commentators now say at Ascot, with coral gloves and hand-bag.

She was genuinely admiring and in awe of this great Blakean figure, but possibly wondering why he wasn't clad in one of Lord Sandy's left-over leopard skins. Eventually, at the main course, she spoke up in her most strangled, ingratiating-the-headwaiter voice: 'Oh, Mr Robinson. It's such an honour for us to meet you.' Mr Robinson beamed kindly. 'My son is such an admirer of yours. You see . . .' She looked around the restaurant, then said with deferential confidence, 'You see, Mr Robinson, he's always been very *sorry* for you darkies.' The smile never left his eyes.

In those days, innocent of racial policing, cheerfulness did have a way of breaking in. Perhaps I should have tried her on a Hampstead Hostess, if I had known one then.

THE LITERARY MANAGER — known as a Play Reader and paid thirty bob a week when I did it and took home fifty scripts a night; now £10 per script, or £2 a minute — at the Royal Court Theatre told me not so long ago that she had in her possession 100 plays, all produceable, by women writers. Michael Hastings, the male playwright, publicly attacked Sir Peter Hall with possession but not production of twenty such feminist works. Sir Peter promptly burst into tears. Where are all these works, the size of the century's entire dramatic output? What became of these treasures? Buried in a sexist vault?

'WHO WOULD YOU Rather Sleep With' is not the title of a Ray Cooney farce but an ideal game Tony Richardson and I have enjoyed since our earliest Royal Court days. I hate 'games' but I find this one agreeably trivial, even soothing. Historical change and the caprice of fashion cannot affect its simple appeal, enlivening the most right royal traffic tailback or fractious railway journey, a diversion from the receding shadows of A-levels in bored or travel-sick young minds. Played strictly to the rule that you *must* reply affirmatively to either choice, it endorses Ken Livingstone's assertion that we are all naturally bisexual.

33

Who would you rather sleep with?
Hilary Clinton or Nigel Dempster?
Peter Hall or Edwina Currie?
Fay Weldon or Salman Rushdie?
Glenys Kinnock or Boy George?
Andrew Neil or Kenny Everett?
Joan Collins or the Bishop of Durham?
Woody Allen or Caryl Churchill?
Gazza or Margaret Beckett?
Ian McCaskill or Ben Elton?

And so on – pastoral, tragical, comical. As the Aussies say, put a paper bag on their heads and think on it as you sweat to the seaside. Only remember, never break faith with bad taste.

Spectator, 13 July 1985

[2]

Plays

Henrik Ibsen, *Hedda Gabler*

I have been fascinated for a long time by *Hedda Gabler*. By this, I don't mean merely the character, but the play itself. For, like most great plays, the apparent central character exists only by the favour of the other characters in the play, however small. I have read the play many times and seen several productions in English, including the lamentable Scandinavian one by Ingmar Bergman.

The first production I saw was that of Glen Byam Shaw, with Peggy Ashcroft as Hedda. I only managed to get into the theatre by convincing my Pakistani lodger that we were, in fact, going into the Hammersmith Palais de Danse to pick up some girls.

Seeing the play then, and having seen it several times since, it seems clear to me, although this may be a glib assumption, that Ibsen did not set out to write one great part for an actress. Again, as in all good plays, all the parts are good and relevant and essential. Take, for instance, the tenacity of Mrs Elvsted. Hedda Gabler cannot begin to cope with it. Hedda is a *victim*. She is not tragic but desperately needs to get the minimal rewards of life.

She is petty, puny, frigid and clearly unable to carry through any relationship.

The last straw is Judge Brack, who uses her, or intends to. She is immediately aware of this situation and compounds it. She is indolently evil and lives off her own fantasies, absorbing from people better than herself.

The idea of being made pregnant – by anyone, even Lövborg – is repellent to her. Her tragedy, if it can be called one, is that of being born *bored* and that is what is fascinating about her in the annals of dramatic literature. The very concept was unique at the time. She is a loser, whereas Mrs Elvsted is an odds-on favourite.

35

The important point about the adaptation and production of the play is very simple: the complexity of the character of Hedda Gabler is richer only if the other characters in the play are also seen to be made as rich as they are.

They are all, by any standards, a pretty shabby lot. Hedda is a born victim but she does have the gift of energy, while Mrs Elvsted is a very cold cookie indeed.

What would happen after the last scene? These speculations are always intriguing but, of course, fruitless. The situation is not nearly as open as that of the end of *A Doll's House*. But Nora is stronger and less distracted and commonplace and unable to create her own timing.

As I see it, Hedda Gabler has her fun at the expense of others. She has a sharp wit but no authentic sense of humour. She is a bourgeois snob and a walking waste of human personality. What, for instance, about her honeymoon? What did she really *do*? Of course, she was bored. But, tied to her timidity, she also *chose* to be bored and I think that outset of the play is the core of her tragedy, if that is what it is. Like many frigid people, her only true feelings are expressed in jealousy, possessiveness and acquisitive yearnings.

For instance, she is completely unable to initiate situations in her life. It seems quite clear, to me anyway, that the Gabler house would be furnished and decorated by Juliana and that the horses would be bought by Tesman himself.

She always has to be the centre of attention, would like to be a great lady and would be bored whatever she did or whatever happened to her. A great, largely misused play.

from *Hedda Gabler: An Adaptation* (1972)

August Strindberg, *The Father*

In July 1988 I was asked by the National Theatre to produce a new English version of *The Father*. My immediate response was to refuse. For one thing, after having worked on an adaptation of *Hedda Gabler* some years before, during a far more fugitive period of my life, I was disinclined.

It seemed to me that adaptations of this kind, often of 'unperformed European masterpieces', were best left to academics and those who have at least a linguistic familiarity with the intricacies and translation puzzles of work originally written in a tongue familiar to few. Besides, apart from the constant appeals of theatrical journalists, hot-foot from the base camps of dramatic literature with their discoveries, these unperformed masterpieces had remained unperformed for one reason. They were, in the words of my old friend George Devine, 'bloody boring', of no interest to anyone except professional theatre critics, desperate for some respite from their one hundred and twenty-third viewing of *As You Like It*. Their livelihood is possibly made more safe or acceptable if a certain cultural cash flow is maintained. Otherwise, even more might begin to doubt the usefulness of their pension-rated calling.

In the case of these two particular, more accessible works, they had most certainly not gone unperformed. Indeed, there are times when Ibsen's play seems rarely out of the general repertory, constantly being seized upon by actresses who complain that the English canon contains a meagre selection of parts 'written for women'. This absurd grumble fell upon eager, rallying ears by the sort of men who like to flatter such ladies by referring reverentially to them as Ms, rather than Miss or the simple old Dame. One wonders how, if this example of a wicked male conspiracy were the case, so many female actors had managed to achieve such huge reputations. How had the likes of Mrs Siddons, Ellen Terry, Bernhardt, Duse, Dames Edith, Sybil and Peggy become so famous, loved and admired? And all in the face of such paucity of material? The range of parts written for women by men didn't seem to sustain the myth of women being systematically ignored or ill-served by playwrights during five centuries. Shakespeare (admittedly constrained by the contemporary use of boys), Congreve, Wilde, Chekhov, Shaw, Coward, to name only a smattering of the First Eleven, seemed to have provided a list of famous opportunities. This did not include the Alpine heights offered to them by the likes of Corneille and Racine, enabling them to boom mad bluster in Gallic glory for a century and a half of rapturous male applause. For various reasons, all the lady writers with time on their hands, Jane Austen, the Brontës, George Eliot, old Auntie Virginia and their successors, seemed to reject conspicuously the public power of the stage in favour of the novel or poetry.

Now, in spite of feverish inducements and campaigning for the last twenty years, no woman playwright seems to have set us on our heels with a revivable vehicle for an actress. They are all, and continue to be, written by, yes, men. Feminism, like socialism, hasn't added much more than the merest pinch of season to the pot of world literature and least of all to drama. Hardly at all, unless you include the works of a considerable army of popular lady dramatists like Enid Bagnold, Esther McCracken, Dodie Smith, Lesley Storm, Mary Hayley Bell, Bridget Boland, Clemence Dane, Ann Jellicoe, Shelagh Delaney and, more recently, Caryl Churchill.

Some may have difficulty in remembering the parts they wrote for women. Still, they all enjoyed their support and admiration in their day. Their appeal to audiences surely disposes of partisan claims of male domination or conspiracy. Earnest liberalism, the shameless eunuch of feminism, had become so pushy and noisome around the sixties and seventies that a moratorium on further productions of, at least, *Hedda*, would have been a relief to even the most rabid enthusiast for our old friend the Neglected Masterpiece.

The Father is altogether a different case. I read the play quickly in an eighty-year-old translation by Edgar Bjökman and N. Erichsen ('Nelly' Erichsen, an object of Shaw's several early, virginal passions). I say 'quickly', because even in this rather crusty version with its stiff Edwardian cadences the sensation was like being pitched headlong from page to page astride an unstoppable beast of pounding dramatic energy. Once mounted, there was no question of getting off, remounting, and putting the brute back on the bit. Although I was in the process of saddling up my own latest entrant for the theatrical stakes, the 'challenge', as ambitious actresses are prone to say about their latest unremarkable enterprise, was irresistible. It was more than a challenge. It seemed to me a special, beholden duty to be honoured. Incorrectly or not, I was convinced that I was uniquely placed by temperament, tradition, similarities of experience and personal style to render the play into a convincing modern English version.

If anyone was to carry the Strindberg torch into the arena, I knew I was destined to be the undisputed chosen runner. I had never felt such proprietary instincts for the work of another playwright, and I was determined that if anyone were to become the keeper of that unpredictable flame the task should be recklessly entrusted to me. I was Strindberg's Man in England. He had been done such grievous disservice in his own land and time and after, I hoped that I could make some petty reparation for his sufferings, vilification and enduring exile.

To my dismay, the casting of the National Theatre revival had already been completed. Most of the actors were unknown to me, as was the director. However, all theatrical enterprises are more or less calculated exercises in compromise, and I felt that the opportunity of acting as Strindberg's guardian was not to be passed over because of my immediate practical reservations or misgivings, particularly because I knew that these were certainly coloured by my remembrance of Wilfred Lawson's legendary performance thirty-five years earlier. Like many of my generation I had been mesmerized by that occasion. Young actors and directors who had been fortunate to witness it were indelibly influenced by its hammering impact. It was to become part of the common currency of cherished theatrical memory, like the first half of Wolfit's Lear, the echoing excesses of Ernest Milton, Peggy Ashcroft's Hedda or more famous landmarks, like Olivier's Richard III. It seemed timid to be hag-ridden by the possibly esoteric shadows of past monuments. Other heroic actors had, after all, brought their undoubted powers to bear on the part, including Redgrave in 1949 and Trevor Howard in 1964.

Almost more surprising than the fact that these three productions seem to have been the only major London revivals in over forty years was that Olivier never took on this role himself, particularly while he was director of the National, when he did indeed most successfully play the lead in *The Dance of Death*. It would have seemed the perfect vehicle for his own famous animal demon. Other tantalizing candidates would have been Richardson, Scofield, Finney in his prime, Denholm Elliott. And so on. You can make your own list.

Anyway, the text remains, I hope, to be restored to a regular place in the popular repertory and, no doubt, possibly improved upon by other hands. Most of all, I hope that Strindberg's reputation will be freshly valued and experienced. It is painfully susceptible to wilful and modish misinterpretation.

Firstly, there is the charge of misogyny, branded large upon his name, to which he is more than ever exposed today by tooth-and-claw feminism, far more insidious and virulent in its accusations than in his own time, and supported by the craven conceits of men, themselves intimidated by the displeasure of liberal mob-ups.

Strindberg's sweeping power of humanist imagination has been adjusted to accommodate the pinched political orthodoxies of the day. This habit of political reductiveness diminishes us rather than him. His posture, and often it is a posture, and sense of rage at women manifestly exists in *The Father*, but to conceive of it as a fundamental condition is to miss the point of his prodigality and art, illuminating nothing. The ferocity of the battle between the Captain and Laura apprehends far more than an isolated account of the battle between the sexes. His constant reversion to lyricism of agonizing power, his astonishing modernism, his sense of the nineteenth century receding and, with it, the disintegration of structures of faith, moral philosophy and accepted notions of romantic love, put him, as the director of this present revival [David Levaux] said to me, 'in the Great and Unreasonable camp of the humanists'.

Often he takes up these unremitting postures of confrontation because it was a way of getting most accurately at the heart of something in all its stark awfulness. His men strike a note of unwelcome battle which puts the fear of benighted godlessness into the ranks of the faint-hearted and pussy-footed. He gives off a shocking smell of a pervasive and longed-for notion of innocence that has been irredeemably replaced by knowledge leading to turbulence, opposition, deception and, finally, a flight to the death. A profoundly religious romantic, he wades up to his ears in opposites of almost neurasthenic proportions and makes assaults on anything and anybody who seeks to threaten his capacity for conquering the world. Such men, such poets, are not to be easily forgotten.

from The Father: An Adaptation (1988)

After Oscar Wilde, *The Picture of Dorian Gray*

The Matter of Dorian Gray and the Staging of It

Why Dorian Gray? And, if so, how? One can certainly hear the questions and even some of the answers at the outset. I shall only attempt here a few answers to the questions and problems raised by dramatizing this work for the stage. First of all, I have called it simply but deliberately 'A Moral Entertainment' because that is what it is. The original is a superb entertainment; notwithstanding all the things that one knows about it and have been said so many times. It is, of course, melodramatic and steeped in the personal but painful yillery-yallery of Wilde himself. One is constantly reminded of some of the flabbiest fat-boys' vainglory of the early fairy stories. Like them, it is also overlarded, full of false patches and almost sublime vulgarity, and overweening in its grasping after an exquisitely splendid absurdity.

I remember reading it as a boy of about eleven, and it went a long way towards dispelling the fatty image of those fairy stories which I had read earlier and which offended a small, ulcerous reticence within me even then. I had always admired overbold gestures in the service of style in writing and in everything else, and I have continued to do so. But the fairy stories were too much for my schoolboy stomach. The voice was plummy and florid, decadent but unexciting, sybaritic but ultimately tasteless and unselective. Naturally, my reaction was not as lucid as this, but I think I was already aware that there are figures in art who dominate an age by the power of their creative personality rather than by the fact of what they actually create. It is obvious, but it is always the obvious that has to be restated, that Wilde, the man, is a much more powerful and significant creation than anything he actually wrote.

It is a proposition he would almost certainly have approved himself. For, while second- or third-rate artists often put their best work into their lives and are more interesting as people, they seldom reach a pitch of perfection which stamps itself permanently on the English consciousness as did Oscar Wilde. He was his own best creation. Good writers are mostly dull dogs. Other writers have made 'legends' part of their lives – one thinks in our times of the Dylan Thomases, the Scott Fitzgeralds, the Brendan Behans, the Hemingways and so on. Certainly, their influence on literature itself may have been more significant and more lasting, but it seems to me that Wilde opened up a free style to a general public who never even saw or heard any of his work. And in a manner itself nearer to the effect on the whole area of the Western sensibility in which the twentieth century has been inhabited – as did Marx or Freud. This may seem sweeping, and no doubt it is. However, almost everything there is to be said about Wilde seems to have been said by somebody (including himself, naturally) and I dare say the same goes for this. It is pursuable but not enough I suspect to do so at any length. It is a semi-proposition, and one may take it or leave it.

The fact remains that *The Picture of Dorian Gray* is not only a remarkable achievement of its time, given all its faults, but the geminal story is an inspired one like, say, that of Jekyll and Hyde. The story itself is what sold out the issues of *Lippincott's* and intrigued its Victorian readers. It is a variation on the Mephistophelean bargain with the devil. But in art ideas are two a penny, as I have repeatedly told Producers, pregnant with outlines, and Writers, heavy with plot, many times.

It is the carrying through of the exercise, the form that an idea takes, which makes it take off rather than languish over a lunch-table, a bar, or the front office. Execution is all, which, as the programmers of Television

Companies never seem to realize, is a very different thing from 'packaging'.

One of the things that has struck me about the original book is its feeling of wilful courage and despair, the two qualities only too clearly embodied in the spirit of Wilde himself. It is an infuriating work, often misleading, sometimes deadly serious when it should be self-mocking, and so on. For example, there was a time some years ago when the ethic of effortless physical beauty might have seemed no more than a camp, tiresomely self-abusing piece of attitudinizing.

But today? What are the things most valued, sought after? Beauty, yes; youth, most certainly. Youth has become, like death, almost a taboo subject. Everyone is not merely afraid of losing it but of even admitting that such a possibility exists. Again, youth is all-important, all-reaching, all-powerful. It is obligatory to be trim, slim, careless. The lines of age on Dorian Gray's portrait are a very modern likeness in all this. Such a bargain with the Devil, which to Victorians seemed bizarre as well as wicked, in that they thought it thwarted nature or attempted to deny the Natural Order, is incipient in our world devoted to energizing, activating, promoting, jetting away. What prolongs active life? Why, a shot of Dorian Grays! Dorian Grays to you, man. Sin may not be the scene any longer. But *evil* is different. You can at least identify it negatively as that thing you don't like, is not to your tastes, conflicts with *your* interests. Of wrath, envy, lust, greed, avarice, pride or sloth, only pride might get a flicker of recognition on the charts. Pride has no place in a property-owning democracy any more than on a mind-blown cloud or among the freedom-killers of unknowing.

So then, we enter into a world which is without a sense of sin but acutely aware of something vague but daily threatening which might even still be called evil; like the present interest in occult sciences and astrology, for instance, it is a world in which the truth of opposites is clear, if not always understood; where duality is usefully all. The only principle is that of ununcertainty. In such a world, the Charles Mansons with their manoeuvrings, killings, bombings, hijackings and growing sophistication of horrors make the mild eccentricities of an Aleister Crowley seem almost spinsterish in their innocence. So far has the liberal ethos had to adjust itself to the idea of contending with, if not recognizing, such sources of evil. As I write this, one of the lame jokes around is that of the new theatrical hazard of an audience, or members of it, at least, being in danger of getting venereal disease from facial or bodily contact with actors.

The same kind of thing goes for the homosexual mobbery of 'gay' movements, with their mags and ads. Indeed the very separatism of sexuality itself has been derided as oppressive and clubbed over its limp head by the remains of Adam's Rib. Years ago, Simone de Beauvoir coined what I thought was a memorable phrase about the menstrual cycle, which she described as the monthly building-up of a nest being torn down. The fragments of that nest are scattered everywhere.

All this may seem a long way from what most people will regard as a piece of *Yellow Book* melodrama. Or, indeed, whether such an enterprise as this dramatization is desirable or has any point at all. Presumably, by this time, someone will have decided one way or the other.

I distrust the method of open analogy as much as anyone but it is not difficult to find paraphrase in the world of the *Pall Mall Gazette*, Wilde, W. T. Stead, Shaw, Dilke, the Oxford Movement, the Pre-Raphaelites and Grosvenor Gallery; of self-help and opium; of laudanum and Fleet Street, of leisurely walks in gardens and dallyings in conservatories with freakouts and happenings.

It is my own belief that the part of Dorian Gray should preferably be played by a woman. As many people know, this was one of the parts cherished by Garbo. Despite, rather than because of this, the very ambiguity would help enormously to defuse the camp or period of the acting style and enable it to be played as straightforwardly, if ironically, as possible. The parallels with the historical consciousness of the last 100 years are, in fact, endless.

Having said as much, I would like to make it clear that the play should be in no way overemphatic in any of these directions. They are merely guidelines.

The set, for example, should be an all-purpose hole-in-the-ground world, reflecting only some of the aspects outside it. It is the world of Dorian Gray, clearly described and envisaged by Wilde himself and also almost pathetic in its dingy vision of the hemp trail that now leaves from the Far East and into Europe and beyond. Not a pretty sight, then or now.

from *The Picture of Dorian Gray: An Adaptation* (1973)

John Osborne, *Look Back in Anger*

May 8th, 1956, is one of the few dates usually quoted in accounts of modern theatrical history, and generally regarded as the commencement, for good or ill, of a tangible change in the climate and direction of the English theatre. It was the first performance of *Look Back in Anger* at the Royal Court Theatre, an occasion I only partially remember, but certainly with more accuracy than those who subsequently claimed to have been present and, if they are to be believed, would have filled the theatre several times over.

The compilers of these histories have deduced all sorts of theories about the consequences of that sparsely attended first night and its social, political and even revolutionary implications. Some of these fanciful inventions are fairly wild, based on speculative and disordered hindsight, but they refuse to be swatted or blown away. And all this has served to draw attention to the piece as an historical phenomenon, while the play itself is passed over under the weight of perpetuated misinterpretation.

People cling stubbornly to their fallacies, particularly those who feel constrained to illuminate or 'explain' the intentions of others who are reckless enough to embark upon an act of original creation. The damage such commentators inflict is difficult to restore, even with the refutation of the most authoritative and authentic performance. I will try then, without much hope, to dispose of the most crass misconceptions about *Look Back in Anger*.

First, I would ask anyone reading the play for the first time to disregard anything they may have heard about it. Reading the text of a play is not easy, especially for those who have little experience of playgoing and, most specially, those who have never worked in the theatre itself. It requires the rare gift of technical insight and, above all, imagination. In forty-five years, I have come across barely half a dozen people who could study a script with the instinct to interpret in their heads as a conductor or musician does when reading a score.

I am often asked by students, expecting me to hand over the 'input' of my past to some examination chore, the impatient question: 'Why did you write *Look back in Anger*?' Why does one wish to breathe, hope for laughter or fall in love? There seems to be an insistent demand for 'motivation' in such things, something concrete and explicable, like an Arts Council grant or the prospect of quick fame. The answer is fairly simple. I was a twenty-five-year-old actor, out of work and separated from my first wife. I had been thinking about the play for a year or more and wrote it over a period of six weeks. The actual writing, as always the most pleasurable and easy part, took a dozen or so days, interrupted halfway through when I went up to Morecambe to play a small part in the local repertory company. Most of the second act was written in a deck-chair on the end of the pier, which inspired one speculator to advance the theory that the original title was *On the Pier at Morecambe*.

Look Back was to insinuate itself into theatrical perceptions, poisonously some might say, but it has survived and no one has yet found an antidote to what may be its principal ingredient – vitality. The other claim I would make for it after all these years is honesty. I tried to write it in a language in which it was possible only to tell the truth. When I began to write plays, it seemed to me then (as it does now) that most writers dissemble. They are not to be trusted. They look for intellectual respect, approbation; they flatter, indulge and offer false and easy comfort.

The pursuit of vibrant language and patent honesty, which I always believed the theatre and the now abandoned liturgy of the Anglican church could accommodate, was my intention from the outset, although I never articulated it to myself. The language which actors were called upon to speak when I first began to work was thin and inexpressive. There seemed to be an acceptance that dramatic language shouldn't get above itself, that it was no more than a supernumerary branch of 'Literature'. The *placement* of the most successful playwrights, Priestley, Coward or Rattigan, was well below the salt of the Novelist or Poet. The scholarly efforts of Eliot or the self-conscious high spirits of Fry added to the confusion, while the purple blarney of poesies by O'Casey and, inexplicably, O'Neill, were admired as attempts to elevate English, the world's most defiant and irrepressible language, into a command it had given up with faint heart under the towering shadow of Shakespeare.

Some had tried and acquitted themselves honourably, Congreve for one, but most – Farquhar, Sheridan, Wilde or Shaw – were Irishmen, a race literally allowed to get away with murder. For a long time there was a prevalent feeling that distinguished men of letters who entered the theatre were slumming. Henry James, who tried persistently to invade this lowly brothel, was spectacularly unsuccessful. Somerset Maugham, on the other hand, appeared to have the trick of it and entertained middle-class audiences for a quarter of a century. As a young actor I did a lot of Maugham – *Lady Frederick*, *The Breadwinner*, *The Circle*, *The Sacred Flame* – and one of the things I discovered was that they were

45

extremely difficult to learn. It is one thing to read a play for pleasure, but quite another to study it for commitment to memory. Maugham's language was dead, elusively inert, wobbly like some synthetic rubber substance. The actor's expression 'D.L.P.' ('dead letter perfect') had an impossible application to Maugham because it didn't really matter about the precedence of words or punctuation. You could approximate with little difference in meaning or nuance.

Slovenly writing invites slovenly performance. Later, more skilful dramatists cannot be presented so wilfully, though actors and directors, God rot them, often do their best, protesting that they don't 'feel' a line. And there still prevails a common assumption that a B Flat or C Minor here or there is no matter except to be left to the improvised hindsight of the interpreter. You can't or shouldn't do it to Pinter, Beckett or, I hope, myself. The notations are indicated for meticulously constructed reasons. The 'ands' and the 'buts' are the map-markings of syntax and truth, not the stammering infelicities of another's haphazard personal selection.

A play is an intricate mechanism, and the whole mesh of its engineering logic can be shattered by a misplaced word or emphasis. The most famous example of a playwright preventing an actor from crashing the gears of his fine-tuned machinery is Noël Coward's reproof of Edith Evans when she insisted on inserting the word 'very' into the line: 'On a [very] clear day you can see Marlow.' Having repeatedly corrected her, he exploded: 'No, Edith. On a clear day you can see Marlow. On a *very* clear day you can see Marlow, and Beaumont, *and* Fletcher.'

Many people made the mistake of claiming that the language of *Look Back in Anger* was naturalistic, whatever that means. The language of 'everyday life' is almost incommunicable for the very good reason that it is restricted, inarticulate, dull and boring, and never more so than today when verbal fluency is regarded as suspect if not downright 'elitist'.

They also missed the point, which may not be obvious on the printed page to the uninitiated reader, that it is a comedy. At the Public Dress Rehearsal on 7 May, the mostly young audience had laughed where I hoped they would, to the dismay of George Devine and Tony Richardson, the directors of the theatre and the play. 'But why are they laughing?' Because it's *funny*, I replied. They were not reassured. I remembered that Chekhov had the same trouble. True, the following evening, there were very few laughs indeed. The First Night audience, if they were conscious, seemed transfixed by a tone of voice that was quite alien to them. They were ill at ease; they had no rules of conduct as to how to respond. The obvious one was to walk out, which some did, but with only a vague idea of why. Boredom and anger may have contributed, but mostly they were adrift, like Eskimos watching a Restoration comedy. A performance of *Look Back* without persistent laughter is like an opera without arias. Indeed, Jimmy Porter's inaccurately named 'tirades' should be approached as arias, and require the most adroit handling, delicacy of delivery, invention and timing. This is no play for amateurs, although they frequently attempt it.

In spite of the attention to the play at the time, amounting to something like crazed tumult, it did not transfer to the West End. The misgivings and private distaste of the presiding managements were unpersuaded. Timidity prevailed over agonized avarice. The one producer prepared to compromise his reputation insisted that all references to bears and squirrels be excised. This, I was told, embarrassed the customers; it made them squirm. Even the play's most quoted supporter, Kenneth Tynan, had described them as 'painful whimsy'. A few years on, whole pages of respectable national newspapers would be devoted to Valentine's Day messages from 'Snuggly Bouffle Bears' to 'Squiggly Whiffly Squirrels', far more nauseous than my own prescient invention. In my profession, the surest road to penury is to be ahead of your time.

It took thirty years for the piece to achieve a production which I found satisfying and fulfilled my intentions, dispelling the misunderstandings which had blurred its impact over the decades. None of the interim revivals had done much to challenge the nonsense about the play being a 'monologue'. It still seemed to induce a benighted myopia. Where there were five clearly defined characters on stage, only one was acknowledged as visible. The conspiracy had it that Jimmy Porter occupies a vacuum, talking without pause to himself alone. His wife, her father, his temporary mistress, his closest friend, contained no reality, no substance, no impact. Porter was an abortive, loutish Hamlet, who has no Gertrude, Claudius, Polonius, Ophelia or even Horatio to distract the eye and ear of those unwillingly gathered to behold his tedious presence.

If I still sound peevishly impatient after all this time with such commonplace incomprehension of the work whose reputation I am doomed to be buried beneath, it is because I am mystified by the myth. Indifference is the most blithely cruel and effective of weaponry. Hamlet is almost devoured by the inefficacy of those who surround him. When Emma Thompson played Alison in Judi Dench's 1989 revival, I tried to explain that it was she, not her husband, who was the most deadly bully.

Her silence and her obdurate withdrawal were impregnable. The ironing-board was not the plaything of her submission, but the bludgeon and shield which were impenetrable to all Jimmy's appeals to desperate oratory.

Kenneth Branagh succeeded in taking the rant out of the part. He tried to take it trippingly on the tongue. I gave him the same advice I have given actors in other plays of mine (often with dire consequences, as in the abysmal revival of *Inadmissible Evidence* at the National Theatre in 1993): 'Let the text surprise you, as if it took you off-balance, and lift you up even further into the battle of defeat and confusion. Take the words *out of the air*.' I said it again to Peter Egan when he was faced with the same technical problems in *Déjàvu* in 1992. He triumphed, but the attempt was lost on those who had a robot Porter forever fixed in their responses. There seems no remedy against the perception that J.P. is a one-man band, addressing himself in a world of shadows. The facts are there on the printed page, but if you are determined that the play is an unrelieved monologue, not even a perusal of the text will dissuade you.

I once described *Look Back* as a 'formal, old-fashioned play'. I should have been wise enough not to fool about with irony. Certainly it is 'formal' in that it follows a simple narrative impetus. Where it was not 'old-fashioned' was in its deployment of, yes, language and in its indifference to the puny constraints which involved conciliating the audience by confirming their prejudices and not mocking their expectations. This was the school of 'the drama's laws, the drama's patrons give', one of Dr Johnson's few nonsensical pronouncements. It was also in the Moss Hart American tradition of slavishly obeying the playgoer's direction instead of the playmaker's; the Dramatist as the conniving servant of his master, the Box Office. 'The audience gets restless, just about here, in the middle of Act Two.' Attention had to be paid.

I have never been a 'popular' writer. Nothing I have ever done has had a London run of more than six months. However, I think that *Look Back* has had some influence, if only in the sense of arousing powerful feelings, hostile or resentful though they may have been. And what *did* happen after 1956 was that attention was no longer necessarily paid. The writer could renounce the obligation to bear the chains of approbation, although there are still plenty left hovering to kiss them.

But that is enough of refutation. Somewhere in the world the play is performed every night. People are bemused, dismayed or, I hope, exhilarated by it and driven to laughter. There have been homosexual and black versions. The lesbian angle must surely be to come. Misogyny is attached to it forever, and the American–Freudian view of Jimmy and Cliff as lovers is still irresistible to academics and feminists alike. It's an old war horse that has paid my rent for a lifetime, and seems able to bear the burden of whatever caparison is placed upon its laden back.

from *Collected Plays Volume 1:* Look Back in Anger *and Other Plays* (1993)

Dear Diary . . .
===

I HAVE A possibly dubious tip which may be useful to anyone enduring hospital menus. Recently sprung from Intensive Care, I remembered Somerset Maugham's advice that the only guarantee of eating decently in England was to consume three breakfasts daily. Hospital food, of course, mugs all description, violated by bland dietitians and working-class cooking. But breakfast, on the whole, defeated their ingenious dislike of quite decent materials provided by a proper butcher and wet fishmonger. The poached eggs were pale pink and flowered open, Ritz-like, at the first incision. The grilled bacon was cured locally; cornflakes or grapefruit, wholemeal toast, Hotel Convention marmalade and drinkable coffee. Like British Rail on a good day. I was elated at my too simple discovery. Ditch lunch and dinner and go for three breakfasts.

For two days I got it. Everyone was astonished and even discomfited by this eccentricity. Nurses from other wards visited me in secret, curious and giggling. Was it really true that I didn't want lunch or dinner? 'We've never had any complaints before.' I explained that I wasn't complaining, just exercising a whim. True, it became boring by the third day but it provided a refuge from the hourly dread of what the lid on the sick tray will reveal next.

It's worth a try, before some NUPE nark decides to put a stop to your subversive attitude to the cultural eating rights of workers.

'THEY ARE SCUM,' was also Maugham's verdict on the class of state-aided university students represented in the early fifties by Lucky Jim and his like. Since the eruption of the Heysel Stadium, the effect has been like the aftermath of the Lisbon earthquake with philosophers, politicians and clerics uncertain where to apportion the blame. If only there were a black box which could be recovered and examined to establish where the nation's flight went wrong. What would Maugham have thought of the New Scum palpably responsible?

First, schoolteachers, progressive and dominant. The schoolteacher is certainly underpaid as a childminder but ludicrously overpaid as an educator. Teaching, in Maugham's time an escape route for intelligent proles denied access to university and the more esteemed professions, is now a bolt-hole for those who have failed to make it in the media, advertising or ICI. The PT (Progressive Teacher) is an inadequate who, whatever facts he may have accumulated in his 'specialism' (a beloved word of his, like 'Texts' and 'Scripts', by which he means books and answer papers), will almost certainly be as semi-literate as a football manager. Failed in the 'real world' of company cars and expense accounts, he flashes his *professional* status and third-class degree like a stadium Neanderthal's tattooed arm. PT also prides himself on his 'radical' approach, the introduction of Black and Political Studies, courses that confound reactionary notions of 'learning' and substitute all-purpose sloganteach, polished and perfected in the Sociology Department of North Eastern Polytechnic.

PT so abhors 'value judgments' attributed to what he quaintly regards as still the Establishment (of which he is now a bastion) imprinting its values on the young that he abandons all critical standards. The thought of presenting Mozart as 'superior' to David Bowie is unthinkable, even if he knew the group's name in which Amadeus played. His total inability to control a class is an exercise in 'progressive methods' and 'free expression'.

Devoutly anti-authoritarian, he makes virtues out of his inadequacies so that each time a child treats him with total contempt, he claims this as one more expression of the 'rapport' he has established with his pupils and the 'positive' aspects of their relationship. He is not discouraged to use or be abused by four-letter words in class because this would be 'inhibiting' and a 'denial' of working-class culture, black culture or Leon Trotsky. The generally appalling standard of work is proof that his charges are 'enjoying' the 'learning process', a technical term for lounging about, feet on desks, and spitting. In fact, the dedicated PT is so eager to identify with his pupils that he will take on their mode of dress from their earstuds to the Dr Martin boots, their accents, tastes in music, the *Sun* and 'streetwise philosophy'. The key word is 'enjoying', everything from graffiti to raping the domestic-science mistress. Indubitably Scum.

SCUM PRODUCTIONS excelled last weekend with the Live Aid concert, devised by 'Saint' Bob of the Boomtown Rats, who is nominated for the Nobel Peace Prize by the Member for Bradford South. Mr Geldof may well be on the royal road of preferment that through 'charity' leads to knighthoods and beyond. A generation of self-besotted yoof that can be gulled by such dismal stuff deserves the fine mess they've gotten us into.

A SIMILAR GOLDEN SCUM AWARD must go to Nancy Reagan embracing the prone President at the operating theatre door. 'I love you,' were the last words from the First Lady's lips close to his shell-like. Lady Dorothy never carried on in public like this to Harold.

I HAVE BEEN reading the recent biography of Tennessee Williams, *The Kindness of Strangers*, by Donald Spoto. I didn't know Williams well but spent some very agreeable hours with him, once in the company of Brendan Behan in his last New York days. (Another sweet-natured man but almost comically alien to Tennessee, who became quickly bored by a barrage of Irish and Colonial Boy songs.) He had the most intriguing rasp of a giggle which could strike an irreverent and rattlesnake blow, particularly on famous actors' entrances and exits.

At supper in Sardi's, I watched a Very Warm Human Being come over to his table and address him warmly, and loudly. 'Mr Tennessee Williams?' The playwright looked up defensively. 'My wife, Hortense, and I have just been to a performance of your latest play, *Period of Adjustment*.' (Not one of his best but certainly not insubstantial.) 'I have to tell you, Mr Williams, that we thought it just great. Truly great. Congratulations, sir. May I shake you by the hand?' And so, meaningfully on. Tennessee smiled a Southern Belle's shy, courteous smile.

'Now your last play, and I just hate to say this,' boomed VWHB, 'Your last play was just *awful*. We really *hated* that. Just awful.'

Tennessee, blood draining from him, spat at his long-time companion, Frank Merlo, a fearsome Sicilian. '*Hit* him, Frank!' he shrieked. 'Hit him. For God's sake.' The creator of an evening's warm, human experience was chattering with pain and outrage, while the grateful recipient of this bounty returned to Hortense, baffled by such ingrate bad manners. It happens all the time.

Spectator, 20 July 1985

[3]

Playwrights

==

Bernard Shaw

Pecking Order

Sir – Michael Billington cannot have read the plays of George Bernard Shaw since his Oxford days. To call him 'the greatest British dramatist since Shakespeare' (20 June) is close to having a critical brainstorm, as well as perpetulating an exam-crazy classroom myth. Having recently seen *St Joan* in London and *Caesar and Cleopatra* in Sydney, it is clearer to me than ever that Shaw is the most fraudulent, inept writer of Victorian melodramas ever to gull a timid critic or fool a dull public.

He writes like a Pakistani who has learned English when he was twelve years old in order to become a chartered accountant.

From childhood I have read these plays, watched them, indeed toured as an actor and stage manager in them on one-night stands. Apart from this experience, any fair decent writer I know could put his finger on the crass, vulgar drivel in any of them.

Simply read the stage directions of *Candida* (opening this week). I had the misery of once playing Marchbanks in this ineffably feeble piece. This is Shaw's idea of a 'poet' (having no poetry in *him* at all). The Poet, a ghastly little cissy, is bullied interminably by an idiot Muscular Christian Socialist who, in turn, is mothered by an insufferably patronizing bully of a woman. As a ten-minute sketch on BBC2 in 1898 from South Shields it would do. But as a full-length stage play it is hard to think of anything more silly, apart from the rest of the so-called 'oeuvre'.

The one possible exception is *Pygmalion*, in which I toured the Welsh valleys in 1954 for the Arts Council. But the miners were still better than the play. I, however, was very funny as Freddy Eynesford Hill, which does go to prove that you can't make bricks entirely without straw – something play-reviewers can never grasp about plays or actors.

But 'the greatest British dramatist since Shakespeare (?)'. Ben Travers could have had G.B.S. before breakfast in Australia watching the Test.

By the time I was twenty-five I had been in admittedly bad, but no matter, productions of: *Arms and the Man, Candida, You Never Can Tell, The Devil's Disciple, Caesar and Cleopatra, Saint Joan, Major Barbara* and, perhaps worst of all, Chekhov-for-philistines, *Heartbreak House.*

Try *learning* them. Mr Billington; they are posturing wind and rubbish. In fact, just the sort of play you would expect a critic to write. The difference is simply: he did it. – Yours faithfully,

John Osborne

Guardian, 23 June 1977

Type casting

In July 1977 Gay News *and its editor were found guilty of blasphemous libel for publishing a poem by James Kirkup in which the crucified Christ was depicted as having homosexual feelings.*

Sir – I was engaged the other day in a friendly correspondence about the merits of George Bernard Shaw as a dramatist. A lot of good-natured banter ensued. Particularly after I had given some chapter and verse to make a point about Shaw's total lack of poetry as a writer. I cited Marchbanks, the poet in *Candida.* I wrote:

– I had the misery of once playing Marchbanks in this ineffably feeble piece. This is Shaw's idea of a 'poet' (having no poetry in *him* at all). The Poet, a ghastly little cissy, is bullied interminably by an idiot Muscular Christian Socialist who, in turn, is mothered by an insufferably patronizing bully of a woman.

Now I read part of Professor Kirkup's statement:

– I heard the grisly, gory details of the Crucifixion for the first time at Sunday School at the age of five. I was so overcome by revulsion and fright that I fainted with the shock of those gruesome, violent images. When I heard of the fires of hell and the torments of the damned my horror expressed itself in outbursts of uncontrollable giggles, my knees shook and I wet the floor.

What perfect casting Professor Kirkup would have made for Shaw's ungifted, cowardly, posturing 'ghastly little cissy'.

Yours very truly,

John Osborne

The Times, 22 July 1977

Michael Holroyd, *Bernard Shaw: Volume 1: The Search for Love*

Like the Victorians, the English lower orders continue to discourage ambition in their sons. The Scots, Welsh and Irish, with their simple faith in erudition, are a different case. The English to this day cling fiercely to membership of the gutter, insisting only more implacably that it be made cosier: a high-tech slum-heaven enlivened by annual trips to the sunny slum-resorts, created and custom-built for their unchanging tastes and prejudices. Celts regard self-improvement as a natural moral imperative. To the English, it looms like the vampire threat of garlic-eating, having dinner at night or being dragged from Cilla Black to Maria Callas. Literature and drama, from D. H. Lawrence to Dennis Potter, is strewn with examples of working-class boys who have striven to escape the bookless, pictureless cells of three-piece suites, where any attempted rejection of the torpor of the working and lower depths is viewed as a heartless presumption and betrayal of family and class. Getting Above Yourself is not a commendable shift to possibly enviable vantage but a treacherous folly, going over to the enemy and repudiation of decent, working people's sacred inertia.

Such ingrates are given short, unforgiving shrift. When my paternal grandmother heard unavoidably that, at the age of twenty-seven, I had two plays running concurrently on Broadway, she made it bitterly plain that it was a humiliating exhibition of my failure even to hope to become an assistant branch manager of Lloyd's Bank. Only my maternal grandfather, himself a failed class renegade, ever encouraged me to nip over the wall to a more favoured world. In his Fulham back parlour, reciting from the Bible, *News of the World*, and the *Watchtower*, he would bellow at me, 'You *see*, Sonny, you mark my bloody words. You'll end up one of two things: Prime Minister of Bloody England or George Bloody Bernard Shaw.'

I didn't know then that Sonny was Shaw's childhood nickname. It would have been about as helpful as grandad's hectoring bombast. Nor, indeed, did I know it until I read *The Search For Love*, the first volume of Michael Holroyd's superb, Freud-free and moving biography. This is an enthralling account of self-improvement on a scale of grandeur, and executed in the style this huge endeavour demands.

Mr Holroyd is a relaxed, wary, unassertive analyst, gently correcting Shaw's own self-accounting and assessments without ever dismissing or destroying them in dissection. He grasps his subject below the head in a tender vice. Like a soothing snake-handler, he grips this sidewinding, slippery streak of paradox and holds him aloft, untamed, trapped or diminished in critical presumptions.

These flashlight glimpses are no less moving or instructive for being presented so easily and stylishly, one upon the other. It is a masterly exercise in biographical magic, like a conjuring performance, demonstrated dexterously and unassumingly to a serious purpose, some Orson Welles presentation of word and wizardry. The method, for all its fluent grace and cunning, pursues not illusion but, triumphantly, powerful and chastening illumination.

Under the glare of Holroyd's magic show, what always seemed to me examples of Shavian banalities and chilly posturing reveal themselves as the weapons of a lifelong struggle against loneliness and imperfection, of heroic persistence and courage. Despair, which seemed inimical to Shaw, begins to reveal itself as the power injecting an otherwise dotty fancy, the Life Force. If this was a systematic campaign of self-help from childhood to the grave, it owed nothing to the smarmy Samuel Smiling school of endeavour but to the Promethean flights of the will, pursued in Christian mildness by Bunyan and Blake, then by the man-in-the-street's heroic longings of Carlyle, to the obliterating finalities of Nietzsche himself.

The Victorians had a lot of time for the will, though, as we have seen, a little of it does go a long way. But Shaw, with his ineffable kindness and good sense, was an imperfect Wagnerite in performance. The range of his fantasies was jauntily contained in his British Museum kind of Marx-trained, frock-coated, silk-hatted socialism. His voracious gifts riding gunshot on whirling tumbrels of intellectual fantasy induce constant and severe attacks of old-fashioned brain fag just to read about. The frenzy, discipline and rapaciousness Shaw embodied personally in the climate of late-Victorian, post-Darwin ferment – inspiring, eccentric and valiant as they often are – make our present ill-natured clamour and supine morality masquerading as compassion seem almost tolerable by comparison.

In spite of my grandfather's gratifying endorsements, I always disliked Shaw's plays intensely. They produced the same feelings in me as Gilbert and Sullivan: a parade of Victorian front-parlour frolicking, thin, amateurish and depressing recitals of claustrophobic archness. They pandered slavishly to the feeble middle-class notion of 'laughing at themselves', a form of theatrical charity virtuously dispensed to clowns posing as insurrectionist dreamers.

Shaw, of course, played up to this applause like the court dwarf who's fallen into a tureen of malmsey. As a schoolboy I went through the complete Penguin edition, looking for the formula that would clinch grandad's prophecy. Like many people, I found the plays a bewildering disappointment after the prefaces, like the one to *Androcles and the Lion*, twice as long as the play and twenty times less tedious. As a young actor, I found myself in half a dozen of them, playing among others, Shaw's idea of a poet, the cissified, moony Marchbanks, and the insufferable lady almoner, Candida. I was rebuked, not for critical judgement, but racism, presumably by *Guardian* readers for suggesting that his post-Sardoudledom style resembled English as written by Pakistanis studying for accountancy exams.

Only once did I feel that there was a missing Shavian key, the massive anchor which Mr Holroyd now so magnificently salvages. It was during a fit-up tour in the Welsh valleys when I was playing, with huge success, Freddy Eynsford Hill in Shaw's one undoubted masterpiece, *Pygmalion*. Every night I found myself compelled to watch Eliza throwing Higgins's slippers at him in the scene after her triumph at the ball. It always moved me, and now I see that maybe for a few moments I had detected the unuttered howl of a searching love. In that search for love, he turned inexorably to socialism, which is a little in the manner of Cranmer turning to *The Good News Bible*.

The book touches the furthest boundaries of biography as a historical memoir of the years 1856–1898 in its unfolding of the details of Shaw's life: his Anglo-Irish middle-class poverty, his lively and eccentric relations, the mesmeric Vandeleur Lee, apex of the Shaw ménage and the model for du Maurier's Svengali; the passionate complexities leading up to his *mariage blanc*, which was perhaps fitting to a life some might consider a vocational *vie blanche*. Then, of course, there was Lucinda, his mother. Mothers can be a lot of trouble, perhaps especially for playwrights, Jewish or Gentile, and Sonny drew a poor hand on Mother's Day. Lucinda neither admired nor reviled him. She was merely indifferent to him. To his parents, 'I was just something that happened to them.' Some sons do 'ave 'em.

The section on Shaw's friendship with the critic William Archer is one of many, to me, astonishing revelations. 'Both', says Holroyd, 'had made one awful error. Shaw in writing plays, and Archer in not writing plays.' Archer 'saw through Shaw's optimism; he did not see Shaw's need for optimism.'

Archer, as a devoted friend, was very sharp about Shaw's deficiencies as a playwright. He believed that his suspension in fantasy, sliding 'along a slice of invisible air', would forever limit both his appeal and his influence. Holroyd adds, 'He would never get a ducking. His audiences might not be able to ignore him, but, resenting his superiority, they were resolved never to take him seriously. He was a light creature.' 'He does not live in the real world,' observed Archer.

'His prose reeks of certainty,' writes Mr Holroyd in one of his many crisp felicities. It was the certainty of an unloved heart, enabling him to believe an artist must love his work more than people.

Encircled as we are today by a new Cromwellian army of prigs, when cupidity passes for 'concern', it is a relief to be reminded of the G.B.S. trick of being Puritan but not Prig. Scarred by the spectacle of his father's pitiable excesses and so driven to a lifelong teetotalism, he informed an outraged Temperance movement that tea was more harmful than beer. A Roundhead all right, but topped off by, yes, one's forced to it, cap and bells.

Spectator, 24 September 1988

Noël Coward

The Noël Coward Diaries, ed. Graham Payn and Sheridan Morley

I drove away to Dickie's [Lord Mountbatten] and Edwina's house in Chester Street, where the King and Queen were. I sat next to the Queen at supper. It was all very family: only the King and Queen, Princess Margaret, all the Mountbattens and me. We talked about many things, from the Labour Government to E. Nesbit. The King was gay and relaxed. After dinner I sang a few songs. It was all very lovely and I felt most proud to be there. [1947]

I deplore the lack of style and elegance in most modern plays. I long for the glamour of great stars who used to drive up to the stage door in huge limousines. In my younger days I was tremendously keen to be a star and famous and successful. Well, I have been successful for most of my life, and if at this late stage I were to have another series of resounding failures, I believe I could regard them with a certain equanimity. [1959]

I have a Ritz mind and always have had. [1960]

A vast and violent fire broke out in Beverly Hills and frizzled up a great many houses both gracious and ungracious, including those of poor Zsa Zsa Gabor, Burt Lancaster, Walter Wagner, etc., all of which goes to prove that God's in his heaven and not just sitting there either. He's *doing* something. [1961]

Cole [Porter] and I had a long cosy talk about death ... We discussed what would happen if I died and what would happen if he died, and we came to the sensible conclusion that there was nothing to be done. We should have to get on with life until our turn came. I said, 'After all the day had to go on and breakfast had to be eaten,' and he replied that if I died he might find it a little difficult to eat breakfast but would probably be peckish by lunchtime. Well, enough of that. The Queen is in Ghana. Princess Margaret is presumably nursing her baby and as happy as a bee. [1961]

I have been quoting from these diaries for three weeks, to an insolent, cowering wife and baffled, jeering friends. I first met The Master in 1959. Tony Richardson, the stage and film director, rang me from Nottingham, where Coward's *Look After Lulu* had opened before coming into London's Royal Court. Mischievous, hectoring, he pleaded: 'I *mean*, you've got to come up. Noël's *determined* to be WITTY. All the time.' I did go, saw what he meant immediately, but didn't fail to be somewhat transfixed.

It is impossible for outsiders to realize what ill feeling, bile and even wayward hatred existed in those days among those who practised my trade. Reading these diaries confirms, often ludicrously, what I merely suspected. Fear and puny malice abound. Sheer camp silliness and grandiose self-deception prevail over every page. And yet the blithe, overblown posturings and evasions, the often successful striving after style, the amazingly naïve parody take over, movingly sometimes, and establish themselves unmistakably as genuine and *lived* history. A night's frivolity in Philadelphia can seem more becoming and momentous than a week in Westminster or Washington.

About seven years later Coward and I had supper – *à deux*, as he would most certainly have said – in London's Chesham Place. My anxiety to observe good manners was foiled by a fatal lapse of a few minutes' tardiness, and I was immediately subjected to a light finger-wagging about my personal and sexual life over a very, very light omelette.

I had expected an onslaught on my professional ineptitude and a jolly old tongue-lashing about the damage I and others of my ilk had done to the English Theatre and life generally. But I was unprepared for the calculated tactic that The Master had prepared. Shrewdness and low instinct led him to instant shrewish catechizing. It was a wretched, nerve-failing period of my life, and he pounded on it with unerring irrelevance.

His second or perhaps third question was 'How queer are you?' A baffled depression overcame me as I felt that both of us deserved better than this. 'How queer are you?' The fatuous game was afoot, and I played it feebly. 'Oh, about 30 per cent.' 'Really?' he rapped back. 'I'm 95.' That was it.

'Never, never trust a woman,' he went on. 'But most of your friends have been women,' I said. 'Never mind. Don't, *don't* trust 'em. Above all, never marry 'em. You've been a very silly, silly boy.'

I had almost – yes, I *had* forgotten – the waning tyranny of the theatrical producer Hugh 'Binkie' Beaumont and his like, no more now than a footnote in theatrical history, but powerful, pushy and lilac-ruthless in his day. Noël himself was in thrall to this irredeemably boring, tasteless, calculating buffoon. The last time I saw them together Binkie had his face in the fireplace, and his tail in the air, having abused me aimlessly for several hours. As I left, Noël said, 'What a disastrous evening!' It was indeed an offensive occasion and a blasphemy against all the felicities that Coward held dear – in manners, hospitality and good humour.

It is difficult to be clear or honest about these diaries without seeming sanctimonious. The tone incites priggishness, and Noël himself has a dominating line in governessy stricture that is, all and entire, his own, imposing the constant spinsterish ethic of Rising Above It. He challenges heterosexuality as a failure of style – implicit in his question to me – yet his feelings about the grossness of Fire Island queens or those 'miserable little tarts', Christine Keeler and Mandy Rice-Davies, of the

Profumo scandal, are passionate in their contempt.

Almost by accident Noël survived what he and Binkiedom saw as the onrush of squalour and despair and the end of 'riotous glamour'. Like Coriolanus he was author of himself and knew no other kin. The twentieth century would be – I can only parody him – quite, quite incomplete without him.

He affected to despise most of the writers in the world. See him on Proust, Greene, Dickens, Pinter ('a sort of Cockney Ivy Compton-Burnett'). *Three Sisters* 'always rather a tiresome play'. *Lear* 'far, far too long'. Strauss, Verdi, Shakespeare all far, far too long. Most of all he vented himself on Oscar Wilde. Noël would never have given himself away under cross-examination. 'Did you kiss the boy?' He would never have said, 'No, he was far too plain.' He would never have given away the world for a witty answer.

However, he was a genius.

You Can't Help Liking Him. There'll Never Be Another. There Never Was. Self-deluded, reviled by an envious and eternally crass British press, he was a consummate Royal clown, poetaster, author of three of the best comedies in the English language – *Hay Fever, Private Lives* and *Blithe Spirit* – who also penned five of the finest lyrics to be read rather than spoken – 'Mad Dogs and Englishmen' and, cream of them all, 'There Are Bad Times Just Around the Corner.'

Merry as a grig. Fooled as he was by starry dullards, he may well have been merry. It seems so, in spite of the baffled tone of later years, when his plays were so often poorly received. Self-invention may have disabled him, but curiosity never deserted his talent, that deluding ethic which transported him. Noël's diaries reveal his taste to be often shrewd and ineffably bad, as he would have had it. They are far, far too long but inescapable and potent, like his own cheap music.

New York Times Book Review, 3 October 1982

Noël Coward, *Autobiography*

It would be a most fanciful spirit that could imagine Noël Coward at prayer. But then the spectacle of the Prime Minister on her knees or even a sharp, briefcase Methodist like Mr Paul Boateng would be equally unseemly. Humility becomes none of them. The Master delighted in a lifetime of unholy clowning for the likes of kings and assorted queens, but the prospect of his singing for a Last Supper would have reduced him to giggling embarrassment and it is a tribute to his nannyish courage as well as his obstinate and myopic timidity that it should seem so. Confronted with the Ascension, his only response could be to rise above it.

Reading through 500 pages of his three volumes of autobiography (*Present Indicative, Future Indefinite* and the uncompleted *Past Conditional*, with an introduction by Sheridan Morley), now collected together, it is hard not to return a little gratefully to Cyril Connolly's verdict on the first volume: 'Almost always shallow and often dull ... What are we left with? The picture, carefully incomplete, of a success; probably of one of the most talented and prodigiously successful people the world has ever known.'

This is generous and accurate. But the words 'carefully incomplete' contain the meat of it. Autobiography is necessarily incomplete, as selective as any other form of fiction or drama. However, it is the clamped rigidity of its evasion that makes Mr Morley's claim for these volumes as being 'one of the greatest autobiographies ever written about a life dedicated from an early age to the theatre' as patently flighty as Coward's perceptions of his own achievements.

Connolly, a more troubled critic than Coward's fulsome editor and disciples, continues: 'He is not religious, politics bore him, art means facility or else brickbats, love wild excitement and the nervous breakdown. There is only success, more and more of it . . .'

Well, critics, alas, die too soon to be force-fed into vomiting on their own unwholesome words. Intellectuals get most things all wrong about recognizable human behaviour and frailty, but in this case Connolly got it just about all right. Though not quite. Success is *not* all there was, but it was The Master's voice, as he recorded it himself, that made all duller dogs believe it. We know also that the bequest of some of his plays and his finest lyrics is not a temporary gift to the nation but a unique and abiding one. He did indeed invent himself, but these autobiographies confirm rather than disown the fact that it is inspired invention, facility (as Connolly rightly spotted), that enlivens them rather than any passing concern for frankness. Self-invention, even of a very high order, is not the same thing as life itself, adventurously and tortuously lived, and without recourse to an existence of day and night dissembling.

As Morley acknowledges, the books are barricaded behind the barrier of the then prevailing theatrical love that mercifully dared not speak its name and which now cannot be restrained from shrieking itself silly.

These self-deceiving gestures of freedom would have been most abhor-rent to Coward's inbred, fastidious caution. It is hard not to hear his voice pleading from the grave for everyone to just jolly well shut up and get on with the whole absurd and quite maddening thing we all call living until we drop down hilariously and finally dead. The homosexual appetite for love is usually predatory, evasive and, at its most treacher-ous, as approachable and malign as a cat caught with a sparrow in its mouth. All this is scarcely glimpsed and can only be guessed at in these pages. The moggie life, notwithstanding Morley's sales-manager's talk, remains concealed in the undergrowth, beneath the shadow of invention and pretence.

Present Indicative is almost maidenly arch about its baby-on-the-hearthrug author and the tone as vainglorious and sentimental as any modern belt-and-braces radical playwright's, although it is good on the vanished days of the boy juvenile and prodigal. This first volume is particularly marred by containing more than anyone not stricken with Mander and Mitchenson's disease could want to know about provincial tours, casting sessions and long-gone unremembered names. The unrelenting show of very shifty self-analysis, the self-addressed confiden-ces, the mostly successful pursuit of adulation from actresses and friends cloys and deadens both curiosity and sympathy. A pretty foot becomes a giant ingrown toenail of monstrous insubsequentiality. All this, with its closet peepshows of Jacks, Jeffs and Davids, on boats, beaches and the boys-in-waiting at Goldenhurst, is more palatable and amusing in Mor-ley's own edition of the Diaries and, in my opinion, Cole Lesley's excel-lent 1976 *Life*.

It should not be forgotten that Coward, whose love correctly dared not speak its name, proclaimed his love for the theatre in his every breath, giving it a very bad name indeed. That reputation has been painfully lived down until it is now descending the slope of seriousness into the solemn-ity and preposterousness of plays about the idiotic phantoms of sexism, racism and any populist intellectual rot you care to put a fancy-boy's name to. The Master's ghostly ho-hoing at one's agony under the lash of ill-politicized playmaking and paltry sedition does indeed make one parched for frivolity and downright inconsequence.

But in the midst of all this present, overbearing dullness, it should not be forgotten that Coward and H. M. Tennent and the entire Lilac Establishment of Shaftesbury Avenue were as ruthless in their determina-tion to deny a hearing to their opponents as any Polytechnic loonigan today. That part of the story can only be inferred from this account of the British theatre and is quite unknown to most. Before one is tempted to succumb to despair and cry, 'Come back, Binkie, put a blessed torch to the Royal Court,' that story should be first told.

Sheridan Morley has certain access to archives probably denied to those of us who might appear in them. If the name 'Binkie' raises an eyebrow, he could surely fill us in, if only partially. It was Binkie, the big impresario and small-time Judas, who once said to me with naked ingratiation, 'The trouble with Noël is, he's so terribly uneducated.' Morley would be more usefully employed to students of theatrical history pursuing the elusive mask of Binkie than his projected Olivier 'dig'.

Tatler, June 1986

Clive Fisher, *Noël Coward*

There is a quotation in this book which, quite literally, stopped my breath with dread identification. It is from a letter, written in 1935 from Noël Coward's loyal secretary, Lorn Loraine, to his mother:

> We have got to go very, very easy on money and economize rigidly wherever it is possible. Mind you, I am pretty sure the shortage is only temporary and would never have arisen if it were not for the fact that all Noël's personal earnings have to go into a special tax account as soon as they are received. Still, the fact remains that money is definitely tight and has been for some months. Both bank accounts have overdrafts and there is very little coming in just now.

'There is very little coming in.' How often have I myself been subjected to this gleeful accountant's verdict. The author of this dull and artless biography adds his own jeering stricture:

> Unfortunately, these reversals in prosperity [the poor devil was as good as broke] coincided with a lean period of creativity. There was no drop in the quantity of work Coward produced in the middle and late Thirties, but there is a fall in its level of invention.

A familiar tone of voice, and one that was addressed to me directly the other day when a man at lunch asked me what I did for a living. Usually, I say 'writer'. 'Playwright' sounds rather presumptuous, like calling yourself a poet. Then he asked my name. Perhaps I should have equivocated and said Noël Coward or David Hare, but I owned up. 'Oh yes,' he said, with all the dislike and distrust my odd profession inspires. 'You've just had a *comeback* haven't you?'

Coward was a working-dog of his calling as actor and writer all his life. By the end of a retrieved career in cabinet he was also, in the unkind words of an American tabloid, 'the highest paid British tulip ever imported into the United States'. It may seem that he had achieved the most enviable life, doing all the things he wanted with minimal effort, hopping on and off steamships as he pleased. But behind it all there lay prodigious effort, and the rewards often seem rather meagre. After a lifetime of what young men today would regard as masochistic drudgery, he was still unable to earn enough to appease the Inland Revenue and assure himself of some reward and comfort in a rather cruelly induced old age.

The reminder of the master of self-invention, limping finally off to a forwarding address in Switzerland with the consolation of a last-minute knighthood confirms the impression of a rather inelegant exit from the world's stage of his own creation. No wonder he was perhaps over-effusive in his gratitude to America:

> My own dear land which for years has robbed me of most of my earnings, withheld all official honours from me and . . . frequently, made me very unhappy.

The predominantly lower-middle-class English press could never restrain their spite against someone who must surely be of their own kind (from Twickenham, for God's sake), who had sustained a legend about himself and whatever such hacks think are the rewards of fame – ill-imagined debauchery, I suppose. But Coward's physical appetites were constrained by a thirst for work. He lived on chocolate and cigarettes. No gluttony there. As for sex, Mr Fisher's book promises revelations which simply don't exist, and for very good reason. Old Noël, whatever his protestations about 'being no good at love', was too busy and self-preoccupied to *be* any good at it.

There simply isn't much left to be said about Coward, as this slovenly and pointless rehash confirms. (Although I did learn that he wanted to play Madam Arcati himself and that the Blithe Spirit of Elvira was named after Binkie Beaumont's housekeeper, the one who denounced my social promotion so roundly, when it was suggested I might move to Lord North Street, with the words, 'No, 'e's not ready for it yet.' She was right.)

I had thought that Fisher or someone might come up with some insights about the nature of homosexual deceit and dissembling, but that now seems too much to expect. Coward's spirit of evasion is, at the last, impenetrable. Concealment was first nature to him and, most of all, he lacked any sense of awe, except at the prospect of his own next achievement. 'It's my best, it has "smash hit" written all over it,' he wrote to Beaumont, his treacherous ally. Such a statement, on any terms, seems incomprehensible, no, meaningless.

As to my own feelings about him, I find that they have changed. For a long time I thought I had perhaps behaved churlishly and with not much lustre or imagination in the face of his own generosity to me. Then last year I came upon the telegram he sent to me from Switzerland: 'I LOVE YOU – NÖEL'. What may have prompted it, I can't remember, but I was strangely astonished by its very lack of either implication or obligation.

We had many things in common: social backgrounds, more or less; professional progress; even the same slugging out with the Lord Chamberlain. The insulting assessments on his plays from that office almost defy belief. But I still feel that The Master did irreparable damage to my profession and all those in it. No one has yet managed to dispel the aura with which he surrounded the very word 'theatre', an abiding synonym for superficiality and deception. Intelligent people who read new novels if they can afford them and study the form carefully in their film-going remain wary about setting foot in the perfidious playhouse. I see only too well what they mean.

I once said that it was impossible to imagine Coward at prayer, let alone on his knees. That may not be a fault, after all. Pride has never seemed to me to be a great sin, unlike avarice or envy. But I do believe he gave theatricality a bad name for good. The term 'kitchen sink' was a lead weight from the outset. The silk dressing-gown won the day, as the present applause for *The Chalk Garden* revival makes plain.

Finally, one of the recurring tediums of the chafingly offhand *Sunday Times/Independent* know-all, imagine-nothing style in which this book is written is the author's repeated reference to Coward's lack of education. He is not the first to seize upon it. Binkie used to relish saying, to myself of all people, 'Well, of course, you know – Noël's quite uneducated.' Mr Fisher went to Oxford. It is clear enough from this sneering and inept stab at diminishing a talent which informed and altered the century, that slickness will get you anywhere these days, and with pretty paltry effort.

It is also plain that Noël Coward could put a sentence together better than any cocky little detractor from Academe or wherever. Perhaps those who seemed obsessed with what they call 'racism' or 'sexism' might now turn their attention to this bizarre 'educationism'.

Spectator, 2 May 1992

Tennessee Williams

Four Plays [*The Glass Menagerie*, *A Streetcar Named Desire*, *Summer and Smoke* and *Camino Real*], *Cat on a Hot Tin Roof* and *Baby Doll*

There are too many critics. I have no intention of setting up in the appraisal business. A playwright should never try to make – or pretend to make – objective critical judgements on the work of another. He can't. He will merely tell you how he would have written the same play. He will usually manage to tell you something about himself. Having said this, what are my reactions to the plays of Tennessee Williams?

To ignore these plays is to ignore the world we live in. Every serious British dramatist is indebted to them. Firstly, they are a kick in the face of the common belief among playgoers in this country that suffering is some form of inferiority. They are an assault on the army of the tender-minded and tough-hearted, the emotion snobs who believe that protest is vulgar, and to be articulate is to be sorry for oneself; the milk-in-first and phlegm boys who will mine meanings from seams that fell apart years ago, but will summon up all their disengaged hostility, all their slicked-up journal-istic tired old attitudes, and get into a pedantic, literal-minded flap over inessentials when they are forced to look at a slum or a bomb-site (these two seem really to hurt for some reason) all the evening – or, worse, at the kind of homes millions of people have to live in.

These are the people who will tell you that Blanche Dubois is just a whore, anyway, and can't understand what all the nasty, sordid fuss is about. This is the adjustment school of criticism, who even look like packing off their own Hedda Gabler to the Marriage Guidance Clinic sometimes.

These plays are about failure. This is what makes human beings interesting. So what do they want? To give Brick a cold bath and Blanche a bromide somewhere before the first interval so that we can all go home and watch a decent, straightforward documentary about mental illness on television? Each one of these plays is an assault on this school of criticism ('Why doesn't he stop loafing about, and try a good job of work?' 'Why doesn't she face up to her responsibilities and snap out of it?'). These are the people who don't care much about what you say, as long as you say it nicely, who believe that playwrights should be like the Royal Family, above the brawl and conflict of life as we know it. I rejoice in Tennessee Williams because I'm sure he never took a cold bath in his life, and he wouldn't have the almighty nerve to suggest it to anyone else.

The argument of the adjustment school is that characters like Blanche and Brick are not 'normal', their surroundings are not 'normal', they aren't like *us*. In fact, they are, yes – neurotics. Now, this attitude is, I believe, built on a complete misconception of what theatre – or, indeed, art – is about. Adler said somewhere that the neurotic is like the normal individual only more so. I believe that theatre is the art of the more so. A neurotic is not less adequate than an auditorium full of 'normals'. Every character trait is a neurosis writ small. I like my plays writ large, and that is how these are written. Those who complain of people like Blanche being neurotic are objecting to theatrical method itself. When one reads that one person in twenty in this country will at some time in his, or her, life enter a mental institution (and what are the other nineteen doing? Going to see *Salad Days* I suppose) one wonders how the adjustment school manages to keep so magnificently fit.

These plays tell us something about what is happening in America, and this is something we must know about. Lacking a live culture of our own, we are drawing more heavily than ever on that of the United States. This will turn out to be the most expensive and burdensome of the American loans, but we can't expect to put up some kind of tariff barrier when they start sending over their own particular anxieties and neuroses. America is as sexually obsessed as a medieval monastery. That is what these plays are about – sex. Sex and failure. The moral failure of Protestant Capitalism has produced the biggest sexual nuthouse since the Middle Ages. And let us remember sex is everybody's problem. Even Aunt Edna has an itch under that tea tray.

Williams's women – Blanche, Maggie the Cat; Alma in *Summer and Smoke*, Baby Doll – they all cry out for defilement, and most of them get it. In Baby Doll, Williams has hit off the American Girl-Woman of the last hundred years – spoilt, ignorant, callous, resentful. But no more resentful than the American male. Make no mistake about it – this Baby Doll kid is a killer. She would eat a couple of guys and spit them out before breakfast. When Archie Lee says, 'You'll get your birthday present all right,' every male from Houston to Boston must want to throw his hat in the air and cheer. 'You and me have had this date right from the beginning,' says Stanley. The female must come toppling down to where she should be – on her back. The American male must get his revenge sometime.

Each one of these plays is more interesting than anything written in this country during the same period, with the exception of *Camino Real*, which is a rag-bag of – often exciting – tricks. Now I have no objection to tricks. If one accepts that theatre is some kind of magic, a dramatist without tricks is like a conjurer without a top hat. But *Camino Real* is full of tedious symbols, and deadbeat intellectualism. If it were in a mean kind of verse, it would almost certainly fool somebody – in the West End, anyway.

This play is the sore thumb on this hand of five plays. It is a fine hand, sensitive, compassionate, gifted, extended. But a little plump and soft, and, occasionally, slightly clammy. The softness does not lie in the pity (*Streetcar* – still his best play – throbs with compassion). I believe it lies buried deep in Williams's personality as a writer, which seems to me to be feminine – with its set mouth of female cunning, its unsure attitudes and moral inconsistency, sedentary, exposed, *underneath*. But this may be a failure in my own vision.

These five plays and one film script make up most of Tennessee Williams's statement to date. It is one worth making, full of private fires and personal visions. It is worth a thousand statements of a thousand politicians.

Observer, 20 January 1957

Arthur Miller

Arthur Miller, *Timebends: A Life*

The trouble with Arthur Miller is that he's so damned nice. Of all the playwrights I know personally, I count nine or ten of the best of them among my most cherished friends. Scattered over the country, we manage to meet or make contact fairly regularly. We carouse, commiserate, correspond and swap despairing jokes. They are all exhilarating and loyal companions, unfeigningly affectionate, thoughtful, amusing, inventive and often inordinately brave. But nice guys, no, I think not.

Not only is Miller palpably nice, he's also American. One of life's mysteries is how American children, generally acknowledged to be more odious than those of other less fortunate and poorer nations, ever grow up to become reasonable, charming, kindly and responsible adults. Another mystery is that, having been born to the very heart of the panic insanity that they describe reverentially as the American Dream, they have an overpowering sense of indebtedness to it.

'Ask not what your country can do for you, but what you can do for your country.' It seems an unexceptionable sentiment only if your country has not become a madhouse. In America it is deemed patriotism, an aberration commonly regarded over here as a modern moral wickedness on a par with the twin evils of sexism and racism, the mere taint of which is enough to invite the social workers' 4 am knock to come and take your children away into protective custody. Any English playwright who wrote of his native land with the aching hurt and wonder expressed throughout Miller's life and now, in his autobiography, would be hooted off the stage.

'The truth is that I always believed that a good man could still make it, capitalism or no capitalism . . . I was an American after all. Who knows – maybe something good was on its way.' Time and again the affirmation is rousing, fervently honest, ringing with the prime rallying American virtue: optimism.

'Despite everything, I still thought writing had to try to save America, and that meant grabbing people and shaking them by the neck.' Necks, rednecks especially, did not care for being shaken. The view of America as a tragedy rather than a dream must be that of an avowed enemy of her people. 'Why do you have to write tragically about America, Mr Miller?', was the final question put to him by the chairman of the Un-American Activities Committee. To write tragically about England might be considered whimsical but not seditious. At least they do not yet take your passport away for it.

'Once I got home I would be tried in a federal court and might go to jail,' he writes after his honeymoon visit to England, adding wryly, 'I wondered how I could be so unmoved by it all.' Throughout his career he suffers monsters and illiterates, senators and prelates. There are the Hollywood thugs, Harry Cohn and Spyros Skouros, who appear hilariously in the book. Treacherous friends follow: Elia Kazan, then agents and overweening phonies like the appalling Lee and Paula

Strasberg. He even had the bad luck to start off with producers like Jed Harris, on whom Olivier modelled his characterization of Richard III. 'Every playwright has to have Jed Harris once,' George Kaufman told him, 'like the measles.' Then, of course, perfidious actors and, finally, Marilyn. If Mr Harris was the measles, Miss Monroe was a killer virus.

Few men should be encouraged to marry actresses, and playwrights should be forcibly prevented from such self-slaughter. Their touted 'vulnerability' is no more than the poison of deadly ambition, and Marilyn was the venomous All-American Flower.

In his play *After the Fall*, written just before her death, Miller made out what seemed at the time a rather sanctimonious case against his ex-wife. It was received with gleeful hostility by audiences and reviewers alike. Knocking the just departed goddess was about as un-American as you could get, and he paid the price. 'I was soon widely hated but the play had spoken its truth.' The great public was unable to accept the proposition that innocence, or good old vulnerability, could be lethal. If his defensive account seems possibly disingenuous, he may deserve the benefit of his unremitting self-doubt. 'I thought there was a kind of greatness of spirit in her, even a crazy kind of nobility. And yet what frightening power she had!' It was a power over him she had exercised remorselessly.

'But I had joined my life with her and still expected to come to believe it one day – it was inevitable. The problem was that permanence with another was a missing part of her.' There were a lot of missing parts, including either pity or esteem for others. He got neither.

Still Miller soldiered on, writing *The Misfits* for her as a kind of comfort offering after her miscarriage. Driven from the hospital bed, he found 'her vulnerability was almost impossible to bear.' It is that word again and, trance-like, he keeps repeating it. 'I realized that this might be a chance to demonstrate what she meant to me.' There are times when such selflessness would seem disproportionate and cloying in someone less than honourable. 'I was prepared to dedicate a year or more of my life to her enhancement as a performer – I would never have dreamed of writing a movie otherwise.' No playwright should offer so much: his precious creativity put to the service of a dubious act of therapy.

It was a sacrifice as indifferently received as a bunch of hot-house grapes offered to a wasting patient. He agonizes himself into knots of expiation. 'If my intention was as authentic as I believed it was, she had the right not to play the part . . . Nevertheless, her caution had to hurt a bit.' Sure enough. Famous playwrights can be vulnerable if they have a mind to it. With all the grace of a voracious pussycat, she accepted the part, and the production of *The Misfits* went ahead, a bitterly joyless enterprise, even by the standards of movie-making. Its unlikely comple-tion was due to the fluke patience of its dying star, Clark Gable, buoyed up over the frittered weeks of Marilyn's turmoil by a kingly daily rate, the professionalism of Montgomery Clift and, above all, the command-ing genius of John Huston. Marilyn did the dirt on Miller at every opportunity, treating the lines he had written for her with contrived contempt, even withdrawing her physical presence from him and moving in with the witch-Svengali Paula Strasberg, her evil and idiotic 'drama coach'.

During all these weeks in the comfortless desert, his almost courtly persistence in the face of harassment and humiliation against the clock and a brutal citizenry brings to mind the dignity and frontier heroism of the marshal in *High Noon*. In any film about the filming of *The Misfits*, the casting of Gary Cooper in the part of Arthur Miller would have been too obvious to be inspired. Over there, in the Big Country, a playwright could be seen as a kind of lonesome marshal who has to do what a playwright's gotta do.

Early on he had decided that 'it can take a long time to accept that celebrity is a kind of loneliness.' After his first Broadway success, *All My Sons*, he worked for a week in a box factory. 'I was attempting to be a part of a community instead of formally accepting my isolation, which was what fame seemed to hold.' Proctor, Loman, Eddie Carbone in *A View from the Bridge*, all seethe with loneliness. It is often a disturbing spectacle, but none of these achieve the heroic magnitude that Miller tries to impose upon them. Tragedy eludes these toppled nice guys, however much his sometimes hollow-sounding brass brings down to bear the apprehension of the gods upon them. Whatever the hieratic lawyer in *A View from the Bridge* says portentously about Eddie being 'wholly known' and other things that go bump in the playwright's universe, the character is a blue-collar slob of inexplicable interest to Miller but little to anyone else or possibly even God.

'When does one cease to work and start to live?' Miller put the question when he was thirty-five. Of his recent play, *The American Clock*, he says,

we should feel, along with the textures of massive social and human tragedy, a renewed awareness of the American's improvisational strength, his almost subliminal faith that things can and must be made to work out. In a word, the feel of the energy of democracy.

Both the style and the sentiment are an almost perfect example of a writer who has never ceased to work most fruitfully and is now more eager and able than ever abundantly to live.

Spectator, 5 December 1987

Brendan Behan

The Letters of Brendan Behan, ed. E. H. Mikhail

Brendan Behan lurched into my life one early Sunday New York morning, pounding on my door at the Algonquin Hotel. He was Irish, a famous drunk and alumnus of the IRA, three things I didn't wish to contemplate at that dark, hungover hour in an already alien land.

His entrance was glorious, and wearisome, like starting the day with pints of stout. 'Is anyone alive in this f— cat house?' he roared, so privy daily to death himself. 'Well, now, what do you think of this town?' he demanded, leaning on me with no time for the feeblest response. 'My name's Brendan Behan. I don't smoke, I don't eat and I don't f—. But I drink. You can always tell the civilization of a country by two things, its whores and its bread. And they're neither of them any good here.' And so it began.

In *The Letters of Brendan Behan* he re-emerges as a woundingly generous profligate. Among the things he threw away, at such cost yet so easily, are the dashed-off lines to his wife, Beatrice. He wrote rarely to her but plagued by his guttering genius, in a typical act of homage and love, he tossed her this sweet trinket:

> Why does any woman double
> give herself the nuisance that
> husbands are when with less trouble
> She could buy and train a cat?

Brendan's life was a ballad, the wild outpour of a pure, forgiving heart, laughing grievously at the tides of coldness which threatened it from every side. Who is there in Ireland or England to take up his matchless song now when it is most sorely needed to be heard? Perhaps only he could sing it. Perhaps he anticipated this in a letter to the editor of the *Village Voice* after the production of *The Quare Fellow* in New York:

Dear Sir,
> Tynan and Hobson are both very well,
> *Le Monde* il fait beau and Brooks Atkinson's swell,
> *Die Welt, The Spectator* all made me rejoice
> But the praise that pleased most was your sweet *Village Voice*.

As poetry it's not very much, only if you heard me sing it.
Ask Ken Tynan.

The range of his attention in these letters (from corporal punishment to school dinners) is dazzling, reflective and hilarious. Above all is his magnanimity to others, though not himself, and his absorption with language, both English and Irish. Take this letter about retitling *Borstal Boy*, which was 'unacceptable' in America:

I don't give a fiddler's f— about the American edition except for the readies, but whether you or I like it or not, London is the capital of the English language. I don't mind standing in the dock and being charged with high treason, for there can be no treason where there is no allegiance, but the language is as much yours and mine as it is the Duke of Edinburgh's and, to be truthful, I'd sooner lose money even, than to be disgraced in London with that [American] title.

This from the John Bull-charging, scourge of 'Horse Protestants', the snorting patriot and poet who begins his letters with endearments in his loving Irish tongue. Elsewhere he can write, a little closer to the cheek perhaps, 'I sometimes think I am a crypto-Englishman.' How the red-nose English comic radicals chanting 'Troops out of Ireland' must wince at such all-drenching mockery. How Brendan would have flinched at their mirthless allegiances.

He had nothing to sell, least of all himself. He gave that away even to the undeserving of his forgiveness. What present playwright, especially an English one, would portray a British squaddie with the Christian grace and forebearance that Brendan did in *The Hostage*?

You see, in the *The Hostage* I have nothing to sell – not religion, not a political system, not a philosophy, and certainly not a panacea for the ills of the world. I respect kindness to human beings first of all, and kindness to animals. I don't respect the law. I have a total irreverence for anything concerned with society except that which makes the roads safer, the beer stronger, the food cheaper, and old men and women warmer in the winter and happier in the summer ... Please come to *The Hostage* to have a good time. Don't come if you expect serious problems and equally boring solutions. My play is meant for fun and for good loud laughing, even though I admit to being an Irishman ... Most of all, *The Hostage* is of live human beings being extremely busy living and striving for a little gaiety and communication with their fellow men.

These letters came upon me with a jolt of remembrance in the deadly dog days of January. Brendan died in 1964 and I've yet to fully absorb their recognitions, to take them up again when the midnight chimes beckon the sleepless soul to the shadows of departed heroes. Back to those days of Theatre Workshop and their rollicking Joan Littlewood nights, the cheeky joyousness and the loving anarchy with which she hurled Brendan's plays at a startled auditorium.

Ideas are two a penny and here's one for nothing. Someone – even an Englishman – should look to this book and seek a way of transmitting Behan's absented spirit back to the playhouse.

It's an idle thought, but I'm sure he wouldn't object so long as it provided a few breakfast pints of porter and, of course, a few weeks regained of sanity and laughter.

Sunday Telegraph, 2 February 1992

Joe Orton

The Orton Diaries, ed. John Lahr

Jenny may indeed live with Eric and Martin but how would she and little Teddy have tucked up with Joe and Kenneth? As even the most unenthusiastic theatre-goer will remember, Joe Orton, the playwright, and his long-time lover, Kenneth Halliwell, were found dead in their tiny room in Noel Road, North London, on 9 August 1967.

The right side of Orton's head had been smashed in with a hammer which lay on his counterpane. His cranium carried the marks of nine hammer blows. Brain tissue and blood were at the head of the bed and on the ceiling. Halliwell lay nude in the middle of the room. The top of his chest and head were splattered with blood. Near him on the floor were a glass and a can of grapefruit juice with which he'd swallowed twenty-two Nembutal. Halliwell died first. On the desk, the police found a note: 'If you read his diary all will be explained. K.H. PS. Especially the latter part.'

Joe's brains peeking out between Jenny and Teddy might have given even the most dim of Brent's social workers a bit of a turn. Certainly Orton would have relished the solemn fakery of sodomite domesticity embodied in the spectacle of Jenny cuddling brain-soaked Teddy between Ken and Joe's own prick-proud, severed body. 'I'm going up, up, up,' he wrote to a friend a few months before Peggy Ramsay, his agent, backed into this Jacobean finale and, with characteristic niftiness, palmed the Diaries from underneath the plodding gaze of the law. Up indeed.

There used to be a chart hanging on the office walls of the Royal Court Theatre indicating the Turkish baths in North and West London patronized by certain of that establishment's directors. Whether this was intended as a warning or an incitement I have never been sure, but Orton's list of regularly visited public lavatories, known cosily to the profession as 'cottages', could have been usefully added. The goings-on in these homo-heavens might seem grim rather than gay, but Orton's cock-happy account of those dark multi-couplings is often hilarious.

'I was never able to imagine myself as ordinary,' he wrote. Orton believed in himself, and was right to do so. He was a lone-star product of the glum lower middle classes who encourage nothing and dote on the defeat of others as well as their own. It was the class that was yet to dominate the style and taste of the nation; the world of breakfast television, *Eastenders*, briefcase office boys lording it from hotel bedrooms with statutory tea-makers at 'conferences', the new Young Executives, and the disc-jockeys who set the volume and babble of present-day English life with its universal down and dead inflection.

He even came from Leicester, a no-hope town if ever there was one, where the three-piece suites huddle round the telly in bookless rooms and nary a picture on the wall brightens up the surrounding slum of inertia, arrested ambition and imagination. 'He was so tense about it, about being *somebody*.' His mother Elsie babbled on about him, pawning her wedding ring to get him into Clark's College. An observer remarks: 'I remember her constant falling inflections at the end of every sentence.

This "dying fall" certainly had a depressing effect on me.' Only those who have grown up with that deadly dying fall of Elsie's class can know the power of its attrition.

Notwithstanding Leicester and his mother, Orton took an almost innocent pride in the gift of his special weaponry. He may not have believed even his own pork sword mightier than the pen, but he enjoyed the cut and thrust of both hugely, voraciously and ruthlessly. No Gay he, rather a ferocious bum bandit, with no time for bleeding hearts – only those parts which, it is now exhorted, should not be reached without benefit of condom.

Halliwell was the almost perfect type of that familiar social hazard, the homosexual 'wife', the unavoidable companion, avid to share his lionized partner's fame and popularity, even to the extent of requisitioning it for himself. They are a nightmare to hostesses and frequently an embarrassment to their other halves, a perpetual *placement* problem, provoking the perplexed response of 'Adore Him – can't *stand* Him!' Class is often helpful in coping with these delicate social dilemmas. The dropped aspirates of surly merchant seamen or sibilant hairdressers are more amusingly contained at the dinner table than opinionated, articulate and pushy Pygmalion amours like Halliwell. Unfortunately, when the Galatea was brought to life by sudden public acclamation, his creator was immediately diminished.

'I couldn't wait to get Halliwell out of the flat,' said Peter Willes. 'I felt I wanted to disinfect the place.' Willes, the respected Binkie-like television producer, strides in and out of the Diaries, changing scene after scene into garish *opera buffa*.

Smiles became rare before bedtime in the stifling Noel Road bunker. 'Kenneth H. and I had long talk about our relationship. He keeps saying he will commit suicide. He says, "You'll learn then, won't you? What will you be like without me?" We talked and talked until I was exhausted.'

No one, in those pre-Terence Higgins days, loved a fairy when she's forty, and Halliwell became doggedly more unloveable, his genteel pretensions and vanities, the fright blond toupée and paunchiness only emphasizing Joe's easy, cherubic swagger. The classic denunciations of a discarded mistress pour from him: 'You're turning into a real bully . . . You're quite a different person since you had your success.' Feeling daily the thrust of the chop from Joe, he was to decide that when it came it was he, Halliwell, who would deliver it first and in perfect triumph, an act of almost banal inevitability.

Orton insists repeatedly in the Diaries that his plays were for real and not just grotesque fantasies. 'Everyone else thinks the play is a fantasy. The police know that it's *true*.' Neither his over-excited liberal admirers nor even his actors would believe him.

I'd taken my mother's false teeth down to the theatre. I said to Kenneth Cranham, 'Here, I thought you'd like the originals.' He said, 'What?' – 'Teeth,' I said. 'Whose?' he said – 'My mum's,' I said. He looked very sick. 'You see,' I said, 'it's obvious that you're not thinking of the play in terms of reality, if a thing affects you like that.' Simon Ward shook like a jelly when I gave them to him.

His realistic contempt for the world and his audience is bracing. 'The public are ignorant shits.' No self-respecting playwright would quarrel with that.

'How did we do last night?' [he asks his pious director.] 'Very good. A most intelligent audience.' – 'I don't give a fuck for their intelligence,' I said. 'How *many* of them were there?' He replied. 'I see you've been corrupted already.' – 'Any intelligent person should've seen the play weeks ago,' I said. 'All I'm interested in now is their money.'

And so say all of us.

In the end, Halliwell's influence had been a destructive one. Orton's fastidious, deadpan gift, so unforced in the creations of Truscott of the Yard and Mrs Welthorpe (for whom alone the book is worth its price) is consistently clogged in its classical allusions and models, piling artifice upon device, so that the plays function in an overworked and strangely clumsy fashion, like Halliwell's own maladroit attempts at teasing the establishment.

'I've discovered that I look better in cheap clothes,' Joe said. 'I wonder what the significance of that is,' replied Oscar Lewenstein, the theatrical producer. 'I'm from the gutter,' I said. 'And don't you ever forget it because I won't.'

Nobody took it in, especially those who linked him with Wilde or thought he might trail clouds of saintly buggery, an English Genet, both writers dismissed by Orton as flabby and preposterous. Neither of them could have improved upon his superb account of a final weekend spent at Lewenstein's house in Hove, where the only consolations were a cold dip in the sea and being sucked off by a dwarf in a lavatory in Old Steine. 'I find people bad and irresistably funny.'

The final comedy of divine and bloody retribution in Noel Road would surely have been irresistible to his uncontrite spirit. Little Jenny's Teddy would have been a good, fat part, no more a fantasy than any of his other works, for ever and for real.

Spectator, 29 November 1986

Dear Diary . . .

WHAT DO THE following divers persons have in common? Chairmanship, directorship or membership of: the Metrication Board; Port of London Authority; Midland Bank; Trust House Forte; ILEA; Working Ladies Guild; Liveryman Goldsmiths Company; Capital Radio; Noise Advisory Council; Royal Commission on the Workings of the Tribunals of Enquiry; Disciplinary Committee of the Lawn Tennis Association; British Motoring Association; Ordnance Survey Board; Salvation Army Advisory Board; Mount Everest Finance Committee; Top Salaries Review Body? Whose recreations (apart from hunting, shooting and fishing) include: mountaineering, ski-ing (fast), Cresta tobogganing, sailing, painting, photography? Whose membership of clubs include: Athenaeum, Royal Yacht Squadron, All England Tennis, Alpine, Royal Thames Yacht, Reform? And, lastly, some who are honoured as Cmdr Royal Swedish Order of North Star, Holder Star of Ethiopia, *Commandeur de l'Ordre de la Vérité*, Order of Rio Branco Class III (Brazil) and *Grande Official de Ordem Militare de Christo*? Who are these distinguished, striving men and women? They are all among those boasted as council members by the boards of our three principal theatres. It makes you ponder.

Last week a selection of these highest achievers offered to sue me over the production of an old play of mine [*The Entertainer*] which they had recently announced. However, they had forgotten to buy the property before tampering with it. It seems to have occurred to none of them that if you buy a used car, even from the likes of myself, you should pay the owner before selling what doesn't belong to you. Now I hear that the same busy souls are threatening to resign over the rejection of an anti-Government play about organizing food parcels for colliers' whippets or something similarly relevant. Perhaps all that downhill racing and strenuous Brazilian relations turns their heads.

78

THE *DAILY MAIL* sent out eight devout reporters to assemble a consumer's guide to contemporary rural churchgoing. The result was something like this:

Church: St Langudoc's, Gormless New Town, W. Midlands.

Congregation: Plenty of collars and ties though one farm worker in defiant jeans with his orange-haired girlfriend. Fine enthusiasm for Family Service with bawling kiddies and youngsters scampering among the aisles. The message? Bread and wine can be fun food for all!

Music: Depressing old organ droning out what may have been Granny's top-pop hymns written by guys with upper-class names like Baring-Gould and Clough. Definitely won't start the Duran Duran generation tappin', yappin' and a-clappin'.

Comfort: Outdated, hard pews. OK for monetarist squires in Savile Row tweeds, but won't get today's bums on seats! No crèche, breast-feeding facilities, light snacks or even coffee vendors! Communion may be fast food all right but so is Chinese take-away and we all know how *that* leaves you.

Sermon: Too long (six minutes). *No* discussion, slide or video show; *no* counselling. Delivered aloft (i.e. down) to the congregation in olde-worlde language. Old-time bucolics, simple ploughmen and negro slaves must have had eight O-levels plus to get through this stuff, but our teenagers aren't turned on by ancient 'thees' and 'thous'. Too much reference to Israel. The Church messes about in politics enough. No mention of make love not war. Saint Bob knows more about Christian Charity and where it's at – Ethiopia.

Welcome: General handshaking during service a short relief from accepted stuffiness. *No* multiracial or ethnic awareness; just Jews and Christians.

Summing up: Off with that dumb dog-collar, Rev! – they're the century before yesterday's gear, didn't you know? Pound those sleepy rural, deprived areas of discontent and get yourself a guitar and a haircut out of the collection plate.

Since writing the above indolent lines I read that the Rector of Stratford upon Avon's Holy Trinity Church has installed a 'liturgical cafeteria' in Shakespeare's old Worship Centre. Having acknowledged the occasional appropriateness of the Book of Common Prayer for sick or dying parishioners ('They knew the words of the Lord's Prayer and some of the Psalms by heart and this comforted them'), his real enthusiasm is for his popular new facility. 'In our liturgical cafeteria . . .

the service of praise is conducted by a splendid team of layfolk and is informal, sincere and has only a simple framework – with choruses, clapping hands, guitars, trumpets and ventriloquist's doll. It possibly makes Shakespeare turn in his grave nearby, but it helps to bring people nearer to God in a world where life can be very difficult.' Indeed it can, particularly for those engaged in this unholy trade. Attempts at art, irony and artifice are left yapping as ever at the heels of life.

A GOLDEN SCUM Award surely to the BBC and Sir John Pritchard for the New English Bible subtitles used in its broadcast of Mozart's arrangement of *Messiah* last weekend. To impose the infelicities of the NEB on the thundering impact of Charles Jennen's 'scripture collection' of King James, so beloved by G.F.H. and known by heart by the sick and dying like myself, seems like cafeteria culture gone berserk. The valleys were no longer exalted but lifted up; all flesh is heave-hoed, though mankind shall 'see it together'; we don't dare 'rejoice greatly', but 'shout aloud'. Downscreen nannyspeak. Next week: Youf Workshop sings Cole Porter: Hallelujah folks! Up with you to the mountain-tops!

THE BOOMTOWN RATS' latest single goes to all those clamorous bums languishing in their deprived areas who have not yet slipped in among the thousands of con artists who have already penetrated Lord Gowrie's [the Minister for the Arts's] door, ever ajar to the persistent phoney. The uneasy inheritors of the Ethiopian jamboree support the insane democratic view that even Rock and Pop are fruit from the tree of the Arts to be picked and paid for by a servile nation. Lord Gowrie said so from their Lordship's barrow. 'Pound of arts, please, and a packet of Duran Duran.' This Theatre of Absurd apart, it might be remembered that no one ever *asked* you to write a poem, novel or play. But, if you must do so, in your undoubted jobless despond, sit down, write it and then shut up. It's a tough world, even eventually for Arts Council-granted bums.

Spectator, 27 July 1985

[4]
Directors

George Devine

Obituary

In my own life, January seems to have a gratuitous trick of springing cruelty. Perhaps it is a personal illusion that life at the beginning of the year, like life at the beginning of the day, is harder to bear or contemplate. For me a year hardly begun that springs the death of George Devine is a harsh one to face. It is a bleak week in the English theatre.

I don't think many people really knew him well. I believe I did. I would like to think I had been able to get at least one foot inside that surprising and moving personality. Like many men blessed with a gift for friendship, he was not easily accessible, although he appeared to have an almost comically natural Socratic persona.

He could appear harsh to outsiders, especially know-alls, and, like most profoundly modest and self-critical people, he could seem most arrogant when he was self-denigrating and felt himself being merely realistic. If he could have dissembled with even a little jauntiness, his career might have been more apparently successful and certainly easier. But he despised flattering and wheedling, which is probably why the relations of the Royal Court with the press were usually a trifle prickly, to say the least of it.

George was a natural teacher. This was because he longed to respect his pupils and learn from them. And he was always fiercely un-patronizing, except to the over-ambitious, dewy-eyed or expedient. On these occasions his contempt could be chilling. He was unfailingly watchful and suspicious of opportunism, ambition, caution and timidity.

People think of the Royal Court as having been a forcing-house for younger writers, but this was not a matter of systematic policy. George

made consistent efforts from the very beginning to bring older, established writers – novelists and poets whom he admired – into what people
assumed to be a charmed circle of youth. The lack of response from his
own generation disturbed him. It seemed like a lordly brush-off of the art
he loved.

He was incapable of sentimentality, and I think it is important to stress
that this was especially true of his dealings with younger people. What
was so formidable was his nose for sham in art and people. I think
perhaps the friendships he prized most were with those more or less his
own age – Beckett, Michel Saint-Denis, Glen Byam Shaw; only three
weeks ago he made a very special effort to entertain Ionesco. It seemed to
me he also had a very rare attitude among men – he genuinely and
eagerly admired and respected gifted women.

In ten years as artistic director of the Royal Court, George Devine was
almost solely responsible for its unique atmosphere, which anyone who
knew him knew to be a reflection of his own unique temperament. Some
people with their hatred of what they believe to be a self-congratulatory
theatrical in-life may think that this became cosy. It never did. It was very
English in its approach – empirical is a respectable word for it, I suppose
– unsystematic, non-manifesto.

In the end he was worn down by the grudging, removed attitude to
decent and sustained effort that is such a recurrent and depressing aspect
of English life. No one can surpass the Englishman's skill of maiming
with indifference. Viewed from outside, his ten years in Sloane Square
may have seemed wonderfully rewarding and exciting, as indeed they
often were for him. But this peculiar native climate of critical attrition
chilled, bit into him and wore him down. I can imagine his special,
amused shrug at the crass newspaper headlines which described him last
week as 'kitchen-sink director'.

If I give an impression of George Devine as someone disappointed or
embittered, I would be quite wrong. His disappointment was minimal, in
fact, because his expectation was relentlessly pruned. This, combined
with his prodigious, hopeful effort, seemed to make his stoicism heroic
and generous, rather than a pinched, carping austerity. These were
exactly the qualities he admired and saw in the work of personalities as
different as Beckett and Brecht. Perhaps it was a kind of reticence.
Strength, gaunt lines and simplicity always excited him. During an earlier
illness he used to enjoy making furniture and it always expressed this
passion in a very touching way.

The sort of people who were dismissive about George Devine's work were the ones who were aware of the Royal Court only when a star or a fashionable revival appeared there. In spite of that dim support he did make its name a household word. Only a tiny minority actually sampled any of its goods, but most people had at least heard of his work.

The two big subsidized companies – the National and the Royal Shakespeare – owe a debt to him that is incalculable. Their existence is directly due to him. Hundreds of writers and actors owe their present fortunes and favour to him. I am in the greatest debt of all. It seems extraordinary to have been quite so fortunate.

Observer, 23 January 1966

Irving Wardle, *The Theatres of George Devine*

Mr Wardle has written a very fine book indeed. It is a sensitive, reticent but shrewd account of the life and work of this massive, unsentimental man. The author's usual spinsterish, evasive style has been agreeably eroded by a surprising seam of warmth, neither fulsome nor lofty. There is no critic's prophylactic prose here.

So soon after the events described in this book, it is certain that many of George Devine's friends – and enemies – will quarrel with the result. That is inevitable. George had quarrelsome friends and unforgiving enemies. For the present, here is an overdue and honourable piece of work, honourably executed.

From the outset, Mr Wardle is disarming about his own remoteness from the events he records. He writes not only as an outsider but, to those veteran guerrillas from the Royal Court – before it became the outlying and egregious banana republic of today – as the natural, considered enemy. Unlike many who write such books, he disclaims at the outset any particular access or insights. It is refreshing to read the four-square declaration in his introduction:

> I met him only three times and always for formal reasons. I can look up what he said, but the remark that stuck in my memory was one he delivered out of the blue as we were crossing the road: 'I do believe intensely in the creative value of struggle.' I understand the passion he put into that statement rather better now than I did at the time, and one thing that clarified it was the picture of that little boy with the sickly smile. Chronology apart, it is a good place to begin.

Earlier, Wardle says, 'Under all the masks he wore there was the one constant element of uncurable dissatisfaction: dissatisfaction with himself, and the theatre to which he had committed his life.' No one could argue with that, even his adversaries and detractors. George prevailed, like the Early Church under Constantine. He prevailed not only because he had the faith, tenacity and courage to survive, but because he proved himself superior to his rivals. The analogy with the Early Church is not a precious posh-paper whimsy. Only George could have strode upon a Rock crawling with such an underside of Anabaptists, Albigensians, Jansenists, Maniacs and odd-ball Loyolas, hieratic and ecumenical, historical, pastoral.

So much for that. A week never passes when I don't find my head trapped in the iron hole he has bequeathed to me in my profession. Or a day when I don't need to mourn and have a good spit. Three personal stories illustrate the kind of legacy George left to me.

Almost exactly two years ago, I returned from the United States to find that the play I had on at the National Theatre was threatened with summary withdrawal. Hurling myself up to the cloud-topped towers of Colditz-on-Thames, I harangued Sir Peter Hall and his soothsayers for an entire afternoon on the reasons why *I* thought we were all pursuing our chosen profession. 'Well, you see, your play is only playing to 82 per cent and here we have to play to 98 per cent.' Or some such ludicrous Whitehall wankery. 'Wouldn't you rather your play was taken off while it was *still a success*?'

I had, in my Royal Court instruction, never been confronted so openly with the sophistry of the new Cultural Mafia Protection Racket. I protested that as far as I was concerned, it *was* a *success*. That, surely, was why I had written it in the first place and the company had put it on. Many of my most enjoyable and enlightening hours in the theatre had been spent watching half-empty and critically despised productions. Was the National Theatre in the Success Business? Not half it was! It had *forecasters*, pensioned men down there amid the bowels and Dobermanns of the Culture Factory itself, hedged in with crystal balls, charts and drawing-boards.

But why were they not investing the taxpayers' money in Failure as well as good old Success? Why *me*, perhaps? But even more – why William Douglas Home, Alan Ayckbourn, Noël Coward? The stuff that Forecasters' (£10,000 a year) dreams are made on? When George began in Sloane Square he was getting £25 a week. Tony Richardson £14. So what, you say – Ancient History. So *something*, I say. Why *Blithe Spirit* at the National Theatre? 'My mother wanted to see it,' replied Sir Peter, with what I thought, at that hideous moment, humourless good cheer. 'Ah, well,' he said finally. 'Back to the Drawing-Board!'

The Drawing-Board was in the forefront of George's career, as Mr Wardle makes fascinatingly clear in his book. But it was only brick blocks of a dream, to be thrown away as soon as painfully mastered. After my session in the National Forecasters' coven, I emerged into the planned wastes of the South Bank, more despairing and desolate than I can remember in my career. G.D. would have swallowed his pipe. Except that he wouldn't of course. 'But what did you *expect*, dear boy?' He was impervious to the rot of ambition and success as a priest to the stench of a leper.

Last year I was in Canberra and happened upon Mr Snoo Wilson – for it is a he – lecturing a group of Australian Playwrights. Such a luckless or doomed minority group beggars the imagination. To add to the spectre of their upended misery was the sight of the Snoo ('Whaur's yr Wullie Shakespeare, Snoo?') telling his audience about the Beginnings of the Modern English Theatre. It appeared that this was initiated in 1968 by a few good folks like old Snoo himself, Howard Brenton and Trevor Griffiths from the BO-scented salons of *Time Out*. Reminding myself that George would have given the whole self-regarding mob the same boot in the crutch he gave to Ronald Duncan, John Whiting and N. C. Hunter, I listened to the Snoo warning the indigent Antipodean lonelies how it was almost impossible to get money from the Arts Council without *actually asking for it first*.

Before the tubes of Fosters rained down with heavy threats about Calvinist work ethics, sexist attitudes and Gestalt (monkeys and bananas – remember?) conspiracies, my companion, less tolerant of fools than myself, reminded Mr Wilson that Devine, so peripheral to himself and other latter-day mediocrities, did *not* coin their adopted phrase, 'the right to fail'. It was my other good friend, Tony Richardson. So much for popular history. Disregard the apocryphal Snoos and embrace synoptic Irving.

Finally, a few months ago, an attendance at the present Management Committee of the English Stage Company at my own request. More than twenty years later, the endless discussions about the state of the roof, the gentlemen's lavatory cistern, the merits of the beer in the theatre bars and the pub next door. The overall preoccupation with money – £280,000 or nearly thirty times the original grant. The fugitive concern with what is actually to Go On The Green. The useless expenditure on administration and publicity. No flair, no imagination, no circus, above all no fun. 'We need a small-cast, one-set play. Or a revival with a star.' Ye Gods, George, stay on your cloud, smoking your pipe and reading *Seventeen* and *Honey* as you did before.

I listened to this sad scene for some twenty minutes and then stumbled out into Sloane Square. These footling, timid amateurs had been talking away my life.

I wish I had far more space to write about this absorbing book concerning a man who really did shape the landscape of his time. Not grappled in the centre of a minority art but in the central nerve of an exhausted, bewildered and great nation. The first half of the book is especially rich and touching in the way it follows the career of the small boy with the sickly smile, finding his way in a loveless, eccentric world. The sweet, curious innocence of the boy became the man I knew. I remember one evening trying to explain to George the state of comic disgrace known as 'camp'. (Yes, he thought he'd kept homosexuals out of the Royal Court. Surrounded by hissing vipers, swinging, as he would say, from his tits!) After an hilarious evening he kept ringing me up: 'Just had an argument here, boysie. What about Mozart? Is *he* camp? Beethoven, then? Well, Wordsworth . . .?'

For those of us fortunate to work with him, John Dexter puts his finger on it when he says, 'We all wanted his approval very much.' I only wish that Mr Wardle's book could go into paperback immediately and be thrust into the hands of every philistine politician, councillor, schoolteacher, *Guardian* Woman, *New Statesman* reader, social scientist and everyone else who ever missed the sweet whiff of careless smoke from Sloane Square before 1968. 'So far as I am concerned the intellectuals of London are a washout.' George's voice to be sure. No surprise there. The phrase I remember he used most was, 'Remember, all problems are *technical* ones.'

Finally, Mr Wardle, in a passage about the Duncan vendetta, describes me, quite correctly, as an elitist. I imagine that he meant the description to be pejorative. George believed in a severely prescribed democracy in art. When I bought my first car, I showed it to him. It was an Austin 10. He looked at it and said, 'Why didn't you get an Alfa Giulietta, dear boy? *That's* a *grocer's* car.'

Observer, 28 May 1978

On the Writer's Side

Nobody else but George Devine would ever have put on that old play of mine: that's the absolute truth. It had already been sent back by about twenty-five managers and agents when I answered the advertisement in the *Stage* and posted it to the English Stage Company. And nobody else but George would have supported it, to the hilt, in spite of a lukewarm reception by most critics; in spite of a slow box office; and in spite of being attacked – and hurt – by a lot of people he respected in the conventional theatre, including personal friends. History very soon began to be rewritten, and nowadays it isn't realized how much hostility George had to face in 1956. Ten years later, I remember, Binkie Beaumont said to my face, '*I* was the only one who really liked *Look Back in Anger. I* thought it was the most marvellous play.' But I knew – everyone knew – that he had walked out of it. Terry Rattigan was vaguely hostile, but so was the entire West End Mafia. So was Larry Olivier, the first time he saw it, although he did a characteristically intuitive U-turn-about later – not exactly about the play but what was afoot. But George was the only one who responded to it, right from the start.

When George and I first met in 1955 he didn't say a great deal but he did make me feel immediately that something very special was about to happen and that *I* was going to take part in it. That may sound now like a bit of ridiculous hindsight but it was true. I had no money, no job, nothing; and he hadn't even got a theatre. But I just felt, I really did, 'This is it. It's all right.' And I lived from then on, for about nine months, on the idea of something that hadn't yet arrived. I already felt looked after. He gave me plays to read – I'd take forty of them home at a time – and got me to stage-manage auditions (at ten bob a time) to keep me going until we actually got into a theatre. I don't believe that anyone, not even George, had a very clear idea of what, exactly, was going to happen. But he had a *feeling* about it, almost Moses-like, and he managed to communicate that feeling to other people. I've never known anybody else who could do this, as he did it. With Tony Richardson he created a remarkable sense of excitement, apprehension, as well as a sense of security, for a lot of insecure people. I don't know *how* he managed to do this, operating as he was on such an uncertain basis.

Both George and Tony were completely unknown quantities to me and, of course, I was to them. We were all out there in an unknown world. Nobody knew at all what anyone's real intentions were. For them to support people like myself, as they did, was a great act of faith, and they both expressed that faith openly. This was very rare indeed at that time. The first time that I met Tony, an exotic-seeming, loping creature who looked about seven feet tall, he said, 'I think you've written the best play since the war.' Immediately, just like that. He was unequivocal about it, and so was George. It gave you an amazing sense of creative trust.

We disagreed about many things, after we'd started at the Royal Court. George knew, for instance, that I despised the Writers' Group. I thought it was committee wanking and refused to take part. George went along with it because he thought there was some value in it, but he also went along with my opposition to it. We used to have running skirmishes about Ionesco's plays and other French work. I used to say, 'George, we're not going to do *another* of those, are we?' And he'd say, 'Yes, dear friend, I'm afraid we *are*.' He thought they were good. I couldn't abide them. But he could contain my reaction patiently, even though he was not a patient man. He could contain and comprehend many different things: that was one of his strengths. It wasn't that he was weak and compromising; he could be brutal and dismissive, and he went for what he wanted. But he had a special kind of tolerance. He suffered talent gladly.

We certainly didn't always laugh at the same things, or have the same sense of humour. I remember that at the preview of *Look Back in Anger*, on the night before it officially opened, there was a packed house – unlike the première – with a lot of students, and people laughed all the way through. Both George and Tony said, 'Why are they laughing?' And I said, to both of them, 'Because it's supposed to be funny.' There was, in fact, a great gap between Tony and George, and a great gap between George and me. And yet there was this web of trust, a feeling that it's now so hard to recapture.

One splendid thing about George was that he gave you the impression that whatever you did, whatever seemed to go wrong, didn't really matter. He said, in effect, 'This is what we've decided to do. It's right and it's good and we're going ahead.' *You always knew he was on the writer's side.* No one gave you that feeling before, and I've seldom had it since. It wasn't indulgent. It was inspirational support. You didn't know what he thought of your work, in any kind of detail, what his reservations about it might be, but you did know that ultimately you had his complete backing and support. This was – and is, I'm sure – absolutely unique. It might have looked overprotective from the outside, but I don't think it was. He had a really passionate concern for certain people and what they were doing, but it wasn't a blind loyalty. He followed his instinct, and it was a very sure one. He made up his mind, I think, at a certain point whether to support somebody or something, and that was that. His decision had nothing to do with what the newspapers might say, or what might happen at the box office. Above all he hated anything that was merely modish. He could be Calvinist in what he dismissed, but he could have the expectation of a small boy at the circus.

I directed a play at the Court by Charles Wood in 1965 called *Meals on Wheels*. It wasn't half bad as a play, but it was a box-office disaster. On the first night, about two-thirds of the way through, George suddenly appeared – he was always there, somewhere in the theatre, or you always *felt* he was – and he said to me, 'They're *hating* it, aren't they?' And he didn't say this at all despondently; he was delighted because they were hating it for the right reasons, responding as we had anticipated. He enjoyed the irony of it. He had known what was going to happen, and he also knew the limited but particular worth of the play, which no one would be able to recognize or acknowledge. He had a wonderful realism in this way about what the Court was doing. He didn't try to convince himself that everything we did there was necessarily the best play or the most marvellous production, but what mattered was that he thought it was basically authentic in itself and worth doing in the first place. George was capable of a *just* enthusiasm, and it's such a rare quality that this is the only way I can describe it. He could demonstrate that enthusiasm to people and inspire them with it, not only for the business of putting on plays. He humanized the whole process. Can you imagine a commercial manager – a Codron or a White, say – taking the kind of real day-to-day interest in a writer that George took? If George thinks I've had a bad week – I still talk about him sometimes as though he's alive – he would worry about it, really worry. But he always used to say, 'My dear boy, all problems are technical ones.' Even now I repeat that consolation endlessly to other people, and myself.

George never harassed writers in the way that agents – or indeed managements – do. 'What are you doing *next*, dear? How many pages have you written?' That sort of thing. He would just ask you out for lunch or dinner. It was like meeting a friend: that's all. And he probably was my closest friend, but in a reticent, almost removed way. Obviously he was thinking, 'Is the old boy writing something?' or 'Is he all right?' but he never made you feel that he was probing. It's difficult to describe how welcome that was, or how unusual it is. But he did ring me up after *Look Back* and said, 'I know you're doing something at the moment. How far have you got?' I said, 'About the end of the second act,' or something absurd like that. And George asked me, 'Have you got a part in it for Laurence?' 'Laurence?' I asked. 'Olivier,' said George. I really hadn't known who he meant, because I thought of Olivier as Larry – it was actors of George's generation, I think, who called him Laurence. I can't remember what I answered but George asked me to send along what I'd written, even though I hadn't finished the play. I would never have done that for anyone else, but he asked me with such a power of tact. When Larry read it he decided he wanted to play Billie Rice, not Archie. When I finished it he changed his mind. Just as well – for both of us.

The Entertainer wasn't any better at the Palace, with 1,400 seats, than it was at the Court with a third of that number. The Court is a marvellous building. I know every inch of it. I don't think that any play of mine could have been done better anywhere else. I don't believe that there are any ideal theatrical circumstances, and I don't care what the constraints of the old proscenium arch are, that people go on about so much, because I think you can do *anything* on that kind of stage. I have never seen anything that seems to me to be all that much of an improvement on it.

For ten years, thanks to George, I had a professional life there that I'd most certainly never had before and haven't since. You were part of a family, which accepted all your frailties and imperfections, a family that most of us don't have any longer. Everyone in that little building knew each other – even if they were at odds. And they were. Almost everyone was involved emotionally in what happened, and it helped to power the works. I knew that particular life was over, as far as I was concerned, when George left the Court in 1965. Bill Gaskill continued the tradition more than honourably, but naturally the succession had to change – personality alone made it inevitable.

At the last ghastly annual Savoy lunch for the critics in 1965, when George announced that he was going to resign, the resounding indifference of the silence was really stunning. I didn't believe it. I *couldn't* believe it. Lindsay Anderson, at least, to his eternal credit, broke that silence and spoke for England and tried to point to an uncomprehending mob of cigar-smoking hacks the significance of what had happened.

One knows now what George had done in those ten years, not just in day-to-day physical hard labour but, what was really important, the emotional and imaginative effort of it all. But hardly anyone in the theatre or outside realized then just how much he was doing, how he hated the administrative load, how much it was weighing him down. He was picking people up the whole time and putting them on their feet again. He had this terrible phrase, 'I wish everyone would just stop swinging on my tits, day after day.' But they did. 'I never want to talk to another actor's agent or draw up another contract,' he would say. But he did. He had to.

I still miss George Devine, every day. How can you really say anything adequate about someone you loved and knew some part of, however small, fifteen years after he died?

from *At the Royal Court*, ed. Richard Findlater (1981)

Peter Hall

Peter Hall's Diaries: The Story of a Dramatic Battle, ed. John Goodwin

I am no nearer making it now than when I came out of Cambridge because one never really makes it. Can't I learn to live again, instead of using my profession as a means of escape from life?

I work hard to earn money in order to have environments which I never have time to enjoy.

Day in Wallingford ... there was a great deal of nervousness in the air, I suspect coming from our inability to feed such quantities of people, and wait on them with no help at all. Jacky and I are not relaxed hosts, to put it mildly.

I feel part of essential services.

It is hard not to quote repeatedly from this numbing record of banal ambition, official evasiveness and individual cupidity. Sir Peter hands down opinions about his experiences rather than illuminating them. Page after page of friendless encounters prevail over even the pretence of some inner life.

Passing acknowledgements to domesticity on the Hall agenda: life, death, children ('Christopher graduated at Cambridge today, I wish I could have been there.') and coy and unnecessary hints about what is apparently the break-up of his marriage can only be hurtful and dismissive to those rating so low on the any-other-business of a committee man's life.

> Today I wandered about disguised in my dark glasses, overgrown hair and casual clothes. It was the first time for months I felt unrecognized.

So speaks Lord Garbo of Bankside. If he had walked down my local high street, clanking in a Hever breastplate and gold-lamé panty girdle, scarcely a head would have turned muttering: 'There's Peter Hall. He's part of essential services.'

Not since Boswell's London journal, Frank Harris's autobiography or the confessions of Maria Monk has such a cloying sensibility expressed itself with such coarse relish:

> Dinner tonight with Peter Brook and Trevor Nunn. It was wonderful to be with old friends ... Who paid for the dinner, all fifty quids' worth? I did of course. That must stop. It was an evening of elation, though.

Like Pope, Sir Peter seems to think he can both equivocate prettily and cultivate an inexplicable reputation as an adept politician. 'I was very charming ... thank God I am good with committees,' he says as if it were some seemly epitaph.

These diaries are an astonishingly winsome account of how the commonplace, workaday lunacies of organizations like the Arts Council and, above all, the subsidized theatres tick over. It is no accident that one of the National Theatre's houses should be named after an actor as secure in the nation's consciousness as Nelson and that the others should immortalize two one-time establishment nonentities, Lyttelton and Cottesloe: one dimly remembered as a brutal colonial secretary and the other, I am reliably informed, as 'the best shot in England'.

Here is the daily record of institutionalized theatre, the senseless turnover and clamour for plays on the production line, the feverish tooling up for the discovery of what was once some blessedly lost European masterpiece, a mediocre revival of a Shakespeare that would have seemed unremarkable thirty years ago. This is the British Leyland cultural whale that we have been gulled into enduring. The critics have here a venal interest: if the new theatrical Sierras or Cortinas don't come rolling out, they will be like motoring correspondents without yet another indistinguishable model to bully the public into buying on spec.

It is difficult to think of a more glum account of the iron dominion of the committee in this country and how it has established itself. Within the National's walls of chicken wire and unweathering concrete, they even speak of a new Venice. The tradition is as stilted as Gilbert and Sullivan, and as unfunny. The casting is like a pantomime: the broker's men and barons, Max Rayne, Victor Mishcon (surely the most opinionated and egregious of them all), and, of course, the Lord High Beadle himself, Lord Goodman.

Sir Peter is openly beholden and apparently grateful to the players in these mediocre knockabout committees: far from being an astute politician himself, he emerges as irresolute and suspicious, yet fawning on press, public and politicos.

These benighted boards are interchangeable. Consider the RSC, the National, The Royal Court. Look up their members in *Who's Who*. Here they are: the *gonfaloniers* of the cultural estate: the knighthood bearers and seekers, the grubbing placemen, the fat delayers of the law. One wouldn't ask one of them for a place winner in the Derby Stakes Trial, let alone what passed for an honest production of a fair masterpiece.

Early on, our diarist quotes, with approval, Nicholas Tomalin:

He is interested in doing a book on the National Theatre because he finds it, he says, a metaphor. He thinks the living organism of a theatre is subject to all the pressure and all the illnesses of society at large.

If indeed it is a metaphor, and it may well be, from the evidence of this volume, it is a detestable one, offensive to solitary imagination and endeavour.

Its institutionalism will surely abide. The author smirks at the spectacle of George Devine 'cackling' at being revered as a saint. The word could not be more ill-chosen. It was the shabby futility of this system that brought about his early death. If he were to read this account of it recumbent on his cloud, I only hope that, like the bird in the book of Tobit, he would remove his pipe from his mouth, collect a mouthful of holy dottle, and spit out a good large mess of black avenging juice in the eye of every theatrical committee, drama panel and Arts Council member still striving and, last of all, in that of the perpetrator of this chronicle of our dull and overweening times.

Sunday Times, 25 September 1983

Ingmar Bergman

Ingmar Bergman, *The Magic Lantern: An Autobiography*

I don't mind being wild and free
If Ingmar Bergman fancies me.

Ingmar Bergman is a rare breed indeed: a director who had a popular song written about him. He has also written an extraordinary, turbulent autobiography, *The Magic Lantern*. It received a rather sniffy dismissal when it was published in England some months ago. Perhaps because of its densely emotional kaleidoscopic shape or, more likely, because of the downright seriousness with which he attempts to define his own creative impulse and process.

And, too, he hated London when he was trapped there directing *Hedda Gabler* for Olivier's National Theatre. With Olivier sorely ill and distracted, and himself rehearsing in squalid, makeshift physical conditions, he was welcomed with general unease, an inedible Javanese meal, and an uncouth actor who informed him, as if it were company doctrine, that Strindberg and Ibsen were unplayable dinosaurs, which 'simply went to prove that bourgeois theatre was on its way out'. Reviling the distinguished guest is no longer a cultural sport confined to Australia. America, most welcoming of lands, has its own charmless cities of the plain and none more stylish in their treatment of strangers than those of California. He didn't have much time for the stars of Los Angeles, or they for him; he fled the joint when Barbra Streisand invited him to cool off at her pool party. Understandably, to Sweden: 'It was past eleven o'clock and a mild evening, everything at its most beautiful and fragrant. And then the Swedish light!'

The Swedish landscape is his lifeblood; Strindberg his god. The country's stark Lutheranism incites his demons; its scolding silences provoke him to wild outpourings. He may describe it as 'our remote cultural landscape', but he has insinuated it unforgettably into the minds of millions across the globe.

94

The Magic Lantern is not, far from it, a literary memoir. Bergman's minute recall is essentially, astonishingly, visual. Description after description stamp out scenes from his films. The man, his memory, his work are one, hammered into the Bergman coinage as indelibly mint as the desert of John Ford. Take this:

> It is always summer, the huge double birches, rustling, the heat shimmering above the hills, people in light clothes on the terrace, the windows open, someone playing the piano, croquet balls rolling, goods trains shunting and signalling. ... There is the fragrance of lily-of-the-valley, and heaps of roast veal. The children all have grazed knees and elbows.

Or again, remembering his first love affair: 'We rowed across the bay, straight into all that motionlessness, the glinting of the sun and the indolent waves.' It's a long, long way from London and Los Angeles.

His father, Pastor Bergman, was a chronic depressive who threatened suicide when he discovered his wife was having a passionate affair with another man. They stayed together, as the homely piety has it, 'for the sake of the children', including an elder brother and a younger sister, both of whom, unlike Ingmar, seemed to be rather crushed in adult life. The Bergman household ethic was severely Scandinavian, focusing in on sin, confession, punishment, forgiveness, and, with luck, grace. 'If I wet myself, which often happened, and all too easily, I was made to wear a red knee-length skirt for the rest of the day.'

The young Bergmans – marked recidivists – were encouraged to long for punishment, specifying how many strokes of the birch they deserved, or how many hours incarcerated in a cupboard, before forgiveness should be bestowed. Unsurprisingly, young Ingmar became a liar:

> I created an external person who had very little to do with the real me. As I didn't know how to keep my creation and my person apart, the damage had consequences for my life and creativity far into adulthood. Sometimes I have to console myself with the fact that he who has lived a lie loves the truth.

Behind what was outwardly an irreproachable picture of solid bourgeois family life was, in effect, 'inwardly misery and exhausting conflicts'. The Melodrama at the Manse was relentless. 'Fear created what was feared.' His brother attempted suicide, his sister was forced to have an abortion, Ingmar ran away from home; the parents stayed and prayed together, burdened down by work, tension, and a permanent state of crisis.

Mercifully for young Ingmar, and perhaps the reader, there was an energizing knot of spontaneity within the family circle. There was Rich Aunt Anna, a kind of benefactress who took him to the silent screen in the days when ladies removed their hats at the cinema. Then there was his grandmother, with whom he spent considerable stretches of time and who provided him with the quiet and orderly relationship he craved. The best of his childhood, as he describes it: 'A sunken world of lights, odours and sounds. Today, if I am calm and just about to fall asleep, I can go from room to room and see every detail, know and feel it.'

Best of all was Uncle Carl, an inventor who besieged the Royal Patent Office with his designs. Two were approved: a machine that made all potatoes the same size and an automatic lavatory brush. He was, it seems, extremely protective about his inventions and they travelled with him in an oilcloth wrapper between his trousers and his long underpants. The oilcloth served a dual purpose since Uncle Carl was also incontinent, or 'urinomaniac' as Bergman puts it: the lure of the self-induced flood. Poor Uncle Carl, an endearing innocent, ended his days cut to pieces on the railway track. Inside the oilcloth they discovered a design to revolutionize the changing of light-bulbs in street lamps.

So: Bergman is a self-confessed liar. (The style is catching.) How much do we believe of these childhood memories? How much does it matter? All autobiography is fiction to a greater extent. Is it true that his first memory is of vomiting over a plate of gruel in a white enamel plate with blue flowers on it, on a grey oilcloth in a dining-room overlooking an outside privy, dustbins, and fat rats? Is it true that when his father was a hospital chaplain the young Ingmar was allowed to see corpses in various stages of decay? Or, as he later elaborated in *Persona* and *Cries and Whispers*, that one corpse was not dead and, as he examined her private parts, opened her eyes on the mortuary slab? Images in the kaleidoscope? All part of the magic of the lantern?

One incident that is undoubtedly true is the matter of the cinematograph (or movie projector). One Christmas, the great and good Aunt Anna gave Ingmar's brother a cinematograph. To Ingmar she gave some tin soldiers (his brother's passion). 'The year before,' he recalls:

I had been to the cinema for the first time and seen a film about a horse. . . . To me, it was the beginning. I was overcome with a fever that has never left me. The silent shadows turned their pale faces towards me and spoke in inaudible voices to my most secret feelings. Sixty years have gone by and nothing has changed; the fever is the same.

That Christmas day, he made a deal with his truculent brother: in exchange for the cinematograph he would trade in the tin soldiers. It is worth quoting the experience, in the incarcerating cupboard, at length:

> A picture of a meadow appeared on the wall. Asleep in the meadow was a young woman apparently wearing national costume. *Then I turned the handle!* It is impossible to describe this. I can't find words to express my excitement. But at any time I can recall the smell of the hot metal, the scent of mothballs and dust in the wardrobe, the feel of the crank against my hand. I can see the trembling rectangle on the wall.
>
> I turned the handle and the girl woke up, sat up, slowly got up, stretched her arms out, swung round and disappeared to the right. If I went on turning, she would again lie there, then make exactly the same movements all over again.
>
> *She was moving.*

At a guess, films would seem to be the most personal part of Bergman's life. Certainly, his personal life is openly reflected in them. He cites, specifically, *Scenes from a Marriage* and *The Silence*. It is wonderfully liberating to be made privy to the tangible relish in his craft. Of course, he suffers the dismal vagaries of actors, the crassness of the money-men, and the transience of power and loyalties. Actors began to say: 'It's no longer so important to keep in with Bergman. He's stopped making films.'

There is an exhilarating, and modest, account of a day's filming on *Fanny and Alexander* in 1982.

> I got out of bed immediately and for a few moments stood quite still on the floor with my eyes closed. I went over my actual situation. How was my body, how was my soul and, most of all, what had got to be done today? I established that my nose was blocked (the dry air), my left testicle hurt (probably cancer), my hip ached (the same old pain), and there was a ringing in my bad ear (unpleasant but not worth bothering about). I also registered that my hysteria was under control, my fear of stomach cramp not too intensive. [We closet

hypochondriacs recognize this diagnosis.] ... It was a day of modest delight ... The rehearsals moved on smoothly and a quiet cheerfulness reigned, our creativity dancing along ... Sometimes there is a special happiness in being a film director. An unrehearsed expression is born just like that, and the camera registers that expression ... That is when I think days and months of predictable routine have paid off. It is possible I live for those brief moments.

Like a pearl fisher.

But the pearl fisher had been an arrogant, ill-equipped fledgling, snapping like a frightened dog, unloving, obsessive and guilty. It was Victor Sjöström, the great silent film-maker, who took Bergman, literally by the scruff of the neck, grounded him in the rudiments, and banished his whelpish arrogance: 'You make your scenes too complicated ... Work more simply,' he said, frog-marching that ill-mannered puppy across the asphalt in front of the studio. 'Don't keep having rows with everyone ... Don't turn everything into primary issues. The audience just groans.'

Bergman listened and learned, from a master. The temptation to quote at length again is irresistible. It is preferable to editorializing. His own words cut to the core of his cinematography.

The rhythm in my films is conceived in the script, at the desk, and is then given birth in front of the camera. All forms of improvisation are alien to me. If I am ever forced into hasty decisions, I grow sweaty and rigid with terror. Filming for me is an illusion planned in detail, the reflection of a reality which the longer I live seems to me more and more illusory.

When film is not a document, it is dream. That is why Tarkovsky is the greatest of them all ... Fellini, Kurosawa and Buñuel move in the same fields ... At the editing table, when I run the strip of film through, frame by frame, I still feel that dizzy sense of magic of my childhood; in the darkness of the wardrobe, I slowly wind on one frame after another, see the almost imperceptible changes, wind faster – a movement.

And then he gave it all up.

This dream world he inhabited so trenchantly and describes so evocatively is a powerfully erotic business. 'It took me many years', he says, 'before I at last learnt that one day the camera would stop and the lights go out.' Light, again.

Most of all I miss working with the cameraman [Sven Nykvist, perhaps] because we are both utterly captivated by the problems of light, the gentle, dangerous, dreamlike, living, dead, clear, misty, hot, violent, bare, sudden, dark, springlike, falling, straight, slanting, sensual, subdued, limited, poisonous, calming, pale light. Light.

He gives the reasons for his abdications as aging and exhaustion. He found, while working on *Fanny and Alexander*, that he was often in physical distress; practical problems became increasingly too difficult to solve and he felt himself becoming pedantic, and the result threatened a creeping perfectionism which was driving the life and spirit out of his films. 'I shall take my hat while I can still reach the hatrack,' he decided, 'and walk off by myself, although my hip hurts.'

And yet he had been, often alarmingly, in some physical distress throughout his life. The most persistent of these demons was a 'nervous stomach', a calamitous and humiliating affliction that has plagued him from childhood, liable to strike without warning and without respect. It would have sapped many a man disastrously, but he accepted it, adapted to it, asking only for his own lavatory in the places where he worked. 'These conveniences are probably my most lasting contribution to the history of the theatre.'

Then there has been insomnia, quite literally the 'hours of the wolf', the predawn devils familiar to those creative spirits who regularly dread a sunrise that may most likely bring them not illumination but a more clamorous and crowded darkness. Characteristically, he adopted a strategy, a technique to outwit them by reading, music, a glass of milk, a chocolate biscuit. 'I give the demons free rein: come on then! I know you, I know how you function, you just carry on until you tire of it.' Sleep, then, and another day of technical problems, actors' problems, producers' problems, money problems.

The demons drew him to Strindberg, passionately and at an early age. Strindberg is his lifelong love-affair and undoubtedly the reason why he went into the theatre. He saw *A Dream Play* at twelve and directed it himself four times. He even imagines, or experiences, some kind of telepathy with the playwright. 'Strindberg', he records, 'has been showing his displeasure with me ... That number of misfortunes is no coincidence ... Strindberg did not want me. The thought saddened me, for I love him.' Later, Bergman moved into an apartment on the site of

Strindberg's house and, on his first night there, Bergman heard a 'friendly greeting, perhaps', Schumann's '*Aufschwung*', one of Strindberg's favourite pieces. A whimsy, maybe, but there is no denying they are, uncannily, Sweden's soul brothers.

The Norwegian novelist Knut Hamsun wrote of Strindberg exactly 100 years ago: 'August Strindberg has formed no party, he stands alone.' In the party-minded conformism of modern Sweden, with its iron imposition of state benevolence, Strindberg's trapped forebodings and headlong, courageous ingenuities must have been a readily natural blood supply of oxygen to exult the heart in the thin, overpurified air of modern Scandinavia.

Bergman's attitude to the theatre is fascinating, being both precise and romantic. His approach to rehearsals is about as far removed from Stanislavsky as the Actors Studio is geographically from Stockholm's Royal Dramatic Theatre. Bergman's method of rehearsal is rooted in self-discipline, cleanliness, order, and quiet. 'My own tumult must be kept in place,' he explains, citing Stravinsky, who, as he bore a volcano within him, urged restraint. 'I want calm, order and friendliness.'

Yet his working methods clearly are not as chilly as they sometimes sound when he elaborates his technique. He describes his early days in the theatre with an obvious joy, one that used to prevail in the repertory and touring companies in England before television killed the gypsy life, making actors at once less technically equipped and irremediably avaricious. 'I loved the theatre from the very first moment ... We were grateful for our incredible good fortune at being able to play every night, and rehearse every day.' Incredible good fortune is precisely my own remembrance.

There is also some sensible, old-fashioned nostalgia for the days when scenery was clanked around by hand, when the scene changes actually worked and there were no computers to blame when they didn't. As director of the Royal Dramatic Theatre he remembers his first visit there in 1930: 'I used to go and sit in my old seat ... feeling with every beat of my pulse that this impractical and faded place was really my home.'

So, contrasting with the laborious film set-up, is his response to the exhilaration of the morning rehearsal and the actors from Universal central casting: the drunk anxious to confide his private problems; the transvestite in crippling high-heeled shoes; the actress arriving late and flurried, laden with carrier bags; another who has lost her script; yet another who must just make two quick telephone calls. Inevitably, the veteran who has forgotten his lines and blames the author.

His days as director of the Royal Dramatic Theatre were, naturally, often irksome, but nothing in his life was as horrific as the tax scandal of 1976. Like most of us in this business, he was woefully uninformed and inadequate about money. He paid inordinate sums to others to barricade himself against the armed forces of both private and state cupidity that encircle the honest, unworldly craftsman. He signed forms he neither read nor understood. So, it appeared, did his advisers. Unsurprisingly, they repaid his trust with rabid negligence, and the tax authority detectives swooped out of a clear blue morning sky during rehearsals and bundled him off like some prized Mafia mastodon. 'I was guilty of only one thing . . . I had approved financial operations that I had no grasp of.' His account of this terrifying business chills the blood. Sweden's brightest star was transformed into its most notorious criminal. He almost, hypnotically, threw himself out of the window, suffered a total breakdown, and endured seemingly eternal sedation. 'There disappeared my life's most faithful companion: the anxiety . . . the driving force was also eclipsed and fell away.' It was a cruel, harsh fight back.

Throughout his life this anxiety, or the demons, or just plain old rage have sustained him. Rehearsing *A Dream Play* again, he found it all, for the first time, impossible and, uncharacteristically, felt like giving up.

> Suddenly I heard myself saying . . . 'I'm about to lose my joy. I can feel it physically. It's running out. I'm just drying up, inside . . .' On that darkening afternoon in my room at the theatre, the attack came quite unexpectedly, my grief dark and bitter.

Then, later: 'I had been overcome by a rage demanding adrenalin. *I am not yet dead.*'

The Magic Lantern is no conventional autobiography, more a scalding stream of consciousness from the pen of a licentious puritan. 'Why were we given masks instead of faces?' he asks his mother in a dream after her death. He certainly has a staggering bout at cracking his own. In one sentence he can be praying 'Do not turn Thy face' to a silent God he may not even believe in. In another, he remembers the white hand with a chipped fingernail of a famous but faded theatre director as he fired him. Or the putrid flowered shirt of the tax detective. Or the Band-Aid on his dead mother's left forefinger.

Though the translation runs none too trippingly, the book is also consistently entertaining, even gossipy at times. Bergman is generous, on the whole, to his many wives and lovers. He is funny and crisp about several of the Famous and unstrainingly vicious about the dread and dismal critics. They, too, like actors at the morning rehearsal, seem to be the same the globe over. As Strindberg would have it: 'The world's a shithole!' A letter, supposedly sent to him by Nietzsche, said that he hardly regarded loneliness as a hardship, but rather felt it 'a priceless distinction and at the same time a purification'. Such a letter, even from such a mad mountain-top hand, must surely have cheered them both. Everyone, indeed.

Let Bergman have the last word: 'Before I am silenced for biological reasons, I very much want to be contradicted and questioned. Not just by myself. That happens every day. I want to be a pest, a troublemaker and hard to pigeon-hole.'

New York Review of Books, 27 October 1988

William Gaskill

William Gaskill, *A Sense of Direction: Life at the Royal Court*

'When Irving Wardle asked me about my policy at the Court, I am supposed to have replied, "Policy is the people you work with."' This succinct illumination of the nature of theatre administration comes from one of its most distinguished and incorruptible practitioners, William Gaskill, in this compelling, breezy account of his own combative regime, as well as the preceding years under George Devine.

As one now passes the filthy front of house of that once cherished building, its grimy glass doors, its sullen neglect of display, aloof box office, surly ushers, reluctant programme-sellers and stage-door *gauleiters*, the palace guard of the self-described undersubsidized and disadvantaged, it must be hard for an outsider to believe that this place was ever a glory-hole of energy, affection and robust and uncomplaining talents. Talents who were united in resistance to personal ambition, covetousness, official hostility and the caprice of fashion.

I don't apologize for retelling the story of Tony Richardson, who, approaching the Court box office not many Arts Council grants ago, proferred a cheque in payment for tickets. This was refused on the grounds that it was against house policy in spite of, or perhaps because, its signatory was recognized as one of the co-founders of the company.

'You wouldn't want us to make an exception, would you?' 'Yes, I would,' came the reply of the uncomfortable past. It is impossible to imagine such an oafish display in the days when Marie reigned as keeper of the box-office flame, reading all the scripts before she attended rehearsals; or Elsie, the housekeeper, who trimmed her cleaning schedule to accommodate the individual anxieties of each production.

Gaskill mentions an incident to which I was witness during the first-night opening of his production of *Epitaph for George Dillon* in New York. The reception had been only just short of rapturous but, through a tip-off from a mole in the *New York Times*, I already knew we were most certainly not a palpable hit. Besides, at the counter of my favourite bar across from the theatre, the hitherto effusive bartenders refused to look me in the eye, and by the time I arrived at the lavish party laid on by the producers, Josh Logan and David Merrick, the waiters were already weaving circles around my leprous presence, skilfully thwarting any hope of a comforting drink.

> Josh greeted us at the party like heroes [Gaskill remembers]. 'The show is a hit,' he announced. 'I thought you could never say that in New York till all the notices came out,' I ventured. 'Look, young man,' he roared, 'when I say a show is a hit, it's a hit.' ... Not long after it was noticeable that the room was emptying or rather that there was a mad rush to the door like water running out of a bath. The notices had arrived. I went over to Josh and said, in effect, 'I told you so,' perhaps not the most tactful thing in the circumstances. 'I knew there was something wrong in the third act. You should have done something about it.' 'Why the fuck didn't you say that before?' I wasn't exactly thrown out but I did hit Walter Winchell's column the next morning.

To Gaskill's everlasting credit, he refused to back down in the face of a recriminating audience, swelled by a bizarre group of British patriots, led by Oliver Messel and a noisy Danish sailor companion and shouting, 'You've let down England!' Such a man would never have connived at the despicable capitulation to the Court's resident Zionist mafia over the recently cancelled production of *Perdition* [by Jim Allen]. Giving offence was a revered tradition in the English Stage Company's unwritten charter. Nowadays, only identifiable, safe bugbears of the left wing may be attacked.

I once heard a playwright of what might be called the Court New

School informing a 'workshop' in Canberra that the company was formed in 1968, which is a little like saying that twentieth-century English history began in 1945. Gaskill's book gives the lie to that bit of popular Stalinist interpretation of the past. I know, because I too was there in 1955, even before Bill accepted Devine's invitation to join as an assistant artist director. 'Oscar Lewenstein offered me a salary of £15, exactly half what I'd been earning at Granada Television. I accepted gladly.' Nevertheless, it needs to be said that the Royal Court's achievement would remain intact even with the calendar-fiddling that celebrates 1968 as the revolutionary dawn. By that time the palace had already been stormed, leaving it open to the looters and cultural carpet-baggers of the following twenty years.

Theatre Councils are always comprised of high-ranking nonentities, dependable busybodies, committee persons, glittering with consolation prizes like life peerages or foreign orders such as the Golden Band of Yugoslavia (Second Class). Just take a look at the luminaries listed on your programme at the Royal Shakespeare or the National Theatre. The English Stage Company was no different in this respect, except that it did contain an eccentric mix which made it occasionally susceptible to artistic pressure from within. In other words, its members included some who actually had practical knowledge of the theatre rather than charity-raising or accountancy.

The Chairman was Neville Blond, in Gaskill's words:

> a remarkable businessman who had steered the Court through crisis after crisis. He was completely philistine, with no understanding of theatre, but he knew about money. He looked like Oscar Homolka as Genghis Khan and trampled over the sensibilities of his Artistic Directors.

(Later, there was also his wife, Elaine, probably the rudest woman outside the staff of British Rail. 'Oh, *you're* still here, are you?' was her habitual greeting to me.)

However, shining like good deeds in a nonentity world were two shrewd theatrical managers. Robin Fox was an erratically successful producer endowed with huge, persuasive charm and wit and, apart from the very different Peggy Ramsay, the best agent in the business. In almost total contrast was Oscar Lewenstein, a wily thirties Golders Green communist who exulted in the Soviet invasion of Hungary.

Two other founders were Lord Harewood and the poet, Ronald

Duncan. 'Harewood could always be relied upon to give a clear and dispassionate judgment,' says Gaskill. 'I saw him shield Devine from the attacks of Ronald Duncan and he supported me through all my crises.' It was true, and an ironic example of the uses of royal patronage. Duncan, who had been at Cambridge with Harewood, I christened the Black Dwarf as he seemed to exude a cloud of black bile. The earliest intended policy was to put on his plays and those of like-minded writers of whom he approved. Time and again, the same names were put forward: Ustinov, Fry, Canan, Whiting, Bolt, Mortimer. Devine and Richardson resisted furiously and, ingeniously supported by Fox, Lewenstein and Harewood, narrowly had their way. Perhaps the most bitter confrontation took place over the production of *The Entertainer*, when the Council was evenly divided between the Nonentities and the iron-fisted liberals led by Commisar Lewenstein. Not even the prestigious and commercial coup of securing Olivier could placate the businessmen. Harewood's casting vote made it possible.

Gaskill's terse record of 'an embattled community' fighting for its existence, its enemies within and without, may come as a revelation to some of the Sixty-Eighters. Certainly it is a rousing antidote to the loveless Hall Diaries. His descriptions of the early improvisation groups (which were to degenerate into those dreaded rituals of democratic frenzy 'workshops', with their smug invocation of proletarian sweat), the uses of mime and mask, the serious attention to the inheritances of the recent past, these are all cool, funny and informative. He reminds us of the prevailing spirit of spontaneous joy in disaster, of George 'brandishing the notices of *Serjeant Musgrave's Dance*, saying with almost a note of triumph, "they're even worse than *Live Like Pigs*!" '

He puts his finger on the heart of the matter, which was never the rattling swill-bucket of subsidy, but simply and squarely that of creating a loyal and attractive audience. When the building was ever packed it was due to the gift of excitement and entrepreneurial flair provided by the likes of George, Tony and Bill himself, neither obtainable on demand from Government agencies.

He swiftly establishes policy equals people, the link with the social storms and furies of the time, the particular battles against the Lord Chamberlain, the tread of policemen's boots in the foyer, the press saboteurs, the threats, financial and legal, the final victory over censorship itself. Among many cheery snippets of memory is the Committee of One Hundred's sit-down in Trafalgar Square in which we almost all took part.

When Big Ben struck three we swept out into the Square. Everyone – but, my dear, everyone – was there. Some arrests were made. The word went round, 'They've got Vanessa!' I ended up in a cell with Lindsay, Anthony Page and Alan Sillitoe.

He was lucky. From that day on, my conviction that the cloud of the H-bomb was infinitely preferable to the company of the strategists of CND was irreversible.

Spectator, 3 December 1988

John Dexter

Obituary

I knew John Dexter for almost the whole of my adult life. From our very first meeting in Derby I was utterly convinced of his driving gift. He was a man of ferocious energy, sparkle and courage. In the early days at the Royal Court, I was able to persuade the administrators, with some difficulty, to take him on. He was always aware of this reluctance and felt painfully disadvantaged by the predominance of Oxbridge directors in the profession.

He shouldn't have been. Not one of them had, or has now, a fraction of his fierce intelligence and invention. The often uncanny boldness and originality of that invention came from the alchemy he could conjure from a devoted exploration of play text rather than playing wilful games at the expense of the actors' resources. He could be harsh with them, but it was nothing to the merciless drilling he gave himself throughout his career. I have always been glad that I had the rarest opportunity to nudge, even in a minimal way, such bright good fortune into the theatre. But the achievement was entirely his own. Such flair was irrefutable.

His theatrical instinct was extraordinary. He could make theatre out of a ballpoint pen and, unlike many contemporaries, without vulgarity. His range was immense: Shakespeare, Shaw, Wesker. It's sad that he was never given his head and encouraged to bring administrative life back to the moribund Royal Court or gaiety to the grim gymnasia of the National Theatre.

Our preferences were usually opposed and we often argued. He was the most stimulating companion and a sharp anecdotist. He once had a nickname for me which I believe was 'Sister Mary Discipline'. I didn't think it appropriate myself, but it had a certain aptness which I found amusing. We once had an extended, fiery disagreement about the merits of a minor but charming John Ford film, *The Sun Shines Bright*. I loved it, but he was quite immune to its sweet sentiment. 'Cornball syrup,' he rasped.

Dexter apparently told people that he was the model for Webster, one of the twenty-seven offstage characters in *Look Back in Anger*. This was the truth, although neither of us ever spoke of it to each other. That description in the play is a poor epitaph to his brave vitality but it is the sincerest dedication to it, from the darkest provinces, long before any intimation of what was to come for both of us in our profession. Written thirty-five years ago, I think he was secretly pleased with it. I hope so. It isn't often you can pass on personal admiration so nakedly under the anonymity of invention:

ALISON: I thought you said he was the only person who spoke your
    language.
JIMMY: So he is. Different dialect but same language. I like him. He's got
    bite, edge, drive.
ALISON: Enthusiasm.
JIMMY: You've got it. When he comes here, I begin to feel exhilarated.
    He doesn't like me, but he gives me something, which is more than I
    get from most people.

Observer, 1 April 1990

John Dexter, *The Honourable Beast: A Posthumous Autobiography*

John Dexter's death in 1990 went almost unnoticed except by those who had worked with him and had been scalded by the heat of his stern professionalism and rigorous powers of self-examination.

His nickname for me – Sister Mary Discipline – applied far more to his own prickly genius than to my own often indolent spirit. To many, and not just Shirley Williams's children who are content to believe that Oscar Wilde was a contemporary of Shakespeare, this posthumous 'autobiography', *The Honourable Beast*, will provide some muddling guidance to the career of a key figure in English Theatre.

Briefly, Dexter's star first appeared at the Royal Court, where he worked magic on Arnold Wesker's trilogy. From then on it was difficult to ignore his special inspirational energies, and he went on to become Associate Director of the original National Theatre under Olivier (directing *Othello* and [Peter Shaffer's] *The Royal Hunt of the Sun*). He spent seven years as director of the New York Metropolitan Opera. His farewell production in London, *M. Butterfly* was an amazing feat of alchemy, which only he could have conjured out of the numinous cloud of theatricality he carried in his head.

He had little gift for friendship, which he defiantly confides to the poet/playwright Tony Harrison in a reverential letter one can hardly imagine any other director addressing to a mere writer: 'I don't relate well to people outside a working situation. That is why I prefer to create and not administrate ... work is the only worship I know and understand.' It was a steely constraint he imposed on himself and others, mistakenly in my view, but one cannot argue with the strategy of such headlong talent.

Yet, in life and in his letters here, he constantly abandons this austere ethic of 'work' coming before personal frailty and affection. In the same letter to Harrison, he abrogates all the arm's-length bluster of before: 'The web of relationships at the Royal Court has always seemed more important to me than the work we did. If you look at the upcoming *Man and Superman* production, you will see that it contains in its substructure a clearly articulated skeleton of the working life I have had so far and the relationships I have valued.' These turn out to be: 'Shaw, the Royal Court, George [Devine], Jocelyn [Herbert], the OLD National, creativity as a Life Force, everything I have learned about language.'

Like George Devine ('George was my university'), Dexter was a born teacher. Intimidated, but not too bowed by the squatting scions of the OUDS (Oxford) and Footlights (Cambridge) in the London theatre, he was impelled by a Pygmalion urge of creation, which transformed plays and players, but involved a gruelling, lifelong reworking of his own spiritual destiny.

If his method sometimes struck people as harsh, sado-Jesuitical even, it was one he applied to himself unremittingly. Within Devine's lofty concept of the Theatre as a Temple of Ideas, Dexter was a chaste self-flagellant who renounced the paths of incontinent ambition, cupidity and rancid orthodoxies.

He talks of discovering a 'play which is bigger than I am', a grotesque notion to most of those who currently practise his craft to such applause and personal profit. If there were any justice, even in a kindless and rancorous world, he would have been Olivier's natural successor at the National Theatre. During recent weeks, protecting my knees from the tiny fists of the dwarfs who scuttle through the darkly correct alleyways of the South Bank bunker, I have often thought of him, of his vitality in particular. He would have booted them all into the Thames. Dexter was emphatically not a smooth man but a most irredeemably hairy one.

Leaving school at 14, his thirst for erudition exploded daily. He passed on his discoveries from hand to hand like an excited prospector. 'Read *this*,' he said to me forty years ago when I first met him. 'You'll learn from it.' It was *The Catcher in the Rye*. All his lovers were shining Galateas, whom he groomed and perfected. So, the Beast was the half-mask he adopted. Honourable he was as far as most of us can ever expect to be.

This is an atrociously edited, confusing book, but, for anyone curious to discover what the English theatre might have become, it is well worth the purchase. Details of costumes, of props and furniture in forgotten productions, of political wranglings, may become wearisome, but they should be taken as part of the lumber of a man of towering theatrical genius. A twitch or twinkle of that driven brain could create a very firmament from next to nothing.

Sunday Telegraph, 20 June 1993

Tony Richardson

Obituary

Tony Richardson was my close friend and partner for thirty-six years. We first met in 1955 when he was living in a flat above George Devine's house in Lower Mall, Hammersmith. George had called up the stairs and Richardson appeared. He had the authoritative stoop of a gangler who is born to master. In what was to become one of the most imitated voices in his profession, he said, 'I think *Look Back in Anger* is the best play written since the war.'

I heard his voice for the last time about three weeks ago, when he rang me from London on his way back to Los Angeles. I had not spoken to him for two years and the strangled cadences came as a shock, a reminder of his impatient, electric presence. The tone was soft, but seductive and firm as ever.

I had known for some time that he was very ill (with Aids). 'And how are *you*?' As usual, he made the opening ploy, delivered with that probe of mocking interrogation which demanded confessional conspiracy and the unwilling yielding up of mystery.

In May 1989, Tony had once again declared himself as the director of my latest play, *Déjàvu*. He had wheedled a copy from the producer, Robert Fox, my friend and his prospective son-in-law. 'It's possibly the best play written this century,' he said this time.

Echoes of that unequivocal declaration in Lower Mall blotted out all memory of the bitter, brawling exchanges between us during thirty years of pain and recrimination. 'I'm the *only* one who understands your work.' 'Better the devil . . .' I said to Robert. But Beelzebub was already condemned to fires of which I knew nothing and which he could not possibly confide. By October, blind acrimony, ostensibly over casting, put an end to what would have been our final shared enterprise.

Yet, here he was, two years later, urging me, 'That play has *got* to be seen. It's the finest thing you've ever done.' He gave a whinnying laugh and, arranging to see me at the end of next month, rang off. I almost believed him.

Déjàvu . . . a quarter of a century ago, on a bitterly cold January night, I learned of the death of George Devine. I wandered through the Saturday-night-drunk streets of Newcastle and then watched *The Sound of Music* in a warm stupor of disbelief, trying to cast in my head the things I felt must be said about my most loved companion. I had ten hours to phone through my copy to the *Observer* from the station hotel.

Tonight I am at home, this time surrounded by domestic comfort, and now Tony is gone, half a world away in Los Angeles. The sybaritic delights of that desert place were milk and honey to him. Desolate and anonymous in the sunshine, the poolside reflections of darkness, celebrated so startlingly by his fellow immigrant, David Hockney, might have been invented for him.

He gloried in his abrogation of England, all the more so because he knew I thought it a folly, a wasteful gesture, a betrayal of his talent. He regarded the Woodfall years in England (the company we formed together, when he made what I regarded as his best films) as his Babylonian exile. The search for an American *laissez-passer* seemed to me as perverse as his earlier attempts to adopt an almost comically French identity. Whatever is the opposite of xenophobia, Tony pursued it resolutely, as a profoundly felt gesture of total rejection.

Months ago, writing the second volume of my autobiography, my pen was guided more truthfully with an artifice and reflection that eludes my uncertain hand tonight:

> During the six years that had followed my first meeting with Tony up in George's workroom on Lower Mall, my love for him had grown into something taunting, mysterious and quite inexplicable. In spite of all my regular, outraged efforts to repudiate and expunge it in the bitter course of a lifetime, I was slowly forced to concede that this was a phantom which had penetrated my heart inexorably and, however fiercely I tried to banish it, I would never be finally rid of its implant. So it has proved . . .
>
> Utterly dissimilar to my passionate friendship for George, it is a chaste, severe love circumscribed by some mutually agreed attachment of alienation. It is cool, circumspect, and no exchange of mockery or disillusion can dislodge its binding brace of respect. No one has inflamed my creative passions more tantalizingly than Tony, nor savaged my moral sensibilities so cruelly. Whatever wayward impulse of torment he inflicted, his gangling, whiplash courage, struggling within that contorted figure, was awesomely moving and, at the last, unimpeachable. The rewards are recorded in scars rather than the stars, but I shall never regret one moment in his company, nor our scabrous *marriage blanc*.

As, once again, I try to piece together yet another memorial as truthfully as I can, I think I hear his playful spirit murmuring, 'The thing is, Johnny, all you think about is those f— old golden words.'

Observer, 17 November 1991

Dear Diary . . .

TERENCE RATTIGAN and I had a desultory, forlorn correspondence for a while. His letters were written in the small hours, usually from Paris or Bermuda. They were cautious, courteous and generous. There was a great deal of regret for his past, confessions of professional dishonesty and avarice as well as advice about not deserting my country to live among tax-reprobates, how to withstand the sustained vilification of reviewers and, worst of all, the desertion of your public. Never having had the last, it was the least useful insight. 'Whatever you do, and I don't think you will,' he said, 'don't write what they expect you to write.' No one knew better that playwrights are especially condemned to the yawn and spite of fashion. Their work lays them open to something like social banishment while novelists and poets are more comfortably barricaded in their studies. If they are successful in their twenties and persist in working on into the decrepitude of their early fifties only uncompensated redundancy faces them until they receive the country's gold watch when terminal illness and death qualify them for reassessment.

No one suffered more evidently from this assault course than Rattigan and Coward. Noël, with his justified arrogance, 'rose above it' in the discovery of his newly acclaimed genius in cabaret. Rattigan, introspective in a manner which The Master would have regarded as self-indulgent, was permanently wounded, exiling himself to Beverly Hills and Colonial golf clubs. The irony is that they were never really out of fashion at all. They simply allowed themselves to be convinced of it by a few hacks and hustlers.

I thought of Rattigan a few days ago when I had a communication from the Royal Society of Literature informing me that I had been elected a Fellow and that it would cost me £15. In one of the more chatty sections of his letters to me, Rattigan had written: 'I've just put you up as a FRSL. I don't think there's much glory to it. You just buy yourself in. And, if you haven't already got any, you can put their letters after your name. It might amuse you.' Well, it did slightly, but not to the extent of stumping up the fee. The Companions of the Society are impressive enough, but the list of Fellows largely includes mediocrities similar to those proclaimed as council or board members on the masthead of your subsidized theatre programmes. I also noticed that most of my contemporaries in the trade had accepted this distinction years ago. Possibly some wordsmiths and academics take pride in appending FRSL to themselves, but there doesn't seem much profit in being a begrudged afterthought in such company. *Not* a complaint, nurse. Just the inmate's comment.

ONE ACCOLADE in my career I can claim exclusively is that of being the only living English playwright to be pursued by the mob down the streets of London. On this particular first-night tumbrel, I fled from the spectacle of several hundred people, including Coward, a motley of theatrical knights and sundry stars, who *stood up* to boo me. I found myself in the waiting path of a pavement full of lynch-happy play-goers. I have had ladies' boots thrown from the audience and been booed by tray-banging customers and what seemed to be a little dog at a matinée in Brighton.

Nowadays we get the real going-over from the management and reviewers rather than the public. Booing has become an unfamiliar sound to this generation of playwrights, official tribunes of the arts. It's an odd, unforgettable sound when it's coming your way, exhilarating, like the tribute ringing in the ears of a wrestler in his corner. No doubt I shall be the one to bring it back.

I HAVE IN front of me a play contract. Paragraph 11.02 states that for attendance at rehearsals the theatre 'shall pay the Author £25 for each day of such attendances and £12.50 for each half day of such attendances'. If the playwright agrees to place himself fully at the disposal of the management for the whole rehearsal period, he will receive a weekly attendance fee of £125 as well as 'reasonable and legitimate' hotel and travelling expenses incurred during preliminary rehearsals.

This is the aggrandisement of true timidity on all sides. To allow a playwright to demand *payment* for attending rehearsals of his own play is the flowering philistine folly of those who administer the nation's purse. Pinter, Ayckbourn, Shaffer, or the public scourges of private greed like Trevor Griffiths, Brenton and Hare can scarcely be said to be in need of a few bob for the bus-fare or a night's lodging for the privilege of listening to their very own and golden words. Those who are so deprived could surely get a chit from the Arts Minister or even a postal order from one of the bank chairmen or downhill racers on the Board – in lieu of royalties, naturally.

WHEN GEORGE DEVINE was Arts purveyor at the Royal Court he received £40 a week and the theatre subsidy itself was the same amount, in some contrast to the half a million handed over presently to the Rons and Lens who preside over that building and its workshops, sweatshops and Yoof theatre. Tony Richardson, as assistant artistic director, was paid £14 a week. Recently, he asked the box office if he might pay for his ticket by cheque. Recognizing the man whose theatre had provided her with a sinecure, the hirsute gorgon behind the counter refused. 'It's against theatre policy,' she said with the smug finality of those prigs and bullies who now have dominion over daily life. In an almost human aside and recognition of a sometime fellow worker, she added: 'You wouldn't expect us to make an *exception*, would you?' 'Yes, I would,' was the illiberal reply.

THOSE WHO WERE dismayed at the demise of the Flavour of the Week engagement photograph in *Country Life* were not reassured by its return when it was represented by Miss Kim Nevill. She was tasty enough, very, very, but her address was 47 Leigh Road, Westbury, and she was to be married to Mr Mark Young of 115 *Station Road*, also in Westbury. Could this aberration be what Mrs Thatcher meant by her own vision of a classless society? Might we look forward to the announced nuptials of Tracey, daughter of Cllr Sid and Mrs Wellfair of Bishop Boateng House, SE1? However, the following week's even fruitier flavour was the daughter of a neighbour. At the wedding, Brigade and Old Etonian ties were hanging from trees and I was the only guest in a lounge suit. High-rise Normans are not yet phoning for the fish-knives for Sharon's do at the Leisure Centre. We blessed reactionaries may breathe again.

LAST WEEK THE Wash-Out-Wife paled again as she slumped in front of Channel 4's latest castration series, *Watch the Woman*. While a harridan in a skimpy T-shirt cracked on about faked orgasms, WOW poured yet another triple malt and moaned: 'It may not be insulting to wimmin but it's sure offensive to the rest of us.' She is now rereading Jane Austen, branded 'a token' by the T-shirt, and, happily, is feeling much better.

Spectator, 3 August 1985

[5]
Players
==

Max Miller

He was a popular hero more than a comic. He was cheeky because he was a genius. All genius is a cheek. You get away with your nodding little vision and the world holds its breath or applauds. Max took your breath away altogether and we applauded.

When I was at school he was popular only with the more sophisticated boys, and girls seemed bored by him although I suspected that the girls I longed to know – big, beautiful Waafs or land-girls – would adore an evening with him. I loved him as fiercely as I detested the Three Stooges and Abbot and Costello. He was not a great clown like Sid Field nor did he make me laugh so much. The Cheeky Chappie was not theatrically inventive in any profound sense. His fantasy was bone simple, traditional, predictable and parochial.

It is said that he hit his insolent peak during the early forties at the Holborn Empire. I saw him there only twice, but during the next twenty years his style slackened very little and he never looked less than what he was – the proper champion of his type. What type?

He was the type of flashiness. He was flashiness perfected and present in all things visible and invisible. The common, cheap and mean parodied and seized on as a style of life in face of the world's dullards. Maxie would have been in his element at the Boar's Head. Just to begin: his suits were superb. My favourite was the blue silk one with enormous plus-fours and daisies spluttered over them. With his white upturned hat on one side and co-respondent shoes he looked magnificent, perfectly dressed for bar parlour or Royal Enclosure. In those days of clothing coupons, I longed to wear such suits, although a weakness for clothes was likely to get you called nancy boy. Someone called out after me in the street once because I was wearing a dull but *yellow* pullover. No doubt he grew up to be a Customs Officer or on the staff of the *Daily*

Telegraph. No one would have dared to jeer at anyone who could wear a suit like Maxie's.

He was constantly being banned by the BBC, then the voice of Higher Court Judges, Ministries and schoolteachers. Sometimes he was fined £5 for a blue joke which became immediately immortal. I knew the truth was that Max was *too good* for the BBC, and all the people like it. But this was just.

He went on telling them from the blue book, wearing his smashing clothes, looking better than anyone else, and smelling of sea air, the open doors of public houses and whelks. He talked endlessly and with a fluency that made me spin. He was Jewish, which made him racy and with blasphemy implicit in his blood. He sang his own compositions in an enviable voice and with a pride I thought both touching and justified. 'This little song . . . this little song *I* wrote . . . you won't hear anyone else singin' it. No one else *dare* sing it!' Nor would they.

He seemed to talk supercharged filth, and no one could put him in prison or tell him to hold his tongue. He appeared to live in pubs, digs, racecourses and theatre bars. Naturally, he never worked. On top of all this, he had his own Rolls-Royce, and a yacht, and was rumoured to own most of Brighton. I discounted stories about his alleged meanness and never buying anyone a drink. He was simply holding on to what he'd got, and he deserved it more than anyone else in the world.

Above all, he talked about girls. Unwilling girls, give her a shilling and she'll be willing girls, Annie and Fanny, girls who hadn't found out, girls on their honeymoon, fan dancers minus their fans, pregnant girls and barmaids the stork put the wind up every six weeks. You always felt with Maxie that he didn't go too much on birth control but if anything went wrong the girls would be pretty good-tempered about it. As for their mothers, he could always give *them* a little welcome present too. In the same way, the Wife was complaisant, just another cheerful barmaid at home reading the *News of the World* till Max felt like coming back for 'coffee and games'. Except that Max could always do without the coffee.

One always acknowledged his copyright to a joke. You could do nothing else. Some of his jokes are still school folklore. There's the immortal story of the man who met a girl on a narrow ledge and didn't know what to do about it. (I can't write the punch line in the *Observer*.) That one cost £5 and worth every penny of it. There are the incomplete rhymes like –

When roses are red
They're ready for plucking.
When a girl is sixteen,
She's ready for – ere!

You could repeat the line but not the master's timing over his swivelling grin of outrage at the audience. 'You can't help likin' him, can yer?' They couldn't. They daren't. He handled his rare shafts of silence as – a word he would have approved – a weapon. When he paused to sit down to play his guitar and watched the detumescent microphone disappear, he waited till the last bearable moment to thrust in his blade with 'D'you see that, Ivor? D'you? Must be the cold weather!' He was a beautiful, cheeky god of flashiness who looked as if he'd just exposed himself on stage. 'There'll never be another!' There wouldn't, and he knew it and we knew it.

As soon as the orchestra played 'Mary from the Dairy' I usually began to cry before he came on. And when he did appear, I went on doing so, crying and laughing till the end. Even his rather grotesque physical appearance didn't belie his godliness. You could see his wig join from the back of the stalls, and his toupee looked as if his wife had knitted it over a glass of stout before the Second House. His make-up was white and feminine, and his skin was soft and like a dowager's. This steely suggestion of ambivalence was very powerful and certainly more seductive than the common run of manhood then. He even made his fleshy, round shoulders seem like the happy result of prodigious and sophisticated sexual athletics – the only form of exercise he acknowledged.

Some people have suggested to me that I modelled Archie Rice on Max. This is not so. Archie was a man. Max was a God, a saloon-bar Priapus. Archie never got away with anything properly. Life cost him dearly always. When *he* came on, the audience was immediately suspicious or indifferent. Archie's cheek was less than ordinary. Max didn't have to be lovable like Chaplin or pathetic like a clown. His humanity was in his cheek. Max got fined £5 and the best of the world laughed with him. Archie would have got six months and no option.

I loved him because he embodied a kind of theatre I admired most. His method was danger. 'Mary from the Dairy' was an overture to the danger that he might *go too far*.

And occasionally he did, God bless him, and the devil with all nagging magistrates and censors and their wives-who-won't. Whenever anyone tells me that a scene or a line in a play of mine goes too far in some way then I know my instinct has been functioning as it should. When such people tell you a particular passage will make the audience 'uneasy' or 'restless' they seem as cautious and as absurd as landladies and girls-who-won't. Maxie was right. And hardly a week passes when I don't miss his pointing star among us.

Observer, 19 September 1965

On the Halls

Whilst watching human nature, having not much else to view . . .

'Having not much else to view.' Shakespeare would not have discarded such a throw-away, and I'd be glad to have it near to hand.

> I saw a lot of people making fun as people do.
> I asked the reason of this fuss
> and how the turmoil grew . . .

Asked. Reason. Fuss. Turmoil. Not a dead word yet. And then:

> They answered with a sneering smile –
> A man who's but a Jew.

Hath not a Jew eyes? Or a Gentile ears. Yes, we have, we had.
   The verse of this song, written and composed by John Lawson and Moses Besso, continues:

> Only a Jew – the insult I'll remember,
> Only a Jew – then why not Christian too?

Such a line: then why not Christian too! Say *that* to yourself in the bath.
   On goes the chorus:

> The same world lies before us, the same sun's shining o'er us,
> And why should they insult a man – Only a Jew! Only a Jew!

I have quoted this song because I feel it is only possible to be *subjective* about the historical fact of the British music hall. This song was the first spark, as *I* remember, of the experience as it later affected my own life and my work. Music hall has established its own pedantry and College of Heralds, much as the movies have. The difference is that the movies *exist*

118

for another generation to re-experience. Film buffs are awesomely academic, frame for frame, and people twenty years younger than myself
know the name of every actor in the Hollywood repertory: who played
elevator boys, bell-hops, *maître d*'s, hotel managers, boxers, gamblers,
small-time gangsters in the films of the 1930s and 1940s. You can't fault
them. What was once a pursuit, like downing a black-and-tan, is now the
crossword pastime of thirsty young 'intellects'.

The music hall has not undergone this arcane scrutiny, for the very
simple reason that the records are not lasting in the way that moving
pictures survive, from picture palace to late-night movie on the telly.
Theatre is theatre and has death at the heart of it, like life itself. Movies
survive. Not only do they survive, but their cultural sense goes into the
general memory of history in a way that no theatrical experience can
match.

Most academics would argue that the golden age of music hall
flowered about 1912, the year of the first Royal Command Performance,
and from then on the rot set in. Managers grew fat and respectable, and
hedged in with family commitments and entertainment knighthoods,
while performers strangely, but often, went off to early graves.

I know of the music hall at first hand only as a spectator and a young
touring actor shortly after the Second World War. But during this downhill period I was able to see many times, and from a very young age until I
was well into my twenties, people like the superb Billy Bennett, Clapham
and Dwyer, Billy Danvers, George Doonan ('That's not funny, old man –
give yourself a kick in the pants'), G. H. Elliott (whose digs I seemed to
use all over England), Norman Evans, the incomparable Sid Field, Flan-
agan and Allen, Nervo and Knox (all much funnier separately than as
part of the Crazy Gang), Monsewer Eddie Gray, Will Hay, Layton and
Johnstone (I don't care what the purists might say), Ernie Lotinga, Max
Miller, Sandy Powell, Frank Randle, Jack Ratcliffe (a Scots comedian
who seemed to appear mostly in Scotland with an alarmingly realistic
deathbed scene as his speciality), Revnell and West, Old Mother Riley
and her daughter Kitty, Randolph Sutton, Vesta Tilley, Duggie Wakefield
(one of my favourites), Nellie Wallace, Robb Wilton, Wee Georgie Wood
and many more. I would have called that more of a golden sunset than a
decline. But decline was built into the first supper rooms, and fall was in
its managers fawning to middle-class attitudes.

I began by quoting the song from a famous sketch, performed by John
Lawson at a time when, according to the serious historian, music hall

was well on the way down its pristine path to revue and 'variety'. My only memory of this famous sketch was provided for me by my mother, whose memory is and was faulty. However, I do feel that I have a firm idea of what this thing Music Hall was, even from such a shaky folk memory.

If, indeed, it is to be remembered, one should be reminded that this was a theatre that knew its Shakespeare, Tree, Imperial Ballet, Shaw, Ellen Terry, Kipling, and Barrie – who actually wrote a piece for it under the statutory half hour. (Music halls were not allowed to produce sketches of more than 30 minutes in length.)

I remember the tale of 'Only a Jew' – incorrectly, no doubt – because of my mother's description of it. It was, according to her, about a highly reputable, rich and – it seemed – wholly virtuous Jew who struck up a full-hearted, passionate friendship with a Gentile who became, quite clearly, his Best Friend. The wholesome Jew leaves home for some reason and his lovely wife to the attentions of Best Gentile Friend. Adultery, Close-Thing, or, most of all, Betrayal takes place before John Lawson, the author of the whole thing, reappears.

Now, my mother, a cruel woman in all things, used to call me John Lawson's son – 'only a Jew!' As she was anti-Semitic in the sense that she thought all foreigners were Jews, I took this to be yet another hammer-blow of hers at my minuscule personality. However, I was not even certain of this, as she would then describe, in great detail, the roof-rending scene in which the Good Jew Thrashed his Best Friend. Quite apart from the horror of such bestial human destruction was the princi-pal Character – the Set. This, or so it was described to me, consisted of a superb sitting-room furnished in Taste-Beyond-Which, Which being mostly breakable – like superb and irreplaceable chandeliers. Glass, blood, antiques, teeth, hair, tailoring everywhere. A ruined palace, a disgraced wife, treacherous friend, destroyed V.J. After the vicious fight between Gentile Snake and Jew, the virtuous one, bleeding in mouth, mud and spirit, among all the despoil, sang this very song: 'Only a Jew'.

The description of it took away my breath even as a boy. I only wish the National Theatre would mount it somewhere in their programme.

Such things were life, such were real. To recognize this is not to be sentimental or nostalgic. It was a hard, unyielding world that gave a lot but took everything. It is unthinkable for a pop group to get the bird. (Never mind the lemon.) It was cruel, but it was cunning and perceptive. Such an audience scarcely exists today, or if it does, has no weight of presence, let alone empire, place and desolation, to make itself felt. It is quite interesting to recall how many of the stars of the golden age died young. Nelly Power, who sang one of the greatest songs ever written, 'The Boy I Love is up in the Gallery', was only thirty-four when she sang that for the last time. Mostly, they died or retired early. In art, oh yes, as in life, events overwhelmed people. Gaslight to electricity, horses to motors, people to bioscopes, sound broadcasting to television.

Sentimental it was not. Sassoon made his point:

> The house is crammed; tier beyond tier they grin,
> And cackle at the Show, while prancing ranks
> Of harlots shrill the chorus, drunk with din;
> 'We're sure the Kaiser loves our dear old Tanks!'
>
> I'd like to see a Tank come down the stalls,
> Lurching to rag-time tunes, or 'Home Sweet Home'.
> And there'd be no more jokes in Music Halls
> To mock the riddled corpses round Bapaume.

Of course, he was wonderfully right. But if the music hall was wrong – as it often was – so was the nation itself. Patriotism was part of the rag-bag, and what a surrealistic (a later name) rag-bag it was, of patriotism, bisexuality, wives, being in love, Irish, queer, a toff, virginal or anything else.

During my early professional life, I played at most of the London and provincial halls that were then left. Perhaps, because I thought of myself as a Londoner, they seemed a very special thing to London. Yet when I went to the provinces, to Sunderland, West Hartlepool, Manchester, Bristol, and so on, it wasn't very different from Shepherd's Bush, Finsbury Park, Kilburn, Kingston, Chiswick, Wood Green, Hackney.

The history of the music hall is fairly well documented, although, oddly enough, there are few books on the subject. But it is memory, it is history, and it is very valuable. It cannot even disappear into the reservoirs of *Thanks for the Memory* or *Good Old Days*. It is abiding and cruel, like the English spirit itself.

One of the greatest sounds of love is the song 'If You were the Only Girl in the World'. Ponder a little and all life indeed is in these songs. 'The End of Me Old Cigar.' What vitality! Compare it with the mid-Western gentility of, say, the Osmonds. But Vaudeville and Boylekue (burlesque) were never quite the same. Another subject.

Years ago I spent a lonely evening at the Chelsea Palace. It was to be demolished, and about ten years later a squalid block of shops replaced it. On the bill was an 'impressionist' who did his Charles Laughton as Quasimodo. I knew then I had to write a play that I subsequently named *The Entertainer*. It was bad, direct and immediate (not the play – the Quasimodo). Reviewers then and now tell me that what I wrote then was under the influence of Brecht. (How one can always be so knowing, without bothering to check up, is one of the fugitive jollities of watching critics at their glum work.) One can only breathe lightly, like Stravinsky, when Clive Barnes made such a predictable ass of himself: 'I was *there*,' said Stravinsky. '*I* was there. Brecht was *not*.'

How odd it is that, since then, the theatre seems to have become patronized mostly by the fascist left and fascist right. Perhaps they both understand 'theatre'. Incidentally, the title of my play came from an old Scott Joplin number actually called 'The Entertainer' (now called 'The Sting') and recorded by a toothless favourite of mine, Bunk Johnson. Toothless he was, but brave! And that's what music hall *was*. Brave. 'Jolly Good Luck to the Girl Who Loves a Soldier'. Silly, perhaps, but bravely expressed (try *saying* it) and bravely done.

If music hall was conformist, this was not so much because of the artists or the audiences, but because of the truckling knighthood grafters, the Mosses and Stolls. It began and declined, but it is not entirely gone.

> So when I tie the knot,
> With the little I've got,
> I hope they all get a fair share.

Music hall is lumbered with literature. It can't be lost. Out of some of that, I once wrote my own epitaph. Which is simply:

Let me know where you're working tomorrow night – and I'll come and see YOU.

If you don't understand that, you will never understand anything.

Observer, 20 April 1975

Rachel Roberts

No Bells on Sunday: The Journals of Rachel Roberts,
ed. Alexander Walker

Rachel Roberts, a character actress, was born in Wales (not something you are allowed to forget if you read this book) in 1927. Fifty-three years later she committed suicide in a 'ranch-type' bungalow at the bottom of a canyon in rightly godforsaken Beverly Hills.

Her father was a Baptist Minister, she went to the University of Wales, she made three good films and married two husbands. Her doped body was found by a Mexican jobbing gardener. She had choked on an English muffin which 'came from the small stock of household food meant to ease the hunger rather than provide regular meals for a couple whose lifestyle tended to be lived in restaurants or at other people's parties.'

So what, if it should matter, went wrong? This book is an adroitly prurient attempt to explain. As a basis, Alexander Walker uses the actress's repetitive and repellent 'journals', which are little more than a catalogue of blame against her life, her lovers, the world and, very occasionally, herself. They are self-consciously addressed like a daring-you suicide note and welded into Walker's narrative with extensive reminiscences from friends and 'famous names'.

The compilation unfolds a grimy chronicle of egotism, resentment and, above all, envy. It is – dare I say it? – the most overweening account of a meagre and loveless existence since the appearance of Peter Hall's Diaries. What might make it interesting to the outsider, happily unprivy to showbiz hysteria, is the cast list which takes part in such a life. Certainly it excites scant pity for its subject, with her preposterous estimate of herself, and only contempt for those who connived at a sad woman's impertinent fantasies.

'Right from the start, she was after a first-class ticket,' recalls one who was witness to the actress's early, odd-jobbing days. Years later, Miss Roberts is still at it, Welsh-warbling into her journals.

I do love Harrods and Knightsbridge and a car at my disposal and to be treated as though I *am* someone ... Yes, yes, I wanted all that Rex [Harrison, her second husband] could give. To meet all the famous people. To stay at the Grand Hotel in Rome and not at a *pensione*. My large personality needed his and his existence. His world was a different place.

She wanted the lot; but, in spite of the protestations of her 'friends', there is no evidence here that she ever gave anything to anybody. The drink and the drugs spiral began thirty years before her death.

I was marvellous as Emilia – a combination of raw emotion and Benzedrine ... I drank Pernod and took Preludin before the matinees ... There was always 'good old Alan' [Dobie, husband No. 1] to go home to, no matter where I had spent the night.

She talks of her 'beloved talent' but reveals eyeless indifference to the decent job in hand. In this she fooled many people, including her bemused Svengali, Lindsay Anderson, who believed work was the answer to her problems. 'I don't want to be Gertrude in Lindsay's Hamlet, drearily travelling from one dreary town to another with Frank Grimes playing the lead.' Like many a flailing star, she wanted merely to be a Celebrity. Even Anderson was forced to concede it.

She was not great, nor unique, simply encouraged by her admirers to believe that hers was a profligate or loving spirit. She was neither. Talking, of course, to an English newspaperman, she said, after her divorce from Harrison: 'This kind of thing happens to most human beings, especially if you're passionate and warm-hearted rather than clear-sighted and cold.' This was not desolate passion but the tantrum of the gilded gutter.

No Bells on Sunday is a recitation of idle cruelty and empty friendships, drunken railing and crafty suicide attempts. 'Rex was in a temper. Abuse flowed. I drank brandy. I came home to emptiness and ice and swallowed Seconal. I came to shouting "Alan! Alan! Alan!".' It is the early-hours record of a life chucked up on the showbiz midden: of clinics and 'sleep' treatments, of wilful and aimless sex ('*Hier soir, j'ai fucké le chauffeur de mon mari,*' she announced to a Paris restaurant), and pools of vomit. 'I stayed in Los Angeles, dolled up, screwed around, drank ... Darren gently picked me up when, dead drunk, I lifted up my skirts and peed on Sunset Boulevard.' Darren Ramirez put up with her to the end, a bewildered and long-suffering young man, working in a fashionable department store. As with all the men in her life, one feels some sympathy for him.

At the end of the book there is a sequence devoted to the disposal of Miss Roberts's remains. In death, as in life, she pursued her avid but

the ashes through Customs, a VIP for-
have licked in a first-class trice, was left
ith them and may still have them even to
other so-called 'gypsy' suggested that they
sandwiches and champagne at the Con-

hristopher (Mrs Richard Burton, Mark 1)
erts's measure. 'She used to say, "If only
o ... " And I'd have to say, "Come off it,
guys to come home to, Alan and Rex."'
are more gullible if not downright dumb:
f all. When we heard of her suicide, we had
eople who hadn't done enough to help and
s could be exactly what the lady intended.
Only those who know little of the delight and gift of friendship could
have been so cheaply deceived.

Observer, 16 September 1984

Laurence Olivier

Donald Spoto, *Laurence Olivier*

It is my own irrational opinion that if you don't believe in God, you
shouldn't waste the time of those who do by writing about him. There is
no common advantage. As most of those who write professionally about
the theatre don't believe in it either, their pronouncements carry the same
weight as the judgment of a Jehovah's Witness on the winner of the St
Leger.

Years ago I made one of many shattered resolutions never to review
a book I could only damn. Writing is far too perilous a trade to tighten
further the miseries of those brave or vain enough to put such heart strain
upon themselves. However, my quaint addiction both to my trade and
the truth presents no choice but to condemn Donald Spoto's preposterous biography of one of this miserable century's unique and most profligate of princes as a bogus and anile concoction.

'Oh God, why don't they leave the poor darling alone,' Olivier once
said to me after the publication of yet another gleefully prurient biography of Vivien Leigh. The intonation was the same one of wounded

125

exhaustion with which he had inflected Archie Rice's 'I wish women wouldn't cry. I wish they wouldn't.'

And yet within a month, his ashes laid at last to rest in Poets' Corner, the Prince, who had indeed proved most royally, is here exposed like Polonius: 'A convocation of politic worms are e'en at him.' Spoto is there first; to post with such dexterity to remunerative sheets!

The dead have no redress against the gross presumptions and preemptive libels of the dull and ignorant biographer, and those who loved them cannot protest the truth without being seen as feeble apologists driven to cover up. They are instant carrion to the wormy speculation of crass archivists like Spoto, intent on giving their dubious verdicts forensic authority by the crushing volume of plodding, dismal detail masquerading as scholarship, and revealing only the Freudian quality of their Disneyworld sensibilities.

Too much has already been made of Olivier's abiding apprehension of his own emptiness and assumptions of squalor. Looking into the glass, he hardly expected the return stare of Snow White, but dreaded that of Caliban, whose make-up at least would have challenged his ingenuity. He was a religious man, superstitious, and if, like St Paul, he died daily, he could live gaudily and in glory twice nightly.

Spoto's lamentably naive allegations of Olivier's sexual ambiguities and his fleeting association with the once revered and pale comedian Danny Kaye can be dismissed at once. They have already been misused to no effect by Michael Korda in a factitious novel, *Curtains* (a surprising lapse into tabloid vulgarity from one who had already written an amusing and sophisticated tribute to his own astonishing clan of gifted, eccentric Hungarians). If *Curtains* is a *roman-à-clef*, all I can say, from a somewhat closer vantage than either of these two incorrigible aliens, is that the locks then have been wilfully changed.

Anyone with the dimmest grasp of Olivier's elusive, foxy personality would have guessed that both Peter Finch and Kenneth Tynan were manipulated none too subtly, as scapegoats to his own defensible devices. As for the supposed Kaye Letters, these can be regarded as the theatrical equivalent of *The Hitler Diaries*. If they exist, why doesn't Spoto quote from them? Untroubled by circumspection or the laws of libel, what holds the biographer's knowing hand from striking two men safely dead? No: Spoto, like Niobe, is all tears and no testimony.

Sometimes it seems that most Americans, however educated and informed, assume − male and female, straight and faggot − that the

Englishman's unassuming, absent-minded effeminacy is deadly proof of his homosexuality. The watermark of icy femininity that is striped across the currency of almost all leading English players mystifies the hygienic demands of Americans in the face of human complexity. They need reassuring safeguards against it, like the cleanliness-guaranteed seal straddling the motel lavatory seat. This epicene tradition in the English temperament, as constant to soldiery and poetry as it is to the playhouse, has them bamboozled.

Even as a tourist guide around a national monument, Spoto's book is myopic and misleading. His attempts to interpret the inaccessible ironies of English social life are as ignorant as the commonplace exegeses of Olivier's performances. I seriously wonder if the deluded fellow ever actually witnessed one. It is as 'unsafe' a conviction as any secured by the bent evidence of an eager detective-sergeant intent on getting his pet terrorist sent down. All this transatlantic nonsense will doubtless soon be forgotten but for one thing: the glum persistence of future pedants and their bemused students. Once some dotty inference is unearthed, even if it is only recorded in the *Croydon Advertiser*, it will be retrieved 30 years later. Sportive fancies by self-appointed dousers of the flame become mythical truths.

Spectator, 19 October 1991

Funeral Note

Sir – I do not know what Lord Olivier's later wishes may have been, nor would one want to encroach upon those of his family. However, it seems astounding to me that he should not be accorded a funeral like Garrick's at Westminster Abbey. This was said to be the most remarkable London had ever seen, with Sheridan in full rig as chief mourner, while Burke and Dr Johnson wept openly as the coffin was lowered at the foot of Shakespeare's monument.

Perhaps, contemplating the low lustre of our own age, it is not so strange. Having had the sometime gift of sharing the chimes of midnight with him, I cannot believe that this embodiment of English pride and heroism would not, whatever his latter protestations, have relished such thrice-gorgeous ceremony.

Yours faithfully, John Osborne

The Times, 14 July 1989

Strutting Players

Sir – Exactly two years ago this week I finished a new stage play
[*Déjàvu*]. Since then I have discovered that it is almost impossible to
persuade star actors even to *read* a manuscript. Should they do so,
passionate avowals of loyal commitment are reneged upon abruptly and
without explanation, but patently for the reasons of expediency Mr
Robin Hawdon (11 April) suggests. Old acquaintances and former colleagues, grown bullish in the lush pastures of film and television, disregard a personal postcard and loftily refer you to their agents.

I assumed that my personal and professional reputation incited such
contempt. I discover this is not the case and that other playwrights, more
popular and successful than myself, find themselves left waiting in the
servants' hall for a summons that may or may not come, for a commitment forgotten as soon as made.

I was merely naive; this is now the accepted behaviour of male 'stars'.
Interestingly, I am informed that the female of the species is less craven.

During my career I have been blessed with the great fortune of having
my work served, as possibly no other playwright in history, by the giant
talents of Ralph Richardson, Laurence Olivier, John Gielgud, Alec Guinness, Richard Burton, Paul Scofield, Trevor Howard and many others.
All of them would have blanched at the prevailing lustreless discourtesy.

Yours faithfully, John Osborne.

The Times, 18 April 1991

Dear Diary . . .

MY RELATIONS WITH the popular press have been bitter and hostile for
almost forty years. Papers like the *Mail*, *Express* and *Daily Telegraph*
have traduced and vilified me consistently. It's no particular surprise. But
recently I have come across moral corruption so bland and remorseless
that it's like confronting an advanced form of madness.

Last autumn I produced the second volume of my autobiography. I
was prepared for the customary onslaught of vulgar vituperation. The
Mirror greeted it with *two* double-page spreads: 'Wot a Way to Treat the
Old Woman!' (This was a reference to one of my ex-wives.) What did
surprise me was that the concerted campaign against both the book *and*

my forthcoming play should start so long before the appearance of either. It all began seriously around April 1991. The *Mail* pronounced that my play had been on the 'scrap heap of history'. I can't afford to sue the *Daily Mail*, as they well know. Their wealth is a licence for calumny. Lawyers shrug their shoulders while their money meters tick away merrily.

Over the next few weeks, various reporters turned up at my house – a four-hour journey from London. I even made the mistake of feeling sorry for some of these novice foot-in-door persons. Not for long. One unmannerly youth from the *Independent* did get a flea in his beringed ear. He turned out to be the son of agony aunt Claire Rayner. So much for her parental wisdom.

Perhaps this is the wretched condition we have come to, one in which intentions have to be vetted and proven by popular consent. There are blundering armies of nosy and interfering 'caring' maniacs. Their compassionate masks conceal a vindictive, retributive energy that arrogantly disputes the possibility of natural decency. Lovers may be blind to gross imperfection, but the truly corrupt cannot recognise the blinding streak of probity in others. It's a form of commonplace moral dyslexia. When the literary (*sic*) editor of the *Daily Express* declared that certain passages in my book were merely a bid for publicity and money, I was confident that even my manifold enemies would find this a dubious interpretation.

HERE IS ANOTHER bizarre, almost comic, example. In front of me I have an elaborately produced invitation: 'The Masters of the United Pack invite you to a Midsummer Ball. On Saturday, 13th June, 1992. Sibdon Castle, Craven Arms. 8.00 pm for 8.30. Black Tie. Dancing to "Cost a Livin 11". 3.00 am Carriages.' A certain Rory Knight Bruce also turned up at my door one morning last summer and introduced himself as a near neighbour. I knew that he ran the *Standard* Diary, which for years had been carrying a knife for me, and was recently responsible for sending up one of his staff plus photographer in pursuit of a non-story. However, he was affable and seemingly contrite. I offered him a glass of champagne. It was an idle day and we had lunch at a local pub. You will by now have guessed the outcome.

Mr KB went on to 'review' my book weeks before its publication. His whole thrust was based upon our desultory meeting. Even for hack work it was astonishing – not so much inaccurate as fantastical. He recorded that The Angry Old Recluse lived in Howard's End (some distance away), with a doorbell 'rammed a full inch and a half into its socket' (it simply doesn't work), dined out nightly and was protected by fierce dogs. 'How is Mark Amory [the literary editor of the *Spectator*]?' I supposedly asked. 'We used to play bridge together.' I scarcely know the good Mr Amory and I've never played bridge in my life. KB trawled the locals, including the landlady of the pub we visited, who, having no idea who I am, merely said absently, 'He's a perfect gentleman.'

This farrago was syndicated to my local paper, where it had no impact whatever except as an example of London lunacy. My wife, whom KB hilariously described as 'a nervous creature', rang him in the full flight of her awesome Geordie fury: 'You worm! You little worm.' 'I know, I know . . .' he whimpered.

Which brings me to my invitation from the Masters of the United Pack. Inside is a note. 'I do hope that you will come to this little gathering as my guests. My olive branch is long overdue and it will be a very local gathering of a wholly private nature.' Sent with best wishes from the Joint Master. His name? You've got it. R. W. Knight Bruce.

HOW I WISH that people given over to 'the Arts' (God rot the word) wouldn't sacrifice themselves to politics. Only Art can be ultimately triumphant. The most revered politician is doomed to the dust of Ozymandias. Actors may indeed become presidents but Americans live, for the present, in a world more lunatic than our own.

I find the spectacle of Miss Glenda Jackson, condemned to spear-carrying in the House of Commons for the next five years, a distressing one. I say this in no spirit of gloating mockery. I always found her fearsome as an actress, a cornered-rat-like but also majestic presence. I only hope that her – to me – overweening attention to 5,000 old-age pensioners in her constituency provides her with the returns that the Theatre could not give.

In the other corner, we have Sir Ian McKellen beaming his homosexuality from every lighthouse. When he broke the news to his stepmother and sister, they apparently replied, 'Oh, we've known for thirty years.' I think they spoke for England. Political stances may make their holders feel better but such shrill interventions must create not illumination but only confusion about the ineffable nature of Art.

My lifelong friend Tony Richardson rang me a few days before his death of Aids, 'explaining' that he had developed a mysterious leg cancer.

He kept up this fiction, to all of us, to the last. I believe that such fierce reticence is more noble and true to the creative spirit than any self-spoiling declarations of political or sexual allegiance.

AS I WRITE, panic is mounting. Our factotum, usually an encouragingly phlegmatic chap, has been mowing and, worse, strimming from dawn to dusk and my wife is behaving like Mrs Danvers with PMT. Why? The gardens are to open on Bank Holiday in aid of – you guessed – the church roof.

A previous owner planted a spectacular azalea walk to thank Winston Churchill for winning the war. Whether or not Mr Churchill was suitably grateful is not known, but the locals were and annually paid their respects. Girls, now grandmothers, recall sunny May afternoons and lemonade on the lawn. The ritual is now adjudged ready for revival. The azaleas are at their heady peak, the rhododendrons ludicrously luxuriant. So why the domestic anxiety? Well, should there be a storm, the blooms, along with all hope, will be dashed. Then, as night follows day, the electricity will be cut off and half a ton of ice-cream in the freezer will be fit only for the cats. I am watching the weather forecast with some interest, as my only useful role in all this is to shovel up any last-minute dog shit.

Spectator, 30 May 1992

[6]

Critics and the Press
====

The Free Press

In February 1961 there were calls for greater powers of punishment to be given to the Press Council following a report in the Daily Express *about the marriage of the Lancashire comedian George Formby and his late wife. In the* New Statesman, *Arthur Christiansen, a former editor and director of Beaverbrook Newspapers, argued that 'a Press Council with "teeth" would trigger off further efforts to censor and to suppress. Where the freedom of the press is concerned the cure for excess may be more perilous than the disease.'*

Sir – The *Spectator* was entirely accurate when it recently described the Press Council as a comic body. Its structure is exactly the same as if the members of the Wolfenden Committee had all been brothel-keepers and homosexuals. Only such a selection could make it possible for representatives of the *News of the World* and the *People* to lift George Robey's eyebrows and wag fingers at the *Observer*, the *Guardian* and the *Spectator*. Don't give it teeth, Mr Christiansen? To give such an animal teeth would be like handing a prayer-book to a goat.

Indolent cant about freedom of the press is exposed every time the freedom of private citizens is threatened by the tactical freedoms of snooping, prying, lying, spying, deception and calumny. 'Cure for excess may be more perilous than the disease,' says Mr Christiansen. Just as penalties for drunken drivers threaten the prosperity of brewers no doubt. If some newspaper reporters cannot observe reasonable standards of decency, then these should be imposed upon them or they will mow down the privacy of every individual who is unlucky enough to get in their path. Burdened as they appear to be by a squalid competitive spirit which they carry about like a house on their back, many newspapermen are pathologically resentful of criticism. For some time the sick prattle of many a column, with its network of hired confidence men, its tip-off pimps and tittle-tattling call girls and boys, has been severely cleaned up, even going back to the dull desperation of toadying aristocrats and millionaires. The reason for this mild reform is not because of the grim, unsleeping eye of the Press Council but consistent criticism from journals like your own and the wit and courage of individuals like Penelope Gilliatt. It is scarcely surprising that William Hickey is still carrying a knife for her; however, he may fumble and drop it.

While the standards of many newspapers and journals in this country are splendid, those of others are often despicable, and we sin against life and liberty when we do not fight their indecencies. Therefore, during that time in which the Press Council exhausts its full comic possibilities, there are some elementary steps which anyone should take to protect himself against irresponsible intrusion on his private life and freedom of activity.

1 Complain to the Press Lord. You may be surprised at the result.
2 Never say 'No comment.'
3 Say nothing.
4 Hang up.
5 It may be that you find this difficult because you are one of those people who can't help smiling back at whores in the street. What a nasty unpleasant job, you think. However, don't worry, if they didn't like it they couldn't stand it for five minutes.
6 If you are bigger than they are, push them out of your way. Moral humiliation is unknown to them but physical indignity stimulates their particular rate of self-contempt.
7 Or, if you prefer, buy a large dog – all teeth and no scruples.
8 Sue whenever possible.
9 If you have friends, enlist their help.

Last week I was staying in a Welsh village. I had gone there to escape from London, to enjoy the peace of the countryside and to work and walk in the company of friends. Before long, by heaven knows what method, the *Daily Express* discovered my whereabouts and sent two members of its staff from Manchester to seek me out. I am delighted to say that they did not succeed. All their questions to milkmen, chauffeurs and hotel managers met with double talk. For example: 'What make of car has he got?' 'Oh, I am not sure now.' 'It's a Lagonda, isn't it?' 'No, an Austin I think.' (Unknown to them, the car being cleaned in front of their eyes was mine.)

Later: 'Did he have any women with him?' (No, they hadn't come to talk about the State of the Drama.) 'Well, he might have done, but I would not have noticed you see. Women don't accost men here like they do where you come from.'

Eventually the *Express* men went away leaving a good joke behind to be enjoyed by all. When they persist as figures of fun, reporters can be fair game too.

John Osborne

New Statesman, 3 March 1961

Narked

In June 1967 Mick Jagger of the Rolling Stones was sentenced to three months' imprisonment for being in possession of drugs obtained legally in Italy. In a leader on 1 July, headlined 'Who Breaks a Butterfly on a Wheel?', The Times argued that the sentence was unreasonable.

Sir, Your excellent leading article (July 1) was a reassuring and welcome contrast to the odd silence from most of Fleet Street about such a newsworthy subject. One would have expected a little more comment, however pious. The subsequent sanctimonious statement by the *News of the World* is surely curious. 'The Editor of the *News of the World* was made aware of the information. He decided that since there was no doubt of the informant's sincerity, our duty was to pass this information to the police.'

Are we to accept the principle that newspaper editors consider it their 'plain duty' to pass random tip-offs from informers about what may or may not be going on in someone's private house? If so, it is an alarming prospect.

Yours faithfully,
John Osborne

The Times, 4 July 1967

Opening Salvo

The following telegram from Mr John Osborne was received by *The Times* after many sharp criticisms of the play, *A Bond Honoured*, by the critics of various newspapers had been listed in 'As it Happens' yesterday:

> The gentleman's agreement to ignore puny theatre critics as bourgeois conventions that keep you pinned in your soft seats is a thing that I fall in with no longer. After ten years it is now war. Not a campaign of considerate complaints in private letters but open and frontal war that will be as public as I and other men of earned reputation have the considerable power to make it.

A Bond Honoured, an adaptation of Lope de Vega's 350-year-old play, opened at the National Theatre this week.

The Times, 9 June 1966

The British Playwrights' Mafia

Report of meeting of the newly formed 1st Battalion British Playwrights' Mafia, held after inaugural Club Dinner on 28 July 1977. Being a shortened account of the above discussion. Present were the President, Osborne, J. (Fulham Welch), and Wood, C. G. (Bristol Pioneer Corps), Secretary, who took the minutes.

The President took the chair and the following were present: Ackland, R. (Agate Turd Award, H. H. Cross & Bar); Arden, J. (F. A. Cantab); Bennett, A. (Armley Rifle Brigade); Bolt, R. (F. A. Manchester Grammar); Bond, E. (Cambs. Young Socialists); Bryden, W. (Glasgow Celtic); Frisby, T. (Dartford Grammar OTC); Gill, P. (Hammersmith Welch); Hampton, C. (F. A. Oxon); Nichols, P. (CSE failed); Wesker, A. (Hackney Rifles).

In attendance: Banbury, F. (RADA); Hall, Sir Peter (Mafia Cantab); Muller, R. (7th Galician Light Infantry).

Meeting begins.

PRESIDENT (OSBORNE): I would like to welcome those who did not find it inexpedient to turn up. As President, I welcome all my fellow Veterans and Campaigners. Now, let it be said first: there are no Critics. Not even to bless them with a name that means only captious, fault-finding, carping, caviller; what we are discussing is Reviewers. Tipsters, form-followers, Shaftesbury Avenue bookies' runners, tic-tac hacks who, without flair or talent, make a book on the real talent of other men, their betters in all things. They are, gentlemen, a dissembling, dishonourable, contemptible race of men. It is not 'rhetoric' to say so. It is the irredeemable truth.

VOICES: Hear, hear!

'You know who the Critics are? The men who have failed in Literature and Art.' (Disraeli)

BRYDEN: Ay, ay Captain. Every one of them is writing about someone who writes twenty times better than any one of them can or ever will.

WOOD: They do keep their underpants clean, they keep everything clean in fact, nails, hair, noses, any filth they might heap on you one time, they disinfect the next time, still leaving it piled on you but smelling sweeter to you under it, and you are expected to say, 'Hello, how nice to meet you,' when you do and of course some of us do. Then comes the day when they find another 'Poet of the Gutter', now more poetic than you were, or less so, poetry having given way to revolution. You might try to remind them that you were in your day revolutionary, dangerous, what you have got to do is do the same thing that you did before to save them time because they are busy men with DRAMA at heart, much more so than you are.

HAMPTON: Asking a working writer what he thinks about critics is like asking a lamp-post how it feels about dogs.

BOND: Critics are the only people allowed to take part in an activity and even become judges of it without any training in that activity. If sport or law or industry were run in this way the situation would be obviously ludicrous. So why does it get by in the arts?

BOLT: It always seems to me that a playwright invited to comment publicly on the critics is in the position of a man in the pillory making faces at passers-by. Prudence counsels the lowest of low profiles in our circumstances.

'Take heed of critics; they bite, like fish, at anything.' (Dekker)

FRISBY: In a programme on BBC2 about reviewers and their victims in which I took part, Michael Hordern was mildly reproving Alan Brien for a particularly vicious remark Brien had made years ago about Hordern's *Macbeth*. Hordern said he still felt the pain of this gratuitous wound. Brien's defence was, 'Oh well. I was younger then.'
(*Pause.*)

NICHOLS: Well, on the other hand, considering what they go through, their cogent verdicts are expressed in prose that is at once readable and lucid, richly funny and deeply moving. Many's the time they've had me rolling in the aisles. Their reviews are only misleading by being so much more interesting than the shows themselves. Obviously most of them could do our job much better than we do if only they had the time or inclination.

BOLT: Well, my mother – who was an alertly respectable woman – told me at an early age that I was not to play with critics.

Luther (*July 1961*): 'Mr Osborne has little feeling for language.' (*J. C. Trewin*)

WESKER: No dramatist baulks at fair comment, only at private spites, ill-will, carelessness and the special journalistic ego. It's not a writer's spirit that is affected. He continues to write – there's enough evidence of that; it's simply that the reviewer, acting as a kind of jailer, opens or closes the theatres' doors.

WOOD: I shall never forgive Harold Hobson, I reckon he owes me a great deal of money. He could so fill an actor's heart with dread that he skips out of the play as fast as he could. I know one famous knight who did just that, although there were queues outside the theatre, and it was bought for a Broadway production. So, they have that kind of power with actors. Actors can actually be hurt by critics whereas in the end if you're any kind of writer at all you can't be hurt. I mean not deeply, in the sense that you repudiate everything you've written because of their astonishing accuracy.

WESKER: Harold Hobson's impact was made not by his powers of perception but by the awesome towers of the *Sunday Times* battlements, from behind which he pinged his flimsy splinters of wooden comment.

GILL: Bernard Levin is my *bête noire*, because he is so unstylish, egocentric and silly. Neither of the Sunday papers is at all serious. What is so nauseating about B. Levin is his sentimental belief in the actor as a kind of child of nature. A terrible thing this, probably derived from his silly obsession with opera stars.

BOLT: Bernard Levin is in my estimation – after his review of my last play – a critic of the most refined sensibilities, a force for the good; without whom the Theatre would be gravely impoverished.

GILL: Have you noticed a recent interest in classical text (instigated, I think, by Levin, with his puerile musical education)? He writes a lot of insubstantial drivel about text. I hate their ignorance. One of their number once complained that the violin in my production of *Twelfth Night* was not a viola (get it: viola, Viola?) when in fact it *was* a viola – an instrument which is rather richer in texture and sounds tones lower than a violin.

Luther: '*Mr Osborne is at once too Brechtian and not Brechtian enough.*' (The Times)

PRESIDENT: Well young Muller here was a critic, once.

MULLER: Only for three years.

PRESIDENT: No excuses, we know that all playwrights are drunken, adulterous hysterics, so could you give us your sober, closely-reasoned views?

MULLER: I don't think anyone can take the job of being a critic seriously. It is by definition a nonsense. He is simply a member of the audience on a certain unreal occasion – who gets free tickets. And whether he says 'masterpiece' or 'rubbish' has no meaning at all. The thing is they – critics – are totally enslaved by fashion. Which means they are always totally confused by anything unfamiliar or new.

WOOD: Have you noticed their shoes? They all wear mean little shoes, except the ones who fancy the Mick Jagger of our profession – guess who, same lips? And they wear totally unsuitable high-heeled things which have them teetering.

MULLER: Exactly, it all comes down to fashion. Which is the main reason why all criticism is useless. It is a ridiculous function, irresponsible and damaging. Critics want to be caressed by their own received ideas.

A Patriot for Me (*July 1965*): '*A terrible bore.*' (*B. A. Young*, Financial Times); '*Overweight, overlong and finally disastrous offering.*' (*Herbert Kretzmer*, Daily Express); '*This ramshackle, top-heavy and profoundly unsatisfying play.*' (*Bernard Levin*, Daily Mail)

NICHOLS: I think it was one of our lot (Oscar Wilde?) who said critics are more important than artists, and who can say him nay? Given the chance, I'd certainly let my daughter marry one, especially if she wanted to be an actress. I expect I'm in a majority of one, but better that than an arse-licking hypocrite currying favour with my fellow-scripters, who can't do me any good anyhow. This refusal to sling muck at honourable men has nothing at all to do with the impending transfer of my *Privates on Parade* to a West End theatre in a few months from now. (*Exit.*)

PRESIDENT: Can't hold his liquor, young Nichols. Noticed it at Frinton in '53. Well, then, the Reviewers. Physical and mental cripples. I don't see why *we* shouldn't get personal.

VOICES: Bad taste! Bad taste!

WOOD: (*Brandishing a soiled copy of* The Times) Alan Coren I intend to seek out and attack one day because of a vicious comment, a personal comment that should be followed up. After berating me for not including the qualities of love, compassion, tenderness in a television play which was about people who totally lacked all such qualities, he ended by saying something like, 'Mr Wood, than whom I can think of almost anyone I would rather be.' And I've never even met the chap. Would he rather be Charles Manson than me; would he rather be that black gentleman he manages to find so funny?

ARDEN: Margaretta D'Arcy and I wrote a play about Nelson. In his review of it, B. A. Young – whom I have never met – wrote: 'I wonder if when Mr and Mrs Arden go to bed at night they look at each other and say, "Are we going up the right road?" '

MULLER: No, to take it as a serious function is patently absurd. They have to be caressed . . .

WOOD: They always seem to want to be assured, to be liked. I suppose they're lonely, and they *ought* to be . . .

MULLER: They can't bear to be baffled. It irritates them and makes them cross. They are the prophets of fashion. I can only say that for those three years I felt like a clown.
(*Incontinent applause. Exit* MULLER.)

The Entertainer: *'Dramatically slack.'* (*J. W. Lambert*, Drama); *'The Rice family: what drivelling, drooling windbags they turn out to be.'* (Evening News)

BOLT: I remember a wry account by Emlyn Williams from his writing days. 'For some time', he said, 'I was very promising. Then I entered my decadence. There was a fortnight or so in which I was all right – and I missed it. I think I was abroad.'

Look Back in Anger (*May 1956*): *'Its total gesture is altogether inadequate.'* (The Times); *'Back street Hamlet talks bosh.'* (Evening

News); *'Mr John Osborne is a writer who at present does not know what he is doing.'* (Harold Hobson, Sunday Times); *'Jimmy Porter should have gone to a psychiatrist rather than a dramatist – not at any rate to one writing his first play.'* (Daily Telegraph)

BENNETT: It seemed to me, giving Clive Barnes his CBE for services to the theatre is like giving Goering the DFC for services to the RAF.

PRESIDENT: Back to home base – what about Irving Wardle? I believe he lives in New Barnet.

BENNETT: I thought it was a pity when he said: 'Christopher Logue [*War Music*, Old Vic] scores some telling images . . . but much of his simile-sodden text might have been the work of Christopher Fry.' I don't think you should use one living writer as a touchstone for bad writing for another. If I were Christopher Fry, in those circumstances, I'd have felt like shooting myself.

West of Suez (*August 1971*): *'An invertebrate piece.'* (*Irving Wardle*, The Times); Sense of Detachment (*December 1972*): *'The word "device" rings through the evening like a death-bell . . . You might almost look at the piece as a terminal point of Osborne's derision.'* (*Irving Wardle*, The Times); Watch it Come Down (*February 1976*): *'There are prevailing idioms; invective and gush.'* (*Irving Wardle*, The Times)

FRISBY: Years ago I was at a party full of eminent people. Somebody suggested a game – 'Guess Harold Hobson's age'. Various figures were donated ranging from fifty-eight to sixty-five. The person who started the game then said: 'Wrong. Fifty-two.' There was a unanimous, spontaneous groan.

PRESIDENT: Well, gentlemen, I think we are all agreed, that these reviewer chaps are, without exception, a bunch of cheap little pension-seekers. They cluster together in packs, or pairs, never daring a majority of one – ('Watch the Pension!') – not even recording an event like, say, Hazlitt or Max Beerbohm, which is interesting in itself, because of the way it is written. Now the The Godfather, Hobson, has retired they are without a focus in Row A to fawn upon.

'My experience . . . is that directors (some directors) and actors (and most of all actresses) are better integrated, fundamentally more self-confident than dramatists.' (Harold Hobson); The World of Paul

Slickey (*May 1959*): '*As usual one felt sorry for the cast.*' (*Felix Barker,* Evening News*)*; Sense of Detachment: '*This must surely be his farewell to the theatre.*' (*B. A. Young,* Financial Times)

WOOD: I have a list of critics that one day I am going to make sure I sit behind, so that I may hit, clip away at their ears and make them pay attention. What astonishes me is that we are expected not to hit them.

GILL: There was the time I proved to myself that Philip Hope-Wallace was indeed prone to leaving plays before the end. I thought it was a myth. People said that if he did the notices were better. So I didn't mind. But once, in that disconsolate and hopeless walk around Sloane Square on a first night (the Orton double bill), I did spy what I took to be P. Hope-Wallace leaving the theatre. I checked his seat. The seat was empty. I followed him all the way up Eaton Square – it passed some of the interminable time – I didn't do anything. What can you do to Philip Hope-Wallace . . .?

WOOD: . . . Better known as Phyllis Hope-Wallace (and I hope he won't take offence).

Inadmissible Evidence (*September 1964*); '*Before the end a feeling obtrudes that a bulldozer is being used where a trowel would have done.*' (*Philip Hope-Wallace,* The Guardian)

BOLT: Just after *Flowering Cherry*, which was my first play in London, had opened, and seemed set to be successful, I was walking with Frith Banbury here, the director, when we met Philip Hope-Wallace who had been sparing in his praise of my piece. I was feeling pretty good of course and ready to be friendly with anyone. I was quite bewildered by what seemed to be his almost personal animosity, not towards the play but to myself.

BANBURY: What you people – playwrights – can never understand is that a lot of them cannot bear to think of the money you make. It really is as simple as that.

BOLT: I still don't know whether it is as simple as that, but it does seem to me that the response of critics to success and failure is of an intensity not to be explained by their concern for the drama.

GILL: Martin Esslin is the worst of the 'serious' occasional reviewers. Old Mr Wise-after-the-event, who's always seen and read the plays, talked to authors, read the reviews and then chastises the other reviewers before he lays himself on the line. He really is a pompous, overpaid – [Censored: President]. He will not face the rough and tumble of ordinary criticism and take the brunt of being criticized himself. He also lectures, if you please, to poor American students, some of whom I know. He is the theatre's George Steiner.

Watch it Come Down: 'John Osborne remains where he has been ever since Hotel in Amsterdam: *at the end of the line. What now?' (John Peter,* TES)

WESKER: There remains a category of serious playwriting which treats the audience as a sensitive and intelligent unity; that category of play can depend on nothing except the sympathetic comments of sensible and informed reviewers. Instead it is, like the Albatross, shot down. And when the Albatross plunged to its death nothing else that was good survived.

Plays for England (*July 1962): 'Tonight was a sad setback. Laborious, embarrassing writing.'* (*Milton Shulman,* Evening Standard)

VOICE: I overheard the following at Miller's *The Crucible*:
    W. A. DARLINGTON (*Daily Telegraph*): Where is this taking place?
    LOVELY WIFE: Salem, you deaf dummy.
    Overheard at Storey's *Home*:
    MILTON SHULMAN (*Evening Standard*): Where the hell is this taking place. Some crummy hotel or something?
    LOVELY WIFE: A loony bin, darling.

Time Present (*May 1976): 'Jimmy Porter with menstrual pains.'* (*Milton Shulman,* Evening Standard)

GILL: Milton Shulman and the Emperor's New Clothes. Like all half-hard journalists his sentimentality is stomach-heaving. He is so obsessed, telling us limeys or pommy bastards or whatever he thinks we are that we're too arty and too big for our boots, that most of the time he does not notice that quite often the Emperor is fully clothed or at least wearing a decent pair of underpants. Incidentally – could I have a glass of water? – it is a little known and totally unimportant fact that the brouhaha over Hilary Spurling was caused because she left the first night of my play *Over Gardens Out* before the end. The audience was restricted to forty in number. The play lasted a little over an hour and she was sitting not a bad breath away from the poor actors. She narrowly escaped being thrown down the stairs, and by the time I got out she had vanished. They do vanish, don't they?

PRESIDENT: Ronald Hayman is particularly unpleasant. He makes a living writing unreadable books about us. I don't know who reads them. Some poor bloody Nigerians or US students who'll actually believe the crass drivel he turns out, I suppose. The damage is that all this critical balls is perpetuated in this way, through academics. Some other dim bookman actually wrote in his tome that *Look Back in Anger* was originally titled *On the Pier at Morecambe*. What *he* must have read or heard was that I had written the second act on the end of Morecambe Pier . . . but, no, he didn't even bother to check up. So now 'students' from all over the world ask me or, worse, *tell* me what the original title was. It's pretty boring.

Watch it Come Down: 'It used to be claimed for Mr Osborne that he did not mince words, but this in fact is precisely what he does.' (Robert Cushman, the Observer); The Entertainer: 'It confronts us rather like a helping from some sloppily-made trifle on which a peculiarly raw quality of sentiment has been poured as from a recklessly decanted cooking sherry. One acknowledges the authentic taste, at once squashy and fiery, but the impression it makes is extraordinarily depressing and seems sadly to lack nutritional value.' (Derek Granger, Financial Times)

PRESIDENT: I like that last one. They often go in for cooking metaphors – 'This sad soufflé failed to rise for me.' That kind of thing.

GILL: One does not know what values these critics stand for most of the time. Which political party does Michael Billington support? Could he let us know? It could be interesting considering some of the politically reactionary junk he praises. The left are as bad. *Time Out* is merely a kind of parish magazine for people in their very late twenties. And the right plays its usual game encapsulating most of what I have been groping for . . .

PRESIDENT: Now is the time to name names and lay our future plans against the infidels. As for myself, [Benedict] Nightingale is the one *I* intend to duff up, gentlemen. He once previewed a play of mine on the strength of merely reading the script. It was slipped to him by an especially dozy PR lady. Naturally I got the shit in advance in a well-known magazine which went to press *before* the play actually opened.

(*Heavy laughter. Shouts of 'Wardle, Wardle, what about Wardle?'*)

ARDEN: At Chichester we tried giving them a copy of the script in advance to read . . .

PRESIDENT: It is a mistake, Arden. If they rarely listen, why should we expect them to read?

ARDEN: As for programme notes –

PRESIDENT: Oh – quite fatal. They'll grab on to them gratefully because they'll think that's what the work is ABOUT. Then they'll resent their gratitude and use a footnote as a kicking boot to beat the play and its author to death – if they can.

WESKER: Now, Sir Harold –

PRESIDENT: You are out of order, sir.

WESKER: Stop being so right-wing.

PRESIDENT: I shall have to reprimand you, sir. To quote myself: 'I may be an old pouf but I am *not* right-wing . . .'

ACKLAND: I thought the subject was Reviewers. The James Agate Turd Award, for instance.

PRESIDENT: Agate? What does it mean now? Who remembers him? Who remembers Clement Scott of the *Daily Telegraph*? He wrote thick volumes on theatre. Listen to him on *Hedda Gabler*: 'It was like a visit to the morgue. What a horrible story! What a hideous play!' Or: '. . . the play is simply a bad escape of moral sewage gas' (*Pictorial World*). Or: 'For sheer unadulterated stupidity, for inherent meanness and vulgarity, for Pretentious triviality . . . no Bostonian novel or London Penny novelette has surpassed *Hedda Gabler*' (Robert Buchanan, *Illustrated London News*). Now *who* was Robert Buchanan? The Benedict Nightingale of 1891, I suppose. Or, what about the general press reaction to *A Doll's House*? 'I never sat out a play more dreary or more illogical as a whole, or in its details more feeble and commonplace . . . It is as though someone had dramatized the cooking of a Sunday dinner' (*The Sporting and Dramatic News*); 'Its total lack of dramatic action is certainly not an enlivening spectacle' (*The Times*, 1891); 'It would be a misfortune were such a morbid and unwholesome play to gain the favour of the public' (*Standard*); 'Ibsen is too faddy and too obstructively unsympathetic to please English Playgoers' (*Sunday Times*). Which brings us to Sir Harold, Ackland.

ACKLAND: Well . . . In 1938, I wrote a play called *The Dark River*. When it was tried out at the Globe Theatre, Agate wrote a favourable piece entitled 'Influences at Work', saying that my work was 'influenced' by . . .

PRESIDENT: Here we go . . .

ACKLAND: Chekhov, then – Shaw's *Heartbreak House*, which I'd never seen or read, and Jean-Jacques Bernard, whom I'd also never even read . . .

PRESIDENT:They *have* to do that. They can't bear the thought that you might be an *original*. Pinter was 'influenced' by Ionesco and Beckett. They all said I was 'influenced' by Brecht when I wrote *The Entertainer*. Naturally, I'd never even seen a Brecht play when I wrote it – nor, indeed, heard of him. I was 'influenced' by the Music Hall, which I'd been to almost every week since I was four years old. But go on.

ACKLAND: Later, after the War had broken out, the play was to be published, and in view of his enthusiasm about the Globe's production, it seemed like a good idea to ask Agate to write a preface. He agreed to do it for £10. I asked him to have dinner, as there were some things I wanted to put to him. He arrived an hour and a half late. I then said that some things were now different in the text from the original, which kept referring to 'before the War'. Of course, by this time, the War had indeed started so these passages had had to be changed. I suggested he might look at the galley proofs. He said these would only confuse him and he couldn't do it. So, he walked out, told every one in the back of the Savoy that I had asked him to dinner but given him nothing to drink, and he subsequently gave the revised play a terrible, destructive and vindictive notice. The management even took box ads quoting his *original* notice. But it was no use, everyone thought we were making it up.

PRESIDENT: And his acolyte Harold?

ACKLAND: Once upon a time I wrote a play called *The Pink Room*, but people thought it was a libel on the British. Tennents wouldn't do it, so Terry Rattigan put up his own money to produce it at the Lyric, Hammersmith, with Frith Banbury directing.

BANBURY: Yes, and then Hobson said we should all be ashamed to put it on at all and that it must be 'one of the least creditable to author, player, producer and management in stage memory'. That it was like being at the serious illness, if not the death, of a great talent.

ACKLAND: It was vindictive. That was in 1952.

BANBURY: Fifteen years later Sir Harold wrote a piece entitled something like, 'What Writer was ever Killed by a Critic?' I invited him to dinner and showed him his notice of *The Pink Room*. He looked at it, said something like, 'That's pretty awful, isn't it.' But he didn't remember it.

PRESIDENT: Like Alan Brien – *he* was younger then.

PETER HALL: I don't mean to sound craven, but I can't remember any anecdotes about critics.

PRESIDENT: I seem to remember that years ago in New York you once told me that, as a director, you dreaded getting play scripts from critics. You named several. A hazard of the job, I think you said. But we are fighting back.

BRYDEN: Yes, [David] Storey tapped Billington gently on the face and said, 'Don't you ever . . . do that again.' He's a big guy, lock-forward or something. Shulman, looking on, looked scared.

PRESIDENT: Good. As soon as this meeting is concluded the action committee will be meeting to discuss Operation Stone in the map room. This new phase of our campaign deals exclusively with the seeking out of certain reviewers on first or second nights. But first, the Honours List.

HONOURS LIST

Knights Bachelor: Peter Hall (CBE, too); Harold Hobson.

CBE: Harold Pinter; Clive Barnes. *Two Tickets to Royal Garden Party* (Buckingham Palace, 1976): Alderman and Mrs Muckybrass (Morecambe); Miss Helen MacTavish (Head Postmistress, Isle of South Uist, since 1927); Mr John Osborne and Guest.

DEVINE: Just a minute . . . All stop shouting and listen – you should choose your theatre like a religion. Make sure you don't get into the wrong temple. For the theatre was really a religion or way of life.

PRESIDENT: But *they* don't know about religion, George. They still haven't learnt.

DEVINE: For me the theatre was a temple of ideas, and ideas so well expressed it may be called art.

PRESIDENT: But they don't want art, George. They didn't want it *then*. That's what killed *you*. They don't want your art or mine. Then or now. They blaspheme against your achievement and your memory by, yes, wouldn't you have guessed it, misquoting even you.

DEVINE: When I started at the Court, *Look Back in Anger* fell into our hands. There was one particular passage: 'It's no good trying to fool yourself about love. You can't fall into it like a soft job, without dirtying up your hands. It takes muscle and guts. And if you can't face the thought of messing up your nice, clean soul, you'd better give up the whole idea of life and become a saint. Because you'll never make it as a human being. It's either this world or the next.' When I read this passage I felt so much in sympathy with it I thought it must be said on stage to a public. It is good luck to find such a thing.

(*Pause.*)

PRESIDENT: Well . . . well, gentlemen, as your President, like the ex-President of our friendly USA, I can only declare the meeting closed and add this: 'If you can't stand the heat, keep out of the kitchen.' It can be hell, in there. You know it. I know it. *They* never will. Off to the map room lads!

(*The meeting broke up in quiet disorder.*)

THE CAST

Rodney Ackland: aged sixty-nine

Actor/playwright/director best known for: *After October, The Old Ladies, Strange Orchestra, A Dead Secret* and *The Dark River*.

John Arden: forty-seven

Playwright best known for: *Armstrong's Last Goodnight, Serjeant Musgrave's Dance, Live Like Pigs, The Waters of Babylon* and *The Island Of The Mighty*.

Frith Banbury: sixty-seven

Director best known for: *Dark Summer, Flowering Cherry, A Dead Secret, The Winslow Boy* and *The Diary of Anne Frank*.

Alan Bennett: forty-three

Actor/playwright best known for: *Beyond The Fringe, Forty Years On, Getting On, Habeas Corpus* and *The Old Country*.

Robert Bolt: fifty-three

Playwright/director best known for: *Flowering Cherry, Lawrence of Arabia, Lady Caroline Lamb, Ryan's Daughter, Vivat! Vivat! Regina!, Dr Zhivago, A Man For All Seasons* and *State of Revolution*.

Edward Bond: forty-three

Playwright best known for: *The Pope's Wedding, Saved, Early Morning, The Fool* and *Bingo*.

Bill Bryden: thirty-five

Director/playwright best known for: *Willie Rough* and *Watch It Come Down*.

George Devine: Dec'd. Late director at The Royal Court Theatre.

Terence Frisby: forty-four
Actor/playwright best known for: *There's A Girl In My Soup, The Subtopians, The Bandwagon* and *It's All Right If I Do It.*
Peter Gill: thirty-eight
Producer/director best known for: *The Daughter-in-law, The Sleeper's Den, A Provincial Life* and *Small Change.*
Peter Hall: forty-seven
Director of National Theatre, formerly Director of Royal Shakespeare Company.
Christopher Hampton: thirty-one
Playwright best known for: *The Philanthropist, Total Eclipse, Savages, Treats* and *When Did You Last See My Mother?*
Robert Muller: fifty-two
Critic turned writer and playwright best known for: *Night Conspirators, Afternoon of a Nymph, Piggies* and *Man of Straw.*
Peter Nichols: fifty
Playwright of TV and stage plays of which the best known are: *Forget-Me-Not Lane, The National Health, Privates on Parade* and *A Day In The Death of Joe Egg.*
Arnold Wesker: forty-five
Playwright best known for: *Chips With Everything, Roots, The Four Seasons, The Old Ones* and *The Friends.*
Charles Wood: forty-five
Playwright best known for: *Cockade, Veterans, Fill The Stage With Happy Hours, Meals On Wheels, Dingo, Jingo* and screenplays of *How I Won The War* and *The Charge Of The Light Brigade*, as the SECRETARY.
John Osborne forty-seven, whose plays include: *Look Back in Anger, The Entertainer, Luther, Hotel in Amsterdam* and *Watch It Come Down*, as the PRESIDENT.

Sunday Times Magazine, 16 October 1977

Golden Boy

The Life of Kenneth Tynan
Kathleen Tynan

'Aesthetic, tall, appealing. I was riveted because you didn't see people like that in Birmingham.' That figure was Kenneth Tynan, the speaker one of his many generously minded female admirers. Birmingham, England's second city, no less, centre of the hardware trade, is generally acknowledged to be its most ugly, unappealing, and charmless.

Its whining accent is the most disagreeable sound to be heard from all the regions in England, being the inspiration for the Australian insult, 'whinging poms'. Between the wars, 'Made in Birmingham' was the recognized trademark for shoddy mass-produced goods. The most distinguished men of the century sprung from this satanic 'cemetery without walls' are Neville ('Peace in our Time') Chamberlain, two comic geniuses, Sid Field and Tony Hancock, and Kenneth Peacock Tynan, born 2 April 1927, who said of it, 'I have no more connection with my early life and Birmingham than I have with Timbuctoo.'

His repudiation's course was swift, natural, and painless. 'In any real sense of the word I was born at Oxford.' It was this patrician forgetfulness that characterized a lifetime of erratic, searchlight enthusiasms, trekking for fixed stars of certainty in theory, ideas and art, and what he announced as 'High Definition' in performance.

Birmingham's only institutions of distinction, King Edward's Grammar School and the Repertory Theatre, gawped and glowed uneasily as they previewed Tynan's capering, mock epicene juvenile debut on their stages. He was an astonishing schoolboy, arguing against the debating-society motion that 'this House thinks the Present Generation has lost the Ability to Entertain Itself', by praising the joys of masturbation. 'He had to take your breath away,' a friend recalled. 'And it went right through his life.' In the school magazine he was writing on Orson Welles: 'He reproduces life as it sometimes seems in winged dreams.' The loveless Black Country midden was no launch pad for winged dreams, either for cock comics or the screech and strut of a lusty young peacock.

The sight and sound of this tantalizing flashbulb creature, ubiquitous, alarming, sometimes absurd and endearing, vexed and delighted a generation, many of them bystanders otherwise occupied in very different galaxies. The nondescript and common diminutive 'Ken' became as instantly identifiable as those of his glittering idols: Orson, Larry, Noël. It was fame without honour on the whole, respected, distrusted, admired, envied; it inspired, above all, puzzlement. The elusiveness of the headlong, self-parodying exotic in what already seems, thirty years on, a decrepit and deserted landscape, looms throughout the pages of his widow's biography, *The Life of Kenneth Tynan*.

Mrs Tynan, understandably, often appears as baffled by her subject as those who did not share the experience of sixteen years within the private and most public cage of marriage. Often she seems to be appealing to outsiders for corroboration or insight ('The closest observer of our life together was our secretary'). By her own rather hapless admission, she confesses to being a poor witness either to his motives or to his inner life. This may be that, although she was a participant in mutually shared events, she was privy to little that was not accessible to the cast of starry outsiders in his life. As a widow, Mrs Tynan often gives her evidence like a passing pedestrian at a street accident. The feeling is not so much of testimony confused by grievous, privileged closeness but of being only another of a lifetime's onlookers. It may be that his life only encompassed outsiders and she was the hesitant holder of a passkey.

The later account of their domestic years together makes distressing reading, not from any sense of being attendant on ill-expressed anguish, but of being held head down into a bowl of prurience. The aftertaste is one of guilt at being both a common snoop and an unwitting prig to boot. One is forced to suspect that there are omissions here that conceal not pain so much as a lack of courage in the telling. That is fair enough, but even a want of frankness should provide its clues and, in this case, it points to self-justification, niggling ambition, a warring lack of trust, and, above all, loyalty in the recounting of these final, unprofitable, and bitterly alienated years.

Mrs Tynan's response to the early discovery of a Pandora's box of Tynan's erotic props, underwear and a collection of pornographic photographs suggests iron-willed naivety rather than innocence. 'The theme of almost every study was of a woman in some stage of undress being spanked by a fully dressed spanker, usually a man.' After chancing on this lot, the new bride reeled from the Bosch-black cabaret gloom of the Mount Street flat and was obliged to walk twice around Berkeley Square to 'get my breath back'. To which one can only reply, 'Come off it.' 'That evening I told Ken. He was visibly affected. We must part, he said. There was nothing else for it.' This is pure Tynan charade, and it is hard to believe that she was so obtuse or unworldly not to have been aware of her new husband's 'quirks', as she daintily describes them. They were common knowledge in a wide circle and put about largely by Tynan himself. Underwear, spanking, masturbation and other fairly common-place English, not so unearthly, delights were as much part of his public portfolio as, at various stages of convulsive chic, were bullfighting, Zen, Reich, and Brecht. He was consistent in his sexual enthusiasms if nothing else. He proclaimed them. Participating ex-girlfriends are admirably discreet on the whole. Not so Mrs Tynan.

Tynan's life and career have a Shakespearian unity to them. First the schoolboy, charming and alarming family and friends. It is difficult to make out whether he concealed the knowledge of his illegitimacy and feigned shock on being told at his father's funeral that his mother was unmarried to Sir Peter Peacock. From then on he dropped the name Peacock, but it is likely that he regarded his bastardy as regally as any medieval pretender. Like his stammer, he put it to skilful use as another item of small-arm weaponry.

After the Birmingham prologue comes the caparisoned entry into Oxford, the triumphal progress to London, the capturing of the Critics' Crown; then hoisting his regent standard beside Olivier above the ram-parts of the new-found kingdom of the National Theatre and the ill-planned battles with the Establishment barons; the turmoil of reckless campaign insurrection over Hochhuth's play *Soldiers* – with its claims that Churchill conspired in the death of the Polish leader Sikorski – and the querulous skirmishing over *Oh! Calcutta!* Last scene of all: the Royal Pornographer across the water, confused exile and jester to the tinsel courts of California ('Here, they don't even wait for me to start stam-mering'); failing body and betrayed heart, shackled to a showbiz type-writer and oxygen machine, *sans* everything but tattered courage. The recording hand that once strove, Hazlitt fashion, to freeze the lightning flashes among theatrical peaks for history's sake was put to dubiously puffing the illuminations of Johnny Carson and Mel Brooks.

'Like me, you're a driven person,' said Tennessee Williams to Kenneth Tynan. Driven indeed he was, and in the torpid landscape of postwar Britain such high spirits and dedicated spontaneity were as rare as civility in the local government offices, still enforcing austerity and food rationing. The nation was tired, run-down, sullen. Bread might be in short supply, but with Tynan sending advance notices of his arrival some felt the circus might come back to town after all, and even turn out to be fun. Oxford was the perfect opening date. Among the duffle coats of the ex-service undergraduates, his wardrobe alone provided mystification, bearing him aloft above mockery and defying indifference. Having stared out social derision and stammered down the Union Debating Society in triumph, he then packed his skip and lustre for the Big One – London – the cheery lament of *Isis* in his ears: 'The Golden Age is finished, gone the grace. / Who now so fit to fill KEN TYNAN's place?'

Many a famous Oxford butterfly has been battered into grey moth under the harsh light of the metropolis, but Tynan was soon buzzing the capital like some gorgeous dive-bombing sky-writer. He changed and recharged the function of theatre criticism almost overnight. Imitators were grounded to their dull spots. There were to be no heirs or successors. A whole generation of undergraduates stumbled out into the Sunday streets of provincial towns all over England in their dressing-gowns to grab their *Observer* and see what Tynan had said this week. Like Olivier, whose unchallenged theatrical kingship depended not so much on a sequence of classic performances witnessed by a cultural elite, he shared a shrewd but sincere conviction that Englishmen were the inheritors of a godlike theatricality unique among nations. Tynan had stormed the old West End fortress of Loamshire and proclaimed a new realm of popular heroic passion. The English sense of drama was irrefutable. Did we not have the finest body of dramatic literature in the world? And players like Olivier, who had the very Nelson touch of common appeal? He turned the idea of theatre into a passionate radical patriotism and apprehension of national divinity acceptable to all but the most obstinately disaffected.

What marvelling boy could marvel so marvellously as the nineteen-year-old writing to the doyen critic, James Agate, about a little-known actor's performance in *Othello*? 'I have watched and become part of a transfusion of bubbling hot blood into the invalid frame of our drama . . . I have lived for three hours on the red brink of a volcano, and the crust of lava crumbles still from my feet.' He 'nearly had a heart attack during III. iii . . . My heart was leaping and thudding about as I have never known it before. I was breathless and beautifully exhausted at each curtain. I experienced full catharsis.'

The prospect of an English reviewer, then or now, ever having experienced the merest pulse flutter in, say, the face of the Resurrection, let alone catharsis, was as unthinkable as a soldiering feminist in the grip of priapic frenzy.

Who but Tynan would daze the catcalls of his peers with the challenge:

'I doubt if I could love anyone who did not wish to see *Look Back in Anger*'? His naked avowal of something as personal as love itself was enough to send his fellow journalists scurrying with embarrassment. Such standard-raising was unknown to a breed of scribblers who prided themselves on their professional detachment and refusal to be raised up by the impact of a mere dramatic entertainment. And yet it worked. He brought to the business of showbiz reviewing the art and fervour of those racing correspondents who declare their actual love for horses and worship of jockeys. In his case the adored objects were actors and the rapture of human performance, what he himself called the literature of testimony.

I first met Tynan a few days after the appearance of his review of my play. He rang me and invited me to Ealing Studios for lunch and to discuss writing a film script. The meeting was, I felt sure, not a success, rather like an audition that had gone horribly awry. Perhaps after the public protestation of love for my work I had expected warmth rather than polite, probing appraisal. My feelings about him, even now, are dominated by regretfulness, at my inability often to respond to his overtures and enthusiasms, for failing to write to him during the last years of lonely illness, and, finally, not attending even his memorial rites.

But, reading through Mrs Tynan's book, I wonder if my spinsterish, self-protective behaviour was not justified. Throughout, people give evidence of an aesthetic avidity on his part, a nymphomaniac spirit which mocked satisfaction and promised unjust humiliation. 'The moment he left you, you were out of his mind and it was as simple as that,' said a Brummie girlfriend. 'He was not brought up to be considerate.'

'He liked notes and hated loose change,' writes his biographer. At Oxford, 'he would stand at the top of St Giles' by the taxi rank, pull the pennies out of his pocket and throw them down the street because he couldn't bear the rattle of money.' He had no time for the common coinage of the masses in spite of applauding the 'language of the man in the bus queue' into the new drama. Tynan would not have known what to say to such a creature. English obsessions like the countryside ('Ken didn't have a blade of grass in him'), dog owning (enemies of democracy and upholders of the feudal system), lonely pursuits, stillness itself, were all beyond our Ken.

When the new Mrs Tynan found herself cast as the ringmaster's wife at the new house in Thurloe Square after the early rounds of being trailed like a handcuffed toddler to the palaces of performing culture, the strain of overseeing the ordering of a Gatecrasher's Hall of the celebrated and mutually besotted invoked her to fits of panic. 'If Ken was bored he could be awful. He never bothered to find out the first name of a wife he didn't consider interesting. And if someone whom he did not find amusing dropped in, he would either walk out or watch television.' One of those approved guests, who presumably did not drive him to the box, describes Tynan guests as

'golden *canailles*', a rabble where you might meet any kind of person ... Ken wanted you to be very clever – which is actually something quite faded in English society now. He created an atmosphere where you didn't want to fall short; you always wanted to glitter and sparkle.

Even Jonathan Miller, a nifty social performer if ever there was one, saw these Tynan Presentations as productions cunningly directed by Ken, his wife acting as a somewhat timorous assistant stage manager. Bull Fever in the drawing-room was ensured by 'bringing together excitable people whose confrontation might provoke a lively row'. Hospitality was a blood sport, enlivened by carefully plotted tricks, traps of rehearsed revelations, and tests of intellectual dexterity. The ingenuity of an Inigo Jones masque even contained its courtly elements, like springing a dirty movie on Princess Margaret and her dismayed entourage, and proposing radical subversions like pee-ins at Buckingham Palace, taking over Covent Garden, and burning down the Old Vic. 'His attention when it was directed at you was charismatic,' says the master reveller Miller. 'You actually felt the less if you weren't the subject of his attention or if you lost it.'

This drive to *s'imposer*, as Tynan detected it rightly in others, the ability to not merely 'impose one's will on others but also to dictate the conditions – social, moral, sexual, political – within which one can operate with maximum freedom', seems to me to be not only disingenuous and insensitive but also banishes the intimacy and trust inseparable from either love or friendship.

As a girlfriend of later years says, 'He wasn't somebody you took your troubles to.' He dropped in on lives and, finding them dull or unoriginal, swiftly left. And yet, for some, the true dog-stars and objects of his abiding admiration – Welles, Olivier, Dietrich – his approbation had a whiff of excess and domination that could produce a snarl of repudiation that would mystify and later hurt him. Like an importunate mistress, he could alarm the wary selfhood of the great indestructibles. Those who might have once feared his scorn would begin to shrink from his praise. As the furious years at Thurloe Square progressed, it is not surprising that its housekeeper often sounds like a plaintive Mrs De Winter forever forgetting where she's dropped Mrs Danvers's old bunch of keys.

'Raise tempers, goad and lacerate, raise a whirlwind.' This was the injunction above Tynan's desk at the National Theatre. It was to prove a disastrous strategy. Like so many intellectual revolutionaries, he was a maladroit practical politician. During the dispute over the supposedly anti-Churchill play *Soldiers*, he rang me to enlist my support. I pointed out that I hadn't read it. No matter. The principle of freedom was the issue. I knew that the play, by its propagandist nature, must be meretricious. He himself had once said, before achieving theatrical power, that nothing was so bad as a bad social play. And nothing is so bad as a bad political play.

Tynan persisted. Would I threaten the National Theatre board and its appalling chairman to withdraw permission for them to produce any of my plays in the future if they did not relent in their opposition to *Soldiers*? I again pointed out that it was not a threat likely to strike much terror in their pharisaical hearts of British oak.

'Come with us, Larry and me, to the National,' he had said to me earlier. 'And make history.' 'Thank you,' I replied. 'I've already made it.' He quoted this afterwards as an example of my peevish arrogance and, indeed, so it may seem. I was affronted by such glib, revolutionary certainty. In the event, the Tynan epoch that followed produced successes that would have been contained comfortably in the existing commercial theatre and some tolerable disasters, all against a backcloth of misspent intrigue and unhappiness. His stewardship was honourable. It was not history.

The rest is a grim tale of wild self-pilgrimage, flailing and grasping for light, air and revelation, of an ever enclosing unfulfilment and, finally, an utter banishment of spirit. His cherished firmament became doused, its stars waned or simply grew tired and older. From the peacock's mirror the image staring back at him made out the outline of some dread dodo.

When Tynan was asked if his first wife's forthcoming novel would be any good, he would reply, 'Oh, I shouldn't think so, just another wife trying to prove she exists.' This Mrs Tynan proves her own existence all right, achieved determinedly in the hideous circumstances of her husband's own dwindling existence, terror, abandonment and dying. Some few film scripts, a clutch of lovers, and liberating trips to political hot spots like Cuba made her point for her. It is hard to believe that the early days could have been so frothy in the light of the last bitter and vicious daily exchanges between them. Some might regard her flights of detachment as a blasphemy against an estate that Tynan revered, however he might have sinned against it himself.

'He was only a boy,' said William Shawn, editor of the *New Yorker*, at his death. Still one of God's children, less happy but gifted and often golden.

New York Review of Books, 3 December 1987

Reel Enthusiasm

François Truffaut: Letters, ed. Gilles Jacob and Claude Givray

As I was picking my way through these confusingly edited letters, I read the dismal news that the post of theatre critic of the *Times* is to be assumed shortly by an East Coast University 'Professor' of Drama. He joins the list of pushy nonentities, like the present incumbent of the *Daily Telegraph* (from the plum pastures of the Arts Council) and the feeble tipster of this very journal, who contribute – albeit peripherally – to the tedious hindrance of a traditionally hazardous and anarchic profession.

The film critics of *Cahiers du Cinéma*, or at least a few of them (Truffaut being the most distinguished), made some sense of what seemed at that time a very Gallic, nit-picking and cliquish exercise in arid academic body-building. This gymnasium, indeed, served for the work-outs of those cineastes who intended eventually to prove themselves in the field and in competition. In England, *Sight and Sound*, with its solemn acres of frame-by-frame exegeses of Welles's or Losey's mirror tricks, read like a pathologist's report from the incarceration of the cutting-room. It spawned forth 'Free Cinema' and impatient advocates like Lindsay Anderson, Karel Reisz and Tony Richardson. However, these were unclubbable, natural dissidents, suspicious of theory and far less concerted in their enthusiasms than the *École* across the Water. It is significant that when Truffaut became a full-time film-maker himself he ceased to comment publicly on his colleagues.

It seems to me that the only justification for anyone to spend their days peering into the darkness at the hopeful endeavours of others is either to encapsulate them for ever for the delight and envy of posterity (Hazlitt, Shaw, Max Beerbohm) or as a temporary discipline embarked upon as a course of self-instruction before taking some part in whatever art has aroused this morbid scrutiny. Enthusiasm is the nose of this form of athletics. Without it, criticism is no more than a soft job for immodest eunuchs hot for a cushy, pensionable sinecure. Kenneth Tynan had it, enthusiasm that is. Rather, he had them plurally, in breathless outbursts: Marxism, Zen, bull-fighting, various stars. He was stage-struck as racing correspondents are horse-struck. All most critics seem to be struck with are outlandish disfigurements and personal handicaps like deafness, delayed acne and surgical boots. Tynan sensibly left the job when his virulent enthusiasm had done its work. To sit uninterruptedly through twenty years of theatre or cinema is a sign not of passion but of torpor. To walk out is a mark of involvement. To sit it out is merely to join the doleful company of zombie scribblers.

I describe the editing of this book as confusing because the letters have been arranged chronologically in annual instalments, each one accompanied by a bewildering appendix of notes explaining the identity of friends, lovers, colleagues, academics, critics, distributors, cameramen, actors, literary figures, past and present, place-names and so on. The trailback of personalities and information tends to lead, unless one keeps one's eye fiercely on the narrative road, to a feeling of being in what would nowadays be impeccably described as a 'contraflow situation'.

Truffaut's letters to his lifelong friend Robert Lachenay, which are the spine of this book, are endearing, importunate, sweet-natured, infectious in their energy and outgoing, curious and, yes, enthusiastic. The voracious appetite for books and films is undiminished from earliest idle teenage until the frantic enterprise of middle years. 'You who enjoy writing so much, tell me about your misadventures since 22 October 1950,' writes Robert, surely expectant of a return tide of detailed exhilaration. Books and more books, from Balzac, Proust and Verlaine, through Dorian Gray to modern pulp; lesser stars like Susan Hayward and Richard Conte (two of my own teenage favourites) to Cocteau, *La Regle du Jeu* and Anna Neagle are all crammed into the overladen grasp of 'dear old Robert' like an assault from a drunken Santa Claus dishing out goodies from his epistolary bran-tub. Truffaut's lame contrition over having nicked dear old Robert's books and sold them in his absence is one of the funniest and most characteristic episodes in the book.

Similarly, his critical prejudices are sparklingly clear and unhedged by the pussy-footing of 'balanced' judgement. He dislikes a Buñuel film because it is simply 'badly acted and that's all there is to it', which does not prevent him from admiring the revered man's *Archibaldo*. And 'I like *Gervaise* because she makes me cry' and Bergman's *Summer with Monika* because 'it's the film every director ought to make when he's twenty.' This is the working insight of the practitioner-to-be, not the moribund pathologist-academic.

In Anglo-Saxon circles, *Cahiers du Cinéma* was often regarded as a fearsome spearhead of spiteful French intellectualism. Its brightest star had none of the myopic stupidity associated with such factions.

> Basically, I am very uninformed, very uneducated. I am not proud of the fact; I just have the good fortune to be blessed with a slight sense of and love for the cinema. That's all. That aside, any attempt at analysis in greater depth goes over my poor head ... As I hate the fact that I am self-taught, I try to learn nothing, or almost nothing; my salvation will be that I 'specialized' very early on in the cinema.

Allowing for Truffaut's bubbling gift of play-acting, that is surely a cheery note, deserving to be slipped underneath a few critical doors.

A magnanimous frankness prevails throughout these letters. Even when 'dear old Robert's' grandmother and mother accuse his prodigally affectionate friend of homosexual inclinations, he responds with almost absent-minded forgiveness, concentrating on what parcels of books, lists, clothes and money he is intent on sending or receiving.

Truffaut's briefs to screenwriters are succinct, modest and quite specific, unlike the plundering process of attrition other directors inflict on their trapped victims. Writing to Maurice Pons, author of the delightful *Les Mistons*, he says warningly:

> I increasingly guess how painful it must be to feel one has been *adapted*, which is to say, betrayed. I say all this to temper your disappointment when you see the film!

Such sensibility would be laughable to the front-office oilmen who buy writers like fax-paper.

To Marcel Moussy, co-adaptor of *Les Quatre Cent Coups* and *Tirez le Pianiste*, he writes:

> My wife embraces yours, while I shake your hand in a very manly fashion, with all that such a gesture, given the circumstances, entails

in gratitude and affection; and I also take this opportunity of suggesting that as soon as you have finished the dialogue we address each other as *tu*, to make it easier for each of us to bawl the other out.

Blimey, Nymie.

Spectator, 23 December 1989

Dear Diary . . .

FELLOW PLAYWRIGHT ARNOLD WESKER recently reproached me about the 'Englishness' felt by aliens like himself who had claimed this land as their home, and referred me to Isaiah Berlin's acceptance speech of the Jerusalem Prize in 1979. He had declared himself formed by three forces: a Jewish background, Russian literature and an adopted English heritage:

> All that I have done and thought is indelibly English. I cannot judge English values impartially, for they are part of me. I count this as the greatest of intellectual good fortunes. They are the basis of what I believe: that decent respect for others and the toleration of dissent is better than pride and a sense of national mission . . . All this is deeply and uniquely English, and I freely admit that I am steeped in it, and cannot breathe freely save in a country where these values are, for the most part, taken for granted.

What eloquent, generous testimony! I then listened to a particularly sullen discussion about the inadequacies of English civilization for the past thousand years and comparisons with Afro-Caribbean 'culture'. It seems we're not doing too well. Almost every speaker expressed contempt for the country in which they had grown up. One girl said loftily, '*What* civilization? I don't see no culture.' Cannot someone direct these aggrieved people from their vengeful obsessions with reggae, rap and their past exploiters to at least begin to address their huge inheritance, rather than perpetually spitting on their good luck? Will an Afro-Caribbean ever speak with such endearment as a Russian Jew?

CIVIS BRITANNICUS SUM. I do find increasingly irksome the foreigners who come here, not to assume the privilege of citizenship through absorption (like Isaiah Berlin), but to colonize unashamedly. They are patronizing, opinionated, unaffectionate and yet possessive. They are mostly Americans, Canadians and Australians, foreigners forever to a person. They talk of 'our society' with a proprietory insolence that would be breathtaking if it were not so ridiculous.

At present the Canadians are in the ascendant, led by Ms Barbara Amiel and Michael Ignatieff, hot-followed by upside-downers Germaine Greer, Des Wilson and Clive James. *Woman's Hour*, TV chat shows and newspapers are littered with their alien, bossy voices. Salman Rushdie would be a sour malcontent wherever he lived. Politicians like Bernie Grant simply hate the country altogether, and all its native white detritus. Screeching-beaked cuckoos all. My own ancestors were carpenters, ladder-makers, servants and ostlers in Tudor times. I think it puts me a few points up on all these uppity carpetbaggers. And yet . . . I've come to believe that Tariq Ali is a truly eccentric Englishman.

ANOTHER VICTORY for the *lumpenocracy*. I'm not much of a one for breakfast television, having been scared off some years ago in Montreal by the sight of Albert Finney singing love songs in grey flannel trousers just as I was tackling the cornflakes. But Sunday is different, when David Frost (despite his perverse insistence on inviting Andrew Neil to review the papers) presents one of the brisker programmes on the box. Perhaps he spikes the orange juice. Now, as a result of franchise barging, he is to be dumped. A Ms Howell of GMTV (wherever that is) says, 'The show doesn't do anything for the ratings . . . It will be replaced by a leisure show on family matters.'

Perhaps Frostie, 'the veteran interviewer' (at all of fifty-three), had it coming. He is increasingly squeezed out in the 'breaks' between matters of state and weight by the ads for plastic baubles for the kiddies, plastic bubbles for mum's washing-machine, and plastic germ-free, rain-free pleasuredomes for all the family.

FROST ON SUNDAY is as Isaiah Berlin compared with something called *The James Whale Radio Show* on ITV, an exercise in troglodyte brutishness and degeneracy, which I suspect is sponsored by the condom industry. It simply should be taken off at once.

Here on Central, still reeling from the *Whale* show, in the nether regions of the night we get something called *Job Finder*. It's rather like looking at cards in a newsagent's window to the accompaniment of a machine-tool beat. The language is a mysterious, factory-floor argot.

'Fully experienced person required by net curtain manufacturer. Must be dedicated.' Who could be dedicated to net curtains in Birmingham, Dudley or Wolverhampton? 'Must have experience within a contract tool environment . . .' It makes you think.

A THOUSAND YOUNG Methodists took part in a fashion show in Trafalgar Square the other day. The Rev. Dave ('Hi, Dave!') Martin said it was a way for young people to express their faith.

I'd once been tempted to put the likes of Rev. Dave into my new play, but thought better of it. The latest Methodist report argues that the language the Church uses to describe God reinforces patriarchy as a 'deep sin'. Bringing back sin, now, are they? How do you dress for that? They have a new prayer, too: 'God, our Mother, you hold our life within you, you nourish us at the breast.' No wonder Young Methodists express their faith in fashion. Holy Spirit unisexed and Christ cross-dressed. The liturgical variations are endless.

FOR ANY OF Knight Bruce's acolyte hacks who venture up to the Marches in search of my buried love-nest or a rent-boy crouching in the summer-house, I make an abject confession. There is a race of men – and women – whom I see whenever I visit London, that I detest more than all other, even those who use portable telephones on the train. Their offence is rank, a blasphemy against the community of man. The Walkman Brigade: I yearn to smash their machines, and them.

But when I return to the empty hills beyond my house what am I wearing? A personal stereo. The Dragoon Guards and the Highland Brigade get me up the lower slopes. Handel may lift me to the peak. On my way down, anything from Elgar to Richard Strauss, Arthur Tracy ('The Street Singer') or Fats Waller. I can already sing the whole of *Don Giovanni, Fidelio* and *Così* with barely a falter. I have started to learn Italian. The dogs are used to me hooting at the sky. But if I see someone coming I whip off the earphones and bury them deep in my pocket. I smile guiltily, high in these blue remembered hills.

In summer, however, there is a problem. How do you hide the thing in your shorts? Please don't send a photographer.

Spectator, 6 June 1992

[7]
The Blue Pencil
==

Grim Chamberlain

Sir – Richard Findlater [*Evening Standard*, 19 October] is absolutely right. The Lord Chamberlain must go.

Don't be swindled by the timid, the boneless and the unadventurous who will try to fool you that the Earl of Scarborough is a jolly good thing for us all.

The alternative is *not* the danger of being raided by the police. The problem is a legislative one, and well within the powers of the politicians to work out.

The censorship is ridiculous and infamous. It is a betrayal of liberty.

John Osborne

Evening Standard, 25 October 1956

Land of the Free?

How free are the British? As free as we wish to be. If we tolerate censorship it is because we feel it protects us from painful things that seem to threaten us.

The truth, for instance. Not the single truth that the friends of censorship thrust on us but the atomic truth that can be split endlessly.

Censorship is the commonest social blasphemy because it is mostly concealed, built into us by indolence, self-interest and cowardice.

The censor's first rule is Please Do Not Disturb. Do not offend, do not hurt anyone's feelings, *don't* get excited.

It is not always easy to impose this code because the British, contrary to what they have been made to believe by foreigners, are an excitable and violent people.

Official censors, such as those in the theatre or the film industry, are always patiently pleading that a certain scene or line in a play or a film is 'unnecessary'.

The public expression of this terrible unease can still be heard in the land from Blenheim Palace to Transport House in variations on that dear old tune: 'There's-quite-enough-suffering/unhappiness/unpleasantness-in-the-world-without-reading/seeing/hearing-about-it.'

Censorship has always selected Art as its principal enemy and rightly, for Art alone attempts utter exposure. There is more revelation about adultery and murder in *Madame Bovary* than in all the Sunday newspapers ever produced.

Art is a danger to the censors because it is dynamic, it helps to disintegrate, it breaks up the pattern of life and puts it together in another shape which may turn out to be harrowing . . . or even apparently anarchic.

Censorship, on the other hand, is unifying, adhesive, soothing, the plaster of all those authorities intent on holding society together.

Modern Art in particular, which has been dispossessed of a common moral or poetic vocabulary, tends to examine human behaviour and experience like a butchering surgeon.

The result often seems to consist of nothing but pain and hopelessness.

The born censor's reaction was expressed very simply the other day by a critic writing about a new Ingmar Bergman film, who said: 'We came away feeling that Art had been *at us* again.'

Art, the eternal nagger – God, the censor, somebody protect us from it! The cry still goes up: 'It's all very well pulling things down and being destructive, but what do you put in their place?'

The only answer to it is Man himself, constantly being pushed off his comfortable wall, like Humpty Dumpty. Somehow he will always get put together again.

Censorship tolerates one view only which *must* comfort, shelter and sustain.

Those who support it are breathtakingly frank about their ruthless belief in authority, from the lunatic viewers who crash the switchboards of television companies every time anyone says 'bloody' to one of the modern masters of the clichés of intolerance, the TV critic of the *Sunday Times*, Mr Maurice Wiggin.

Writing about a satirical programme that plainly disturbed him he said recently: 'As [this] remarkable phenomenon grinds tediously to the end of its run, *even the staunchest believer in freedom may be forgiven an occasional qualm.*'

He then proceeded to berate the show because of its lack of professionalism (which it had in abundance), when he had made it disarmingly clear that what was chiefly distasteful to him was the failure to censor items that were offensive to his own prejudices.

For the Wiggins of this world, the remedy is simple. Switch off, walk out or put the book down. Nobody's twisting your arm.

The press makes a great pantomime of upholding full freedom of expression while being one of the principal instruments of censorship.

Just try to write an uncompromising article advocating an unpopular idea in a popular newspaper.

Let Mr Cecil King, head of the *Daily Mirror* group, give you his answer: 'A newspaper can be a little ahead of its readers, but not too far. To pursue persistently policies which run counter to the spirit of the times is not only disastrous publishing policy. It is quite ineffective. Your readers stop reading and your influence disappears.'

Some influence, that has to depend on the approval of its readers!

Though television has done something towards bringing taboo subjects out into the open, the restrictions of the medium itself often create a built-in censorship.

Issues are oversimplified and examined in an apparently open, enquiring manner but the result is often timid and superficial.

We have all been maddened to death by the chairman with his, 'Well, gentlemen, there I must interrupt you' – just as the first spark of truth has been fired from two devious, sparring politicians.

Politicians, like advertisers, are forced to distort because they are 'in the Market'. This again is a hidden form of censorship.

Thus the Labour Party condemns, and properly, Government brutality in South Africa, but turns its head away when it appears in a place where it is inconvenient to recognize it – say Ghana.

Censorship is rife. Its liars, dissemblers and con men are with us in force. But then there is a censor in all of us. This was one of Freud's great discoveries.

Our best allies against censorship now are the young.

No one could sell them such a tragic hoax as the First World War, which the British people of the time accepted with scarcely a murmur.

On the whole young people now are sceptical, gay, thoughtful and shrewd. They will not be so easily deceived.

Most of them think that the Home Secretary is a poop, that Civil Defence is a farce and that sex is fun. If they think so, then no censors should be allowed to stop them saying it.

TV Times, 31 May 1963

Admissible Evidence

House of Lords Committee, 29 November 1966

Present:

Earl of Scarborough	Mr G. R. Strauss
Earl of Kilmuir	Mr Michael Foot
Viscount Norwich	Mr Emlyn Hooson
Lord Tweedsmuir	Mr Hugh Jenkins
Lord Lloyd of Hampstead	Mr Norman St John-Stevas
Lord Annan	Mr William Wilson
Lord Goodman	

Mr G. R. Strauss in the Chair.

MR JOHN OSBORNE *called in and examined.*

CHAIRMAN: Mr Osborne, my first duty is to tell you how delighted we
are that you have been able to come along and give us the benefit of
your views and advice and experience. We are also grateful to you
for your letter in which you set out very clearly and forcibly your
views about the present set-up of stage censorship. We want to ask
you a number of questions. I should tell you we already have before
us in various documents a very full account of the work of the
censorship during the last few years. Indeed, we have details of all
the cuts made by the Lord Chamberlain in recent years, and the
plays which have been banned, so we are aware of that and there is
no need, unless you want to, to go over the ground. We also had
from Mr [John] Mortimer last week his views which are as strong as
yours about the present censorship and the desirability for a change.
What we are concerned with, of course, is, if we were to abolish the
present system of censorship, what the alternatives would be. I
notice that in your letter you express strongly your attitude to what
you call 'compromise or gradualism', to which you are very much
opposed. You will remember the 1909 Committee to which you
refer did suggest there should be a voluntary censorship which I
think is the only compromise, as far as I know, which is now being
advocated. We would like to know if you would care to expand your
views about the undesirability of compromise or gradualism,
particularly in relation to the voluntary system of censorship?

OSBORNE: Yes. First, I would like to ask the indulgence of the

Committee a little. I am no lawyer like Mr Mortimer and I think, in
the first place, that this ground has been gone over for nearly sixty
years very considerably and also recently by the Arts Council, by the
League of Dramatists and by all sorts of people; the ground is very
familiar to most people and I do not know what I can add except
perhaps answers to specific questions about any concrete thing. I
mean, the ground has been covered from Shaw to Granville Barker
to John Mortimer last week. I do not really know what I can add to
that. This is the sort of ordeal that, frankly, I object to; but why I
agreed to give evidence to this Committee is simply because I do
think that the English theatre is of extraordinary importance and it
is something that the English genius has contributed to the world
that is quite unique. Shakespeare is an English invention; it is a
truism and a cliché that we speak in the language of Chaucer and
Shakespeare and we are not allowed to speak it most of the time.
With your permission, before I answer your specific questions, might
I, to get myself going, just read a slight preamble to this?
CHAIRMAN: Certainly.
OSBORNE: I think first, perhaps, I should say it is quite possible that,
although I have been invited by this Committee to give evidence,
they may be unfamiliar with my actual work in the theatre and I
would like to say very quickly that I have worked in the theatre for
almost twenty years. As a writer I have written plays, not only for
the theatre; I have also worked as an actor and also as a producer
and I am prepared to say quite unequivocally, that I have never at
any time – this sounds like a piety – worked as a dramatist, which is
my principal function in the theatre, for commercial gain but only in
the interest of what I do consider to be this unique English art that
we do excel at more than any other race in the world. We have
produced the greatest dramatic body of literature in the world and I
think that the present system of censorship is making life difficult for
rather serious people. Apart from Shakespeare being an English
invention, I think even in our own day Sir Laurence Olivier has
reminded the English people of their special character and virtue
simply by his work as an actor. I think it is quite ridiculous that this
matter (in a way, we are perhaps venturing into the theatre of the
absurd here in Parliament) should have to be raised at all at this
stage when it has been more than adequately dealt with in 1909 and
ever since by an exactly similar Committee and exactly similar

witnesses. I mean, the record is all too clear: Shaw, Ibsen, Shelley, even, all had plays banned and I do not think anyone can deny that the people who supported the Abolition of Censorship Bill were very considerable men of letters; Meredith, Conrad, Wells, Archer, we all know the names. They all protested and nothing has happened since.

I am utterly opposed to censorship in any form in any art. I think the laws of this country are adequate to deal with any of the abuses which might or might not arise out of the law being changed by Parliament. I am entirely opposed to this familiar and, I am afraid, predictable English compromise which will be in a limited form of censorship. I am no gradualist in this, although I think that there are distinguished members of my profession who may well be prepared to accept some form of grading such as already exists in the film industry. But I feel personally that these problems are completely different. I am not asking favours for myself or for any favours on behalf of some strange or unrepresentative community, but only for the freedom that is enjoyed by all other citizens to express themselves.

In my letter that you mentioned, Mr Chairman, I think I expressed the view that the fact that the Office of the Lord Chamberlain with regard to censorship of plays has on the whole conducted the matter, and this is true, fairly, on the whole, and in a characteristically civilized fashion, is utterly irrelevant, and I think it is high time that both the Office of St James Palace and the Members of the House of Lords should stop congratulating themselves on this fact. I think it is also true that those whom one would expect to be both the reactionary and the conservative elements who respond to this kind of controversy, like the critics and the newspapers, are almost entirely opposed to the continuance of stage censorship. Mr Harold Hobson, who is the distinguished critic of the *Sunday Times*, said in a review of a play of my own, 'If I did not know it to be utterly untrue, I would think that the Lord Chamberlain had gone out of his mind.' Mr J. C. Trewin, who I think is probably the most reactionary man in the country, let alone being a theatre critic, is also opposed to stage censorship.

No matter what Parliamentary or legal brain is brought to bear on this matter, nothing will ever convince me or any serious artist in this particularly special and, I think, important art – and it is a specially English art form – that the world will move one inch if a four-letter word or situation in the theatre or, indeed, in Parliament is uttered;

it really would not make any difference at all, the nation would survive as it did some time ago when this sort of thing happened on television. I think that is all I have to say.

CHAIRMAN: Thank you very much. One of the fears which people express is that, if one abolishes pre-censorship, theatre managers will not dare to put on plays which may get them into trouble, which may result in their having to pay substantial fines and losing all the money that has been put into the plays. I would like to know whether you are worried about that. I put it that abolishing the pre-censorship might mean that the theatre, with the exception of the National Theatre and the Shakespeare Theatre, might become more timid and less progressive than it is today when it works under the umbrella of a pre-censor?

OSBORNE: My own reaction to that would be that the situation would remain exactly the same as before. The subsidized theatres, the National Theatre, the Royal Shakespeare and to a lesser extent the English Stage Company, are all under a certain pressure because they are subsidized by public money. But it does not prevent them from taking these risks. As for the commercial managements, well, I assume that they are usually, and from my own experience they are, moved by commercial interest, so I do not think this will change the situation at all.

CHAIRMAN: Just because they are promoted by commercial interests would not the fear of losing substantial sums of money by putting on a play which might get them into trouble inhibit them from putting it on?

OSBORNE: I think not. I think the situation applies to the publisher who takes the same kind of calculated risk.

CHAIRMAN: You suggest in your letter that anyhow the National Theatre, the Royal Shakespeare Company and the Royal Court Theatre – and you mention the names of the directors there – would relish the opportunity of standing up in a court of law and defending the plays which they had put on which might, in the opinion of some, be obscene or contrary to public interest. You are not worried about the idea of theatres, which receive substantial sums of public money in the way of subsidy, being prosecuted by the public prosecutor for putting on plays which, it is alleged, should not have been put on. That does not worry you?

OSBORNE: It does not worry me, because I am not the person involved and I really cannot in fact speak for those people; that is a personal opinion. But I believe they would be. I, in fact, think the record shows that they have taken that kind of calculated risk quite publicly.

CHAIRMAN: There is only one further question I would like to put and that is this. I assume from what you have written and what you have said that you would have no rules at all governing the production of plays. I am thinking of the 1909 Committee which suggested that certain rules should be obeyed; for example, no plays should be put on which incited to crime or which glorified the criminal and made crime appear to be something desirable, and other categories were mentioned. I assume you would want no rules whatsoever and the matter to be left entirely to the dramatist and the producer?

OSBORNE: Absolutely.

ST JOHN-STEVAS: I would like to ask you, if I may, do you feel that your own work as a dramatist has been handicapped by the existence of the censorship?

OSBORNE: It has been inhibited, yes; not only inhibited but, I think, incited, because one knows that one is having to deal with this situation and so rather unreal situations arise where you are playing a rather fruitless, pointless game some of the time in which points are made and points are taken and a lot of time is wasted by serious people. So one is inhibited in that way and I think, indeed, incited.

ST JOHN-STEVAS: What do you mean by 'incited'?

OSBORNE: I mean when I say 'incited', this. This point has been constantly made, about the courtesy and often, indeed, the helpfulness of the Lord Chamberlain's Office which is perfectly true. But it is also true, quite honestly, that they have very often removed from not only the facts of life but even indeed the English language, and one has to take account of this; so that one is very often writing for a few people or, indeed, one might say performing for a few people, and I think this is an unhealthy and unrealistic situation.

ST JOHN-STEVAS: When you say 'inhibited', do you find as a playwright you would weaken and soften and omit because of the censorship?

OSBORNE: Well, one knows that there are certain things that one cannot do, but on the other hand one knows that it is the political game that one may not be able to win or lose, that is the point, which does not seem to me to be a very serious way for one to approach one's art or to have to.

ST JOHN-STEVAS: If the censorship were done away with and the position was left to be governed by common law as amended by statute, this would mean that living Royalty would in fact be without protection because they could not use the ordinary process of the courts. Would you be in favour of any rule to cover their particular position?

OSBORNE: Well, I would have thought it was not beyond the ingenuity of some lawyer to work out some answer to that. Do you mean some special protection? I have not any special feelings about them myself.

ST JOHN-STEVAS: You would not object to such a rule?

OSBORNE: I think it would be wrong myself.

ST JOHN-STEVAS: When you say that the playwright is placed in a unique category, would you not agree that, in fact, he is in a unique category in that he is writing for public performance on the public stage as opposed to a writer who is writing for private reading?

OSBORNE: Well, one might say the same thing about newspapers. Journalists write for a far wider public than the dramatist ever writes for. One is talking about what, indeed, is not a minority audience and these kind of conditions do not exist for the writer who writes for a newspaper or magazine, for example.

KILMUIR: I would be very interested if you could elaborate on what you say in paragraph 3 of your letter: 'As far as obscenity, blasphemy, etc., are concerned, it seems to me that there are quite enough existing laws regarding libel, public order, sedition, obscenity and so on to protect both the public at large and individuals.' Does that mean that you would like to go back (I do not want to put it technically, but I am sure you have studied the subject) to the common law position? May I just elaborate? The last thing I want to do is to put a question in lawyer's terms. You remember in Mr Benn Levy's Bill he said that one of, I think, three reasons for which a theatre could be refused a licence would be that it was a disorderly house. That has not the meaning which one would think at first use of the phrase, but it means, as we are told, 'A disorderly house is a house conducted contrary to law and good order in that matters are performed or exhibited of such a character that their performance or exhibition at a place of common resort amounts to an outrage of public decency or tends to corrupt and deprave or is otherwise calculated to injure public interest so as to cause condemnation and

punishment'. Is that the sort of situation which you would
contemplate obtaining?

OSBORNE: I appreciate your point. I think this is something that is not
beyond the ingenuity of lawyers to get round if they are serious
about reforming the censorship.

KILMUIR: This is not a question of any pernickety approach to what the
law does. What I am anxious to discover is what would be the law as
you would like it to be. I think that is most material. I quoted that
because it corresponded with what had been in Mr Benn Levy's Bill.
If you take another example, the Greater London Council have told
us: 'As to matters for objection, the Council would see no reason to
differentiate between cinema and theatre, and the only guidance it
would think appropriate would be that which is indicated by the law
and expressed in its rule of management 119 quoted at paragraph 9
above.' May I say in brackets that I am quite familiar with the
argument that there is a difference between the theatre and the
cinema, so that it is merely on this question of what would be a
reasonable law for us to recommend should be constituted.

You remember I quoted that they make no difference for this
purpose between plays and cinemas, but I am quoting, of course,
what is now applicable to cinemas: 'No film shall be exhibited at the
premises (i) which is likely (*a*) to encourage or to incite to crime; or
(*b*) to lead to disorder; or (*c*) to stir up hatred against any section of
the public in Great Britain on grounds of colour, race or ethnic or
national origins; or (ii) the effect of which is, if taken as a whole,
such as to tend to deprave and corrupt persons who are likely to see
it.' I have taken it that they have constituted the paragraph I have
read to you as being their view of the law as it is. Subject to the other
point as to the initiation of the prosecution, is that the sort of law
which you think should be applicable to plays? I put it rather
vaguely; I think I have explained the reasons?

OSBORNE: I think the law should be applied – and I think I tried to make
this clear – to certain responsible people. I am not sure about this,
but I believe in the law of libel, for example, printers are liable to
prosection for printing. Am I right about that? Well, this has always
seemed to me unjust, and in the same way I think one could make
the same sort of distinction if one were framing new laws about the
theatre. It seems to me that someone who simply has the lease of the
theatre, or indeed an actor, should not be in the same position as a

producer putting on the play or a man who has written the play. I
think that a distinction should be made.

KILMUIR: I take your point, which I had in mind, as limiting it to certain
categories of persons. But what I really want to know is, if that
which I have quoted to you broadly – and it is putting it very
broadly – if that is the law as it is, do you want to see any change in
that law or would you accept, subject to the precaution of going to a
judge in chambers, that that should be the law applicable to plays?

OSBORNE: I think the law about films is in complete confusion anyway
at the moment, because, as I remember, local councils are able to
license the showing of films quite independently. That law is
confused already and I find it rather a confusing analogy.

KILMUIR: I wanted to assure you that I personally, as I am at present
advised, would go further in your favour than the law as it is. I
should want to apply what we put in the Act of 1959 with regard to
obscene publications, and that is that it is not an offence if it is
proved that publication 'is justified as being for the public good on
the ground that it is in the interests of science, literature, art or
learning, or of other objects of general concern.' That at present, if I
have it right, does not apply to plays. I was only wondering if there
was any particular point in the law as it exists which you thought
should not be applicable to plays?

OSBORNE: I think what you say is possibly a solution.

KILMUIR: Which you are happy to leave to the lawyers if they decide on
the principles?

OSBORNE: I am simply concerned with my freedom as an artist. I think
art should lead public opinion, just as Parliament should lead it.

ANNAN: Some people who are against censorship are worried that, if it is
completely abolished and we rely on the processes of law, a new
kind of play censorship will establish itself: namely, that whenever a
controversial play appears in a manager's office or a producer is
faced with a play he has got to put on, he will immediately seek legal
advice; that solicitors, and still more counsel if their opinion is
sought, will naturally say that their first desire is to safeguard their
client from risk of prosecution and that they will therefore give
advice to a management or to a producer that this play might be
prosecuted. Did I follow you rightly in thinking that your reply to
this is 'Do not worry, because we have semi-state theatres like the
Royal Shakespeare, the National Theatre, which will always put on

controversial plays; or alternatively that there are little theatres which will do this and revel in the risk'? Is that your answer?

OSBORNE: I do not think the situation will change very much. There have always been cautious commercial managements and there always will be quite rightly; and there will be state-subsidized theatres whose job it is, I think, to take this kind of calculated risk; and there are small commercial managements who will take that calculated risk. I do not think the position will change very much and people can take it or not, it seems to me.

LLOYD OF HAMPSTEAD: I quite understand that you regard this as involving a basic principle of freedom. On the other hand, if you abolish pre-censorship, you are going to entrust that freedom to the courts, are you not?

OSBORNE: This is a situation that journalists have, surely, or the novelist or the publisher. I do not see why the dramatist or the theatrical manager should be singled out in this particular way.

LLOYD OF HAMPSTEAD: Do you think you will be better off leaving this kind of issue to the courts?

OSBORNE: I think one will probably be open to all kinds of prosecutions.

LLOYD OF HAMPSTEAD: One knows, for example, from today's Press that there has been a prosecution relating to a display of some pictures [by the American artist Jim Dine. The Robert Fraser Gallery, in Duke St, Mayfair, was prosecuted under the Vagrancy Act 1838].

OSBORNE: Yes. It is a disgraceful state of affairs that a policeman should be allowed to go into an art gallery to take out pictures.

LLOYD OF HAMPSTEAD: If you leave the law as it is at the moment, which I gather is what you contemplate, is there not a danger that this same kind of persecution perhaps, as you might regard it, will be suffered by serious artists in the theatre?

OSBORNE: I think not, because I think public opinion has advanced; it will not happen. I think there might be a rash of it, but it is a risk that all the people who are taking the same line as myself are prepared to take. Everyone seems very anxious to protect us against ourselves as if we were all alcoholics or something. It seems to me a sort of prohibitionist line.

LLOYD OF HAMPSTEAD: You do not think that where a public performance is concerned there might be an even greater danger of

prosecutions of this kind; that the police might be even more
concerned about what occurs on a public stage as against what
occurs in a book or at an art exhibition?

OSBORNE: I think that depends on the climate of opinion and it is rather
difficult to calculate what that might be. I think the question of
public performance is rather over-emphasized about this, because as
I think I said in my letter, theatre-going has, for this century at any
rate, been largely a middle-class occupation and people who go to
the theatre do not do it in the rather *ad hoc* way that they go to the
cinema or turn on the television. They read about it and they know
that if they go and see an Emile Littler production it is likely to be
filth and if they see something written by myself it is likely to be
rather puritanical and quite different! But I think they are very well
protected. People do not take children to the theatre in the same way
they take them to the cinema. I think this analogy is quite outside
what we are talking about. It seems to me the other great English-
speaking country which has no censorship is America, and I have
had at least six or seven plays produced in America with no
censorship whatever and with the problems of different laws in
different States. I do not know, probably someone here might know,
but I do not think there has been a prosecution for a very long time
in America.

LLOYD OF HAMPSTEAD: You have not encountered any trouble with
plays in America which you have been in trouble with in the English
theatre?

OSBORNE: None at all.

LLOYD OF HAMPSTEAD: There have been things cut out of English
versions for this country which have not been cut out in America?

OSBORNE: They have been reinstated. When things have been cut it has
been for reasons of people not understanding the English language
in America.

CHAIRMAN: May I follow up that point? Certain parts were cut out of
your play *Inadmissible Evidence* and we have before us the part that
was cut by the Lord Chamberlain. When your play was produced in
New York was that part in?

OSBORNE There were so many parts cut out, Mr Chairman, I cannot
remember. I think the cuts were restored when they were
understandable to an American audience, but that is a special
problem and not a moral one. That is a practical one.

LLOYD OF HAMPSTEAD: Can you tell me what happened to *A Patriot for Me* in America? Was that produced in the ordinary commercial theatre?

OSBORNE: It is being negotiated at the moment.

LLOYD OF HAMPSTEAD: But it has not actually appeared?

OSBORNE: It has not appeared, but not for any reasons of censorship.

LLOYD OF HAMPSTEAD: Have any queries been raised about its content?

OSBORNE: Only a practical one again, because there are a lot of anti-Semitic things in the play and, Broadway theatre being what it is, there is simply a managerial question about whether people might take it at its face value. But there is no official view about it at all; it is merely a practical one.

LLOYD OF HAMPSTEAD: That type of question on the managerial level might well occur in England if there were no censorship, anyhow?

OSBORNE: Quite. But the situation in New York is infinitely preferable to the one here, from my point of view.

FOOT: On this question of the police being more likely to take action, if censorship were abolished, against a particular play, is it not the case that in that situation the dramatist would have a chance of defending himself, which he does not have now?

OSBORNE: Quite.

FOOT: Do you not think it would be the case that if, in fact, there were a few prosecutions of this nature which were encouraged following the abolition of the censorship, although that might happen for a year or so, those cases being argued out in public would in fact be a good thing for the theatre generally and for the health of the theatre rather than the present situation where the matters are not open to discussions at all?

OSBORNE: I do indeed. People would understand what the nature of the problem was. As we all know, it is conducted behind closed doors and a great many people think it is not very important and it is a matter of just inserting or taking out a few four-letter words. I think if this were conducted in public it would be very vital to the whole thing. It would be an immense help to us all.

FOOT: May I put one or two questions about *A Patriot for Me*? Exactly what did happen? I understand that your main protest against the whole system is on grounds of dignity and freedom. But could you say what may be the practical consequences to the playwright of a play being banned by the Lord Chamberlain or it being suspected that it would be banned? Is there a great difference between what you might have got or what might have been earned for *A Patriot for Me* if it had not had to be shown in a club and what did you get?

OSBORNE: In one case prosecution, which is what happened in the case of Edward Bond and his play *Saved*, and in my case possible impoverishment, because we had to go through this elaborate farce of turning the theatre into a club. In eight weeks 25,000 or 30,000 people saw the play and they went through this elaborate farce of becoming members.

FOOT: Did that cost the theatre anything or did it help the theatre?

OSBORNE: It cost the theatre quite a lot of money. It cost me seven and a half thousand pounds and the theatre the same amount of money; and it was impossible to transfer the play because, quite understandably, no commercial management was prepared to go through the machinery of trying to involve members in the ordinary commercial West End theatre.

FOOT: So would roughly the same thing, not exactly, have applied to Arthur Miller's play [*A View from the Bridge*] which was only shown at the club? He would have suffered a similar financial loss on what he could get in this country?

OSBORNE: He would have done. My *Patriot for Me* was a special case because it was a particularly expensive production. But theoretically it certainly would have occurred to Arthur Miller.

FOOT: What happened in the case of *A Patriot for Me*? Did you submit it or did you think it was impossible to get it through on the basis of past experience or what exactly did happen?

OSBORNE: I did not know what would happen. It was submitted to the usual channels through the management and the Lord Chamberlain's Officer asked for three whole scenes to be taken out, and a lot of other cuts.

FOOT: So when you got that information you then decided that the game was up and you must go for the club from that point onwards?

OSBORNE: Well, it was an act of desperation indeed.

FOOT: Did they say, 'We should negotiate this' or 'We should have talks about this'?

OSBORNE: There were talks about it, yes. But they were quite adamant,

I remember, about three entire scenes which, to the management of the theatre and myself, seemed absolutely crucial to the whole point of the production.

FOOT: So it is not a case that the present operation of the censorship applies even primarily to matters of particular words, although they may be important; it is a case that it applies to the whole production of plays?

OSBORNE: Oh indeed. My very first experience – not my very first, but one of my earlier experiences – with the Lord Chamberlain's Office, indeed, was about a political matter when I wrote a play in, I think, 1951 (certainly a very long time ago) which involved two subjects. It was principally about the Un-American Activities Committee and there was also a hint of homosexuality in the play as well. Unfortunately, the manager who went with me to the Lord Chamberlain's Office at the time was drunk, so I did not have a very good advocate; and I was young and inexperienced. But it was made very clear that both subjects were ones that could not be countenanced on the stage.

FOOT: So that it is conceivable, certainly, that if it had not been for the existence of the Lord Chamberlain you might have made your appearance as a dramatist in this country in 1951 instead of 1956?

OSBORNE: Yes.

FOOT: That would have made quite a difference, would it not?

OSBORNE: It would for me anyway.

GOODMAN: I wonder if we might investigate what to us is really a crucial matter. The question of principle, of course, is an important matter, but we perhaps primarily, speaking for myself, are concerned about the theatre, not the question of vindicating principles. What I would like to investigate with you, following Mr Foot's queries, is how much better off you would have been with, say, a play like *A Patriot for Me*, if the system you are advocating had been in operation.

I ought to start off by saying, I think possibly you know I did not regard *A Patriot for Me* as an obscene play. I felt very strongly about it. I speak from the viewpoint of someone who thought it was a play that ought to have been shown to the public. Did you take any legal opinion as to whether or not, leaving aside the question of the Lord Chamberlain, that play would have been successfully prosecuted for obscenity under our existing laws, because that seems to me a very crucial matter?

Mr Foot has been making the point that you have been deprived of substantial sums of money through the activities of the Lord Chamberlain and that you had to postpone your career of dramatist for many years because of the activities of the Lord Chamberlain. It is very relevant to see whether in fact all this might not have happened even if the Lord Chamberlain had not been there. Did anyone advise you what the general law would have done, leaving aside the Lord Chamberlain, if your play had been presented to a jury or presented to a magistrate, and considered by them under the general laws of obscenity according to our current notions of morality?

OSBORNE: Lord Goodman, I was not personally concerned. When I say that, I was personally concerned but I was not practically concerned with what happened with the play. I believe in fact that the English Stage Company took legal advice and there was a move to have it passed out to a West End theatre, but it was made, I believe, clear that there would be quite possibly legal difficulties over this. But I was in a privileged position in the fact that I had a special relationship with one theatre for ten years and also that I had been extremely successful during that ten years financially; and I was able to put a substantial amount of my own money (which I lost) into this production which anyone who is unknown would not have been able to do. In that sense I was privileged.

GOODMAN: Yes. That does not quite answer the question. The point really is this. You are advocating, as many of your colleagues are, very understandably, that the censor imposes restraints on you and humiliations on you, which one understands very much and resents. What I am concerned about is how much better off you might be or would be, or how much worse off you might be if there was not a censorship, because this is really what we as a Committee are concerned with. The first point I was concerned with was whether this play would have got on anyway if there was not a censorship, because, speaking as a lawyer with some experience of these matters, I think there would have been a very strong possibility that any legal opinion obtained from lawyers who were advising on this type of matter would have been strongly against presenting this play for fear of a prosecution. If that is so, you are then in some ways worse off because you are not dealing even with an opinion of an institution as public as the Lord Chamberlain, you are dealing with an opinion which is obtained from some anonymous character operating ostensibly on entirely objective grounds, but quite possibly exercising personal prejudices and personal beliefs which lawyers have as anyone else. Do you not think that might be a much worse censorship and more damaging to you than to know that you have applied for a licence to a public body who state their reasons and in the result you find your play is prohibited, whereas it would still have been prohibited if you had had to apply to the Lord Chamberlain?

OSBORNE: My own personal reaction to that is that I and most of the people I know in the theatre are prepared to take that risk. I think in the case of that particular play, historically we got away with it, as it were; in fact, when the next test came up at the Royal Court there were policemen's boots all over the place for quite some time and there was indeed a prosecution.

GOODMAN: You say you are prepared to take those risks. I am sure you are and I am sure you will all go to the stake for it and willingly accept a martyr's fate. I am wondering whether any good would come of it in the result. One of the most touching features of your evidence is the confidence you have in lawyers. This I am personally very agreeable to but I am not sure it is well placed, if I might say so. Now, there was a prosecution today that was successfully concluded, of some pictures. That was a prosecution in which lawyers contrived a situation in which no evidence could be called in favour of the pictures. Quite obviously the lawyers could not have been well disposed towards the art form. They contrived a prosecution under a statute which seems very inappropriate. Or, if you take other previous prosecutions in which lawyers have been concerned and public authorities have been concerned, it is quite clear that there is an attitude that is rather, if I might put it that way, anti-intellectual on the part of people dealing with prosecutions of this type, I think a very dangerous one.

Take *A Patriot for Me*: supposing you had had to rely on the law of obscenity and you may take it from me that there is a sporting chance you would have been convicted; you would have had a long trial, if we take the analogy of *Lady Chatterley*. To defend your case I suggest you would have had to take a caravan of archbishops, of literature and everything else down to the Old

Bailey. You would have had to spend a small fortune and in the event you would have to rely on a jury because the combined solicitude of all lawyers connected with that case, apart from the defence lawyer, was very clear. No one could say that the prosecution or the Judge showed any partiality towards *Lady Chatterley*. If you had emerged from this, having paid the defence costs and the prosecution at that court, and had had your play prohibited anyway, do you think you would have done the theatre or yourself any good or achieved a better result for anyone by removing the censor?

OSBORNE: I think my answer to that is, at least it would have brought it to the public attention. The pictures – I do not know the case you are referring to, I have not read the newspaper today – at least they were exhibited.

GOODMAN: Not for very long?

OSBORNE: Not for very long, no. They were showing for eight weeks. People knew about it; this was not something conducted behind closed doors, it was done in the public arena.

GOODMAN: It was not very public if no evidence could be called in favour of the pictures?

OSBORNE: No archbishops?

GOODMAN: That is a great anxiety here that it might be to exchange King Log for King Stork just for the exchange, and really this has not been brought out in the implications. Suppose there were a voluntary system whereby a man is entitled, if he wants to have a go, to put his play on, to invite prosecution if he wants to; but the managements have a right, if they want to – if they do not want they need not – to go off and get a licence which protects them against all the timidities inherent in commercial managements which you say are not to be found in the heroic state-subsidized theatres, which I am delighted to hear. What is the objection to that, except an objection of principle? Are you not rather throwing the baby out with the bath water by rejecting that possibility?

OSBORNE: I have only glanced at it but I think there is an answer to that in the Arts Council report: the fact that a management has gone to the length of getting a licence would be prejudicial against the management who had not in fact done this, in any action that resulted afterwards.

GOODMAN: This is a technical objection which possibly might be overcome by preventing it being the subject of comment in court. One could put a provision into the statute to say it must not be the subject of comment by anybody that he had or had not applied for the licence. I quite agree, I think this is a problem. Leaving aside that technical question, can you see why one should not really have the best of both worlds by giving the timid manager an opportunity of getting his licence if he wants it and leaving it to the heroic manager never to apply for licences, or to present the play where it has been refused a licence? Apart from the principle, which I am not deriding, but from the point of view of the welfare of the theatre alone, would that not be the best thing to do in everyone's interest?

OSBORNE: I think not. I think it does encourage a climate of timidity.

GOODMAN: You think that this situation should be maintained to encourage a climate of heroism? I do not say this in the least scoffingly. I think we ought to encourage climates of heroism but it is rather a different objective. We are concerned with the welfare of the theatre and not with breeding heroes?

OSBORNE: I think that a lot of us for a very long time have been agitating in the way that we have done not simply for the sake of change but simply, as you say, for the sake of the theatre and people who devote their lives to it; in some cases, literally.

GOODMAN: I think we all accept the total sincerity. What I rather doubt is whether the implications of the change are sufficiently realized. You are a man of the theatre. May I put another point to you? You know that most of the London theatres are controlled, unhappily, by very few managements (a matter, I think, of very great concern), which means that the small management has to seize the opportunity of getting a theatre when it arises for any play that comes along, as you know. If the small management is dealing with a play that is not licensed and an opportunity arises for getting a theatre, which is always very brief indeed, someone else may well, particularly in the case of a popular theatre like the Criterion or the Lyric, get it in literally a matter of hours. Do you not think it would seriously restrict the object of a serious controversial play getting into production if you then had to enter into long arguments about whether or not it was likely to be prosecuted or if it was a question of getting legal opinion to satisfy management on that subject?

OSBORNE: I think on the whole small managements are small

managements because they are small in their outlook and in what they set out to do.

GOODMAN: I think if you look at the history of the theatre that is not so?

OSBORNE: I think recently it is.

GOODMAN: I would not agree with that. I think that is not a very valid comment. Many small managements have put on very important plays that other people would not?

OSBORNE: Not at risk.

GOODMAN: At risk?

WILSON: You tell us that under the present system you are rather inhibited, that it is as if you were writing for one or two persons. If you go back to the old common law, you will then be answerable in the final result to a jury. Will you not then be writing with the thought of the attitude of a jury in your mind?

OSBORNE: I think it is preferable to one or two people behind closed doors, and it is not only a jury but a jury that is observed by the public.

WILSON: So that you would sooner write with a jury in mind in an open court than with a few people behind a closed door, even if the people behind the closed door and their attitudes are known to you?

OSBORNE: Yes. Their views are acceptable to everyone.

ST JOHN-STEVAS: Have you had any of your plays produced in Ireland?

OSBORNE: Yes, I think there have been. I think *Look Back in Anger* has been.

ST JOHN-STEVAS: Was there any suggestion of *A Patriot for Me* being produced there?

OSBORNE: Not as far as I know, no.

ST JOHN-STEVAS: I ask these questions because it is an example of a country contiguous that has no censorship and I was just wondering whether you had found your efforts to put on a play in Dublin, which after all has a very rich theatrical tradition, frustrated by theatre managements there, but it is not so?

OSBORNE: The only country I have had censorship problems with, apart from this country, is Italy.

ST JOHN-STEVAS: You did not try to have a play put on in the Vatican?

OSBORNE: No. But *Luther* was troublesome.

CHAIRMAN: Is there anything you would like to add before I express the
   Committee's thanks.
OSBORNE: No.
CHAIRMAN: Thank you very much indeed for your views and answers that
   have been exceedingly helpful. We are very grateful to you.
OSBORNE: Thank you.

> from *Report of the Joint Committee on Censorship of the Theatre* (1967)

Dear Diary . . .

I THINK IT was the French historian Michelet who said of someone that
they wrote in a style in which it was impossible to tell the truth. Politicians,
naturally have always been adroit at the idiom of deceit. The Watergate
witnesses used a German–American patois which was impenetrable.
Now, almost everyone, not only cabinet ministers first thing on Radio
Four, pours forth a stream of pharisaical logorrhoea, a lingua franca of
joined-up, recently minted clichés, a *peoplespeak*, which is gratefully
plundered 'at the end of the day' in a 'level playing-field situation' of
'bottom-line priorities' by both 'those up front' and the 'insufficiently
motivated'. It certainly is an 'abuse crisis', 'targeted' and 'taken on board'
by 'user-friendly', 'Eurowise' pressure groupies, indolent journalists and,
of course, political correctivists. They rely on a guidebook of cant words,
as invaluable as an Edwardian's list of *Useful Phrases When Abroad*.

Perhaps it was ever thus. I wrote a play, *Inadmissible Evidence*, in 1964
and began with a stylized parody of Harold Wilson's speech to the Labour
Party Conference the year before:

> My belief . . . in . . . in the technological revolution, the pressing,
> growing, pressing, urgent need for more and more scientists, and
> more scientists, for more and more schools and universities and
> universities and schools, the theme of change, realistic decisions based
> on a highly developed and professional study of society . . . the theme
> and challenge of such rapid change . . . in the inevitability of
> automation and the ever increasing need, need, oh need for the stable
> ties of modern family life, rethinking, reliving, making way for the
> motor car . . . in a forward looking, outward looking, programme
> controlled machine tool line reassessment . . .

And so on; all from the then current flow of pharisaical *peoplespeak*. The audience nodded in collusion. At the revival, fourteen years later, they spluttered with laughter. They recognized the language of empty fatuity which they had once accepted, indeed used themselves.

THAT GREAT COMEDIAN Sid Field used to perform a sketch in which, wild-eyed , dressed in tailcoat and bicycle clips and wielding a bell-ringing hammer, he would announce: 'During the course of my performance tonight, I may *inadvertently* . . .' He would freeze as if his tongue had been scalded, then managed to continue: 'Inadvertently . . .' His face bulged like a frog's at the joy of an exquisite discovery. 'I say, do you *mind* if I say that again?' He would exhale the sound once more like a fragrant, linguistic ectoplasm. He had found himself within a *word*, one of ineffable implication. Everytime I hear or read chunks strung together from the *Peoplespeak Phrase Book*, I think of that eureka! 'Inadvertently', and the transport of its utterance.

I'VE NEVER THOUGHT of myself as being an eccentric, but I begin to wonder. I seem to get exercised about things that are of no import, and yet they trouble and even distress me. Why do I get so fretful when people repeatedly misspell my name? I pick up an envelope addressed to J. Osbourne or J. Osborn and my morning is clouded. I have put my true name to all my labour and I swear it never used to be so (honestly, Doctor). But now, everyone does it: banks, accountants, solicitors, *all* tradesmen, newspapers, students (most of all) resentfully demanding I write their essays for them and, of course, university drama departments who compound the offhand insult with the addition 'Playwrite'. And then there are strangers, especially in theatre and television, who address me without affection, sometimes on the telephone, as 'John'. Such things count for little, maybe. And yet it isn't self-importance that makes me stiffen, but a ripple of discomfort and unease. Indifference franked by a postage stamp, I suppose. Jayne Austin, Trollup, Konrad, Cipling, Shore, Dickins, Wild. No, but *they* were famous . . .

WHERE ARE ALL the voluptuous, laughing, bawdy girls of my youth? Nowadays they can prosecute you just for making them feel inadequate, which they probably are.

A few days ago, some legal secretary complained that she was 'touched' at the firm's Christmas party. Another employee 'put an arm

round her waist' and – crikey Moses! – 'squeezed her breast' in the taxi
home. If she'd been touched up in the office, why share a taxi with him?
Anyway, she made an official complaint and the rest of the staff snubbed
this squinny-lipped ice-maiden, who was later made redundant. She sued
the firm for sexual discrimination, saying she was fired because she
objected to sexual advances. Inevitably, she was awarded £5,000
damages and £200 for 'injured feelings'.

Injured feelings – dear God, I have those almost hourly. If you go
squealing to the law every time someone twangs your knicker elastic – a
gambit easily repelled by a sharp, playful slap, a witty riposte or merry
oath – your place is not in this lustful world but a nunnery. There is more
to life than being a power-suited, high-flying executive. And one of them
is being a woman of enough reserve, imagination and good humour to
dispose of male boors without snivelling recourse to Legal Aid.

THIS WEEK, my producer complained of being jaded after twenty-two
years in the theatrical game. That could be to do with me, I suppose, but I
think he's lucky. By contrast, playwrights have miserably short working
lives. Wilde had three years, Sheridan four, Congreve seven, Pinero
thirteen, Priestley sixteen, Maugham twenty-five and Strindberg twenty-
six. Almost all Ibsen's famous plays were written when he was over sixty.
Shaw was nearly forty when he produced *Widowers' Houses*, but after
The Apple Cart some twenty years on he was never taken seriously again.
Rattigan's theatrical career lasted scarcely twenty years before he was
cast into the outer darkness of fashion and caprice. Even Coward was
obliged to find a happier livelihood in cabaret. We theatre scribblers
average about a dozen years or so.

It set me thinking. I had my first play produced (in the glamour of the
Theatre Royal, Huddersfield) when I was nineteen, was running my own
company at twenty and, I suddenly realize, this is my forty-fifth year
working in what Pinero called 'this rotten profession'. But it gets no
easier.

BY THE TIME this piece appears, my eighteenth London production over
a period of thirty-six years [*Déjàvu*] will have opened at the Comedy
Theatre. The crocodile scrawlers will have slithered into my muddied
grave in Panton Street to crunch the bones of a life's work. However, I
shall be ashore, home if not dry; thanks to my dentist, I have a new smile
and my bite now should be as good as my bark. As my half century of

obstinate squatting in the Playhouse approaches, I can look out from the Marches with renewed woof and fang to snap into any straying predators. You can't outstay your welcome when you never had one, I say. Woof. There's rabies lurking in these blue remembered hills. Woof.

Spectator, 13 June 1992

Queen and Country

===

Fighting Talk

It is always a temptation to try to answer the ultimate questions. This enables you to ignore the immediate ones.

It is dramatic to lie in bed with a prostitute discussing the existence of God, but I do not believe it does any of the three parties concerned any particular good.

I am not a politician, and I am not a philosopher; I am an artist working in the theatre. I have never set up as a critic of society, handing down angry commandments, written on tablets of white tiling from the summits of the Royal Court Theatre. But I have been made the founder member of a new stereotype, the Angry Young Men, created by journalists, who are obliged to think in these glib, unreal terms because the easiest way to dismiss anyone is to fix a label on them.

If there are any angry young men, they are mostly employed by newspapers to pounce on people like myself, who are trying to do a difficult job as well as they know how.

Most journalists are so worm-eaten with self-contempt that they are determined to project their own rage on to anyone who has managed to be successful in his own field without offering up his integrity, or beating everyone over the ears with his own compromise.

I have had my shoulder stared at hypnotically by newspapermen who have to walk in doors sideways to safeguard the chips of their chosen profession.

I must make myself clear about this question of identity. I am a playwright, and the only valid statement I can ever make is in the theatre, not in a Sunday newspaper.

Journalism is a poor substitute for art, even bad art. But, unfortunately, most people prefer journalism – and bad journalism at that.

I work in a profession where a great many of the patterns of our society have run wild. The theatre is the happy hunting-ground for the present English fashion in moral toadyism.

Part of the reason for this is that the theatre has begun to attract more and more people from the respectable and conformist sections of society.

Added to this is the fact that the average person who works in the theatre is more of a misanthropic romantic than is even usual in England in 1957.

His instincts are traditionalist, fatalist and superstitious. Brought up on a heavy diet of Shakespeare, he would believe in the Divine Right of kings if he could be persuaded that it were fashionable.

Everything about his circumstances encourages him to believe in magic.

Nobody is more gullible or more easily imposed upon than the average actor. He is an innocent, taken in by the atmosphere he has helped to create around him.

He has carefully inherited the middle-class distrust of group movements, for group loyalty goes against all the lessons he has learnt bitterly in the jungle in which he lives.

He can't see that the way out may be for everybody to start some clearing and cutting down. No, usually he doesn't want the jungle tamed.

He may argue that in this way only the strongest and the most talented survive but, in his own heart, he cherishes the knowledge that justice may not be what he wants anyway.

He knows that the survival-of-the-fittest gag is just another belief in magic. He accepts it, for he is committed to this atmosphere of myth and mystery.

The fact is that the jungle, because it rejects justice, so often protects the weak and the cowardly and the feeble.

I have spoken about the theatre because it is the world in which I work, and I think it is relevant.

It is one in which groups of people who create little or nothing themselves, incapable of imagination or honesty, wield enormous power without responsibility to anyone but themselves.

There is a reasonably adequate word to describe them – they are Tories.

The situation in the theatre is rather like that throughout Britain before 1945. All we have is the Means Test Man in the shape of the Arts Council.

Perhaps this has helped me to keep my faith when all around were losing theirs, and shrugging off Socialism as just another romantic attitude.

The task facing Socialists has never been more difficult, and we are not going to achieve anything by being polite. If you want Socialism, you won't get it without coining some new words.

You can't beat the Tories (and I don't mean simply the Conservative Party) at their own game of politeness and platitudes.

'I believe in Britain!' proclaims the Tory, meaning that what he believes in is a Tory Britain, and that if you suggest that there are a whole lot of things about Britain that stink then you are a cad.

He wants you to shake hands and pretend there are no fundamental differences between us, and when you look at the House of Commons it is difficult not to see his point.

'Let us all pull together!' and then (this is the one to make you feel really shabby and old-fashioned) 'All this class hatred is *out-of-date.*'

This is about the biggest insult imaginable nowadays, to suggest that someone simply has not kept up with 'all the enormous social, political and technological (this word from some smiling Tory is enough to make you feel as if you've been caught taking snuff) advances that have been going on.'

If you are rash enough to mumble the word 'Socialism', you are made to feel that you had said something like 'horseless carriage' – poor, simple, unsophisticated old thing.

It is an effective technique, and it usually works.

This has got to be resisted, and the only way is to stand up, say what you think about whom and what you don't like in our society, and to hell with making a fool of yourself – and the more enemies you make the better.

If you're going to start a battle (and don't think you'll get Socialism without one) you must first know your enemies.

And we mustn't be afraid of starting a battle among ourselves. If we work for Socialism, we have got to work out what we mean by the word.

I do not believe, as the Labour Party seems to suggest, that it means simply better wages, free teeth, and making jokes about witless young men and women who throw strawberries at each other at smart parties. I do not believe that a man can live simply for himself and his family, and this seems to me the essential Tory attitude.

It is an attitude of despair, which insists that human nature cannot be changed or life improved beyond a material level. Above all, it implies a deep-rooted contempt for people.

Socialism is the only political system which believes in human beings. Socialism is about people living together, and the sooner the leaders of the Labour party stop arguing about sugar and cement and wake up to the fact the better.

The Labour Party's miserable failure to provide a valid, workable belief, an attitude to live by, was shown up completely by the Suez affair.

The working people in this country were almost solidly behind Sir Anthony Eden, simply because after fifty years of talking cant about brotherhood and ethics, the Labour Party still had not managed to tell anyone what Socialism meant.

The Labour Party has concerned itself too much with order papers, and ignored human behaviour. It should turn its attention to the things that matter, to the things that make people feel.

Christianity is almost a dead letter in this country, and intellectual appeals to vague religious feelings like Mr Colin Wilson's are frankly dangerous and pointless.

The Labour Party has an enormous opportunity. Unfortunately it hasn't the imagination to see it, or it would be worrying about the things that *do* make people respond, like films, theatre, television.

It would be worried by the corrupt, dishonest symbols that still move people, by the rubbish turned out by the British film industry, with its emotional dishonesty, its false, implicitly Tory values, and idiot heroes.

We live in an island of sanctimony, without any vital culture of our own (this we are forced to borrow from America), without any moral dynamic of our own, and still responding to the same tired, grubby symbols handed out to us by the deadheads who write political manifestos, make films, and produce plays.

Somebody should tell the Labour Party that something has been discovered called mass communications.

Recently, I managed to 'get through' to nearly 5 million people in one evening on television. They may not have liked it, but they responded.

Who on earth is going to respond to pompous, badly written statements about automation or iron and steel?

No, Socialism is about people, and the Labour Party has forgotten it. Or perhaps it never knew it?

Reynolds News, 17 February 1957

The Fifties

It would be easy for me to write about the forties. When they began I was nine years old, and this was the decade of my growing-up. This period has been on deposit long enough, and I am able to draw on it, assimilate and study it. But I am still up to my ears in the fifties, and expect to be so for several years to come.

Decades do not consult calendars, however convenient it might be for the writers of newspaper articles. Nineteen-sixty-nine would be a good time to write about the fifties.

There must be something to be seen from this hardly hewn, rough chunk of history, but what?

How were all those people who threatened to emigrate after the General Election in 1945 to know that their anxieties and privations were to last for no more than a few austere years, and that, before long, they would be happily incanting 'You've never had it so good'; that the lean and sinew of the forties would become the fat and spineless fifties?

The Labour Party's stumbling imagination slowed down to the point where it sometimes seemed to be walking backwards and even disappearing altogether.

As the time grew fatter, so it became like a priest in a world without sin and declined, still trying to remember its native Socialist tongue when speaking to its supporters, but carefully using the new, official language of success and prosperity to the middle class it dare not defy.

Mr Attlee became an earl, and, what with such things as block votes, life peerages, and standing orders, no one could say that the Labour Party did not open new fields for conformism.

In its recent election exercise in unarmed comeback, the Labour Party even tried to appeal to feelings about old age, as hopeless a misreading of the prevailing mood as one could conceive.

For this was the emergent mood of the fifties, not rebellion, as some people seemed to believe.

Out of this decade has come the Illusion of Comfort, and we have lost the sense of life's difficulty.

The techniques of suppression in politics, art, and communications became so perfected that there is no issue which need be allowed to interfere with our individual and national well-being.

If a lion should appear in the streets, we shall not complain. We shall not see him. In this time, we are not keepers of brothers because we no longer believe that we have brothers.

When I grew up in the forties, childhood was private, harsh, and isolated. The world of adult experience was remote, alien, and often painful.

The word 'teenager' had not yet been successfully imported from America, and we were ignored because we were valuable to no one.

We believed we were different and unique, and no one had tried to convince us that we had a common taste, or a profitable mass attitude.

We did not dictate the sales of popular records, and no one was interested in finding out what we thought of God or sex ('What about you, Tom? Do you think there is anything in this idea of saying a private prayer during the firm's tea break?').

Language has become more permissive, but behaviour is no less restrictive, and the outspoken never threatens the unspoken. Words may be free, but conscience is cheap. Some words are appearing in newspapers and being spoken in plays that were forbidden almost yesterday, but these are the mere noises of freedom that the conformism of the fifties kills with its commercial kindness.

We have written our heads off about prostitution and indeed written it off the streets. To save the embarrassment of maidish old men we have lost a sight which was one of the few remaining visible testaments to the stability of the English character.

At last the Napoleonic jibe looks like being confirmed: we are shopkeepers to be sure (or technologists if you like). We could keep little else with our shopkeepers' morality.

Then there has been the telly. The fifties helped to make it, and it helped to make them, creating a new world where everyone watches and no one takes part. It is good to be an audience, but tough to play a part.

When I was a small boy in the forties, it seemed to me that only prosperous people owned cars. Few people I knew had one, and simply to ride around in a car has not lost its novelty for me.

The British motorist with his hopes of an extra car in the garage is a typical feature of the time. With his mean little ego and his flashy ineptitude, the British driver speeds away in the wrong lane, but the right road towards an England that becomes less pleasant and no longer green.

Even the French with their inbred, hard-bitten materialism drive less savagely than the English.

'I am distressed for thee my brother Jonathan: thy love to me was wonderful, passing the love of women.' Today in the fifties these words could not be uttered sincerely or without inhibition.

Marriage has been carefully constructed into the pattern of success, and has even become a secondary profession for many of us, and there are now great holes where there was once passion and identity.

Freud, speaking with his prophet's voice which is so often superb, once said: 'To endure life remains, when all is said, the first duty of all living beings. Illusion can have no value if it makes this more difficult for us.'

I believe we started out with hope, and hope deferred makes the heart sick, and many hearts are sick at what they see in England now.

Perhaps the sixties will begin to turn away from evasion and, although I believe Christianity to be a hearty contributor to that evasion, it was a wise Christian who said: 'He that increaseth knowledge increaseth sorrow.'

Daily Express, 2 December 1959

A Letter to My Fellow Countrymen

In August 1961 the Cold War escalated with the building of the Berlin Wall, and the proliferation of nuclear weapons seemed certain.

This is a letter of hate. It is for you, my countrymen. I mean those men of my country who have defiled it. The men with manic fingers leading the sightless, feeble, betrayed body of my country to its death. You are its murderers, and there's little left in my own brain but the thoughts of murder for you.

I cannot even address you as I began as 'Dear', for that word alone would sin against my hatred. And this, my hatred for you, and those who tolerate you, is about all I have left and all the petty dignity my death may keep.

No, this is not the highly paid 'anger' or the 'rhetoric' you like to smile at (you've tried to mangle my language, too). You'll not pour pennies into my coffin for this; you are MY object. I am not yours. You are my vessel, you are MY hatred. That is my final identity. True, it will no doubt die with me in a short time and by your unceasing effort.

But perhaps it could be preserved, somewhere, in the dead world that you have prepared for us, perhaps the tiny, unbared spark of my human hatred might kindle, just for the briefest moment in time, the life you lost for us.

I fear death. I dread it daily. I cling wretchedly to life, as I have always done. I fear death, but I cannot hate it as I hate you. It is only you I hate, and those who let you live, function and prosper.

My hatred for you is almost the only constant satisfaction you have left me. My favourite fantasy is four minutes or so non-commercial viewing as you fry in your democratically elected hot seats in Westminster, preferably with your condoning democratic constituents.

There is murder in my brain, and I carry a knife in my heart for every one of you. Macmillan, and you, Gaitskell, you particularly. I wish we could hang you all out, with your dirty washing, on your damned Oder–Neisse Line, and those seven out of ten Americans, too. I would willingly watch you all die for the West, if only I could keep my own minuscule portion of it, you could all go ahead and die for Berlin, for Democracy, to keep out the red hordes or whatever you like.

You have instructed me in my hatred for thirty years. You have perfected it, and made it the blunt, obsolete instrument it is now. I only hope it will keep me going. I think it will. I think it may sustain me in the last few months.

Till then, damn you, England. You're rotting now, and quite soon you'll disappear. My hate will outrun you yet, if only for a few seconds. I wish it could be eternal.

I write this from another country, with murder in my brain and a knife carried in my heart for every one of you. I am not alone. If WE had just the ultimate decency and courage, we would strike at you – now, before you blaspheme against the world in our name. There is nothing I should not give for your blood on my head.

But all I can offer you is my hatred. You will be untouched by that, for you are untouchable. Untouchable, unteachable, impregnable.

If you were offered the heart of Jesus Christ, your Lord and your Saviour – though not mine, alas – you'd sniff at it like sour offal. For that is the Kind of Men you are.

Believe me,

In sincere and utter hatred,

Your Fellow Countryman,

John Osborne, Valbonne, France

Tribune, 18 August 1961

The Socialist Once Angry

On 14 March 1962 Daily Herald columnist Dee Wells criticized 'a still-young, once-angry Socialist writer' for saying that he would rather see the Tories elected again than have a Gaitskell-led Labour Government 'because Gaitskell doesn't represent the kind of Socialism I stand for'.

Said Dee Wells: 'In politics, as in everything, half a loaf is better than none.'

I am the 'Socialist, once-angry' (preserve us!) writer who told Dee Wells he would not vote for Mr Gaitskell's Labour Party.

This is true. I would not, and at the next General Election, I shall not.

The reasons for this are based not on personalities but on temperament.

The Tories were always detestable and more so now with their adroit razor-sharp practice and thug success. But the Labour Party is similarly despicable in its mean-witted shambling to keep up the same kind of moral stride with its puny bribes and come-ons to old-age pensioners and unhoused young families.

These problems are important, but they do not go to the root of living.

The Labour Party, with the Tories, says merely: 'Give us power and we will give more people more *things*.' (They mean different sets of people, of course.)

The Labour Party fattens up the general hopes of petty grasping for the petty millions.

Moral good, which is one thing Socialism is about, is club-footed without the imagination, and Labour's is odiously shifty, bourgeois, philistine and self-regarding.

It has consistently shown itself to be so over too many issues, great and small, for too long.

Both your houses are infested with expediency, which is why a plague on them.

This is not irresponsible. Barrenness is preferable to rape by one of two monsters.

John Osborne

Daily Herald, 16 March 1962

Supporting the Cause

The last time I involved myself in any political demonstration was in 1961, when, with a great many other writers or hang-around writers, I 'sat down' in Trafalgar Square. I fully expected to go to gaol but mercifully didn't, although I was looking forward at the time to a legitimate reason for not being able to write. In fact, I was lovingly carried off into a van by eight – I think – kindly constables who called me 'sir'. (All those I saw manhandled asked for what they got. And they wanted it.) Apart from being reviled and libelled by the *Sunday Express*, I was fined forty shillings and went home for a good soak in the bath with a severe headache. I don't regret having done this. At the time it had a kind of national poetic logic that certain of us should make this particular gesture. My sense of timing rarely lets me down and I know I was right at the time. However, I resolved then that I should never engage in this kind of concerted affair again unless some unforeseeable situation should arise. It revealed itself to my simple spirit that there is a certain kind of militant animal which seeks out and exploits political crises for reasons of personal aggrandisement and creative frustration. There is an odour of psychopathic self-righteousness about many of the hardy annual protesters which I find ludicrous and distasteful. I have long ago refused to sign those glib and predictable letters to *The Times*, including the one during the recent Israeli crisis [the Six Day War] when so many of these cause-happy activists leapt to the telephone and their pens.

The same principle applies to the Vietnam War, the very name of which has become a synonym for left-wing sanctimony. I have not been able to come to a clear resolution over this or many other political dilemmas. I do know that I see little to choose between Communist police terrorism and shoddy American power politics. Except that I find the latter minimally less repugnant.

We really do live in a very wicked world. I believe that writers should express their position about this as well as they can and in the country in which they have elected to live. Writers are often more thoughtful than the rest of the community and occasionally more literate. However, they should speak modestly as gifted or admired individuals and not as part of a privileged pressure group with access to revealed truths. The presumption and sentimentality of many of my fellow craftsmen is frequently appalling. May God gag all actresses forever. Unless they are divine, and the ones who are just shut up. Consequently I sign letters no longer.

Friends who were never friends call me blimp. To hell with them. It is harder than they will ever know.

I certainly don't give money. Not to subsidize ungifted people who organize these junkets. Better even to spend it on a subscription to *Encounter*. No, not for all those schoolteachers and pedants and readers of the *Guardian* and the *Observer*. Perhaps to *Horse and Hound* and a girl to read it with.

Encounter, September 1967

Voting Pattern

On 10 October 1974 there was the second general election that year when Harold Wilson, who had led a minority Labour government since March, following Edward Heath's defeat in an election he had called in response to calls for a national strike, sought a new mandate for his policies, particularly the 'Social Contract' agreed with the TUC. (Wilson was in fact re-elected with an overall majority of only three.)

I shall vote Labour once more, but with even emptier heart than usual. Like the historian, our politicians use the language in a manner in which it is impossible to speak the truth. With their ritual incantation of phrases – as if they were *things* – like 'Inflation', 'National Unity', 'Priorities' and 'Social Contracts', they only conceal the nasty reality of the awful brutishness of most of English life today.

It is no use talking of pensions and mortgages when they are mere ideas supported only by the moral and poetic emptiness of all the parties. Jerusalem might yet be built in this pleasant land, but never in the typists' pools and conference rooms of Brussels.

The Labour Party has always been bedevilled by its own rigid philistinism, aided by the unions, and has been largely responsible for the moral slum and squalid climate we have created since the heady days of 1945.

The shabbiness of Mr Heath and his supermarket manager's vision of a cut-price future has been one of the most hideous spectacles of recent history. He has not been dubbed 'The Grocer' for nothing.

As for the Liberals, with their lack of substance and tinkling squeaks of grandeur, they don't even represent an alternative to the left-wing bullies of agit-prop, student unions, the Angry Brigade, the Price Sisters [convicted for involvement in the IRA's London bombing campaign] and Redgraves on the one hand and the right-wing bullies like the National Front, retired colonels, Mrs Whitehouses and readers of the *Sunday Express* on the other.

If I lived in Ebbw Vale I should vote for Michael Foot, and if I lived in County Down I should vote for Enoch Powell. 'Romantic,' I hear. And why not? Politics should be about Principle just as Religion is about Rule, and bauble 'Policies' (the politicians' favourite word) are their substitute. It should not be a series of endless appeals to puny and sectional cupidity. Buy shoddy is the trick of all parties.

Observer, 6 October 1974

Royalty Accounts

Not since the Great Lisbon Earthquake of 1755, when 30,000 people were killed and 11,000 buildings destroyed within six minutes, has a natural, if freakish, phenomenon caused such apocalyptic hysteria as the collapse of the Royal Heir's marriage. The reason for this monumental upheaval has been confidently located as the Windsor Fault. Seismological theory has it that this is partly due to irreversible atmospheric cooling. What is above becomes too large to fit the interior below and must then collapse. The scars then heal and, the theory adds significantly, 'the process repeats itself *with failures* at intervals.'

In the aftershock of Lisbon came firestorms of perfervid prophecy, intimations of wickedness and divine intervention. The first confirmation of the Windsor Fault, with the Abdication in 1936, might be interpreted on the One-to-Twelve Richter scale as Six. 'Felt by all. Some heavy furniture moved. Damage slight.' The next faulting, the divorce of Princess Margaret, scarcely scores more than Two. 'Delicately balanced objects may swing.' The subsequent uncouplings of Princess Anne and Prince Andrew pushed the graph upwards, and the present glum and gleeful forecasts for the Prince Charles Faulting are needling erratically towards Twelve. 'Damage total. Waves seen on ground surfaces. Lines of sight destroyed. Objects thrown up into the air.'

The tidal waves from this turmoil have brought with them a relentless drizzle of Windsor-Richter almanacs, almost blotting out the already dark, recessionary skies, as they buffet and blind the tabloid conscience of a sullen democracy, uneasy with its palpable mediocrity, manifest ignorance and dismal achievement. Fanning the epidemic are what the film producer Sam Spiegel used to call his 'opinion-makers'. In his case, a bunch of Hungarian comfort-stooges who unfailingly read out the runes he wished to hear. This lot are mostly upstart journalists and academics of the dimmer sort.

Opinion-making is this country's most virulent growth industry. Everybody has opinions and everybody wants more. The market is insatiable. Newspapers and television pour out opinion, urged on with the frenzy that stepped up the production of Spitfires during the war. Phone-ins proliferate, choked with calls from the semi-literate, bigoted and barmy. Opinion polls, the entrails of despotic democracy, are picked over for prophetic insights. We are becoming a nation of babbling back-seat cab-drivers. 'What are you giving up for Lent?' I asked my wife. 'Opinions,' she said, adding, 'Permanently.'

At this moment, we are deluged by a cloudburst of opinion-making Windsor books. It's amusing, I suppose, to be told that when Diana informed her puzzled mother-in-law that she needed 'space', the matriarch replied, 'Kensington Palace isn't bijou, is it?' Or that, if you get a gong, the Palace will offer you a £55 video of the great occasion. Your thirty seconds of glory stitched into a standard twenty-five minutes of routine ritual.

But only one is readable, let alone honourable (an attribute inimical to what is known in the earthquake trade as 'seismic prospecting'). The exception, astonishing, considering the below-stairs tattling banality, the seedy snobbery and suburban hypocrisy of this factitious genre, is A. N. Wilson's *The Rise and Fall of the House of Windsor*. It is written in a cool, amusing, plain-dealing style, devoid of the malignity which informs the solipsism and crass speculations of all the other grubbing prospectors. It is not without prejudice but, as Dr Johnson possibly said, 'One good prejudice is worth twenty principles.'

'What's it all in aid of – is it just for the sake of a gloved hand waving from a golden coach?' I gave these lines to a naïve but bewildered girl in a play I wrote when I was twenty-six, and was generally reviled for it. Later, in a volume of essays by up-and-coming opinion-makers, I put in my bit by describing the monarchy as the 'gold filling in a mouthful of decay'. In 1961, I presented *The Blood of the Bamburgs*, a light-hearted lampoon about the trappings of monarchy, and royal weddings in particular. No one realised that this was not mockery of the institution, but of the lunatics who were using it to shore up the debilitating inertia and conformity that dominated life at the time.

My complaints then were against those whom I thought were exploiting something of poetic and symbolic value for their own senti-mental and cynical ends. I was not to know then that those whom I regarded as their victims would ever make the suicidal error of yielding to the alligator smiles of the Fourth Estate and, later, put their heads in its mouth with the expectancy of not mere connivance but loyalty and friendship. Thirty years on, Mr Wilson's harsh and personal judgment on individual members of the Royal Family, particularly Prince Charles (whom he dismisses as a non-runner for the throne) and the Queen, who is damned with the ambiguous praise of being 'uninteresting', will not receive a porchful of excremental tributes as I did. Nor, I suspect, will he be 'targeted' by shooting threats from military men in Bagshot.

Where were all these reckless heretics and seditious opinion-makers when a minor character in a stage play put the plain question about a gloved hand waving from a golden coach? Asleep or unborn, I suppose. Anyway, Wilson provides some eloquently honest responses and, bless-edly, without any presumptuous claims to privileged access or inspired insights. We can know little enough of the interior life of our closest friends. Only Art can penetrate the guesswork of daily intimacy, and kingship is probably immune even to such inspired scrutiny.

The beauty of the British Monarchy lies in the fact that it requires no damned merit in its unchosen head. As Wilson points out, there is no perceptible onus on its holder even to be liked. Queen Victoria was popularly detested. The no-neck little widow spent most of her sixty glorious years skulking behind closed portcullis doors, leading a life of ineffable dullness, snapping at her huge family, foreign relatives and patient ministers. Her husband was convinced she was mad.

The reigning monarch may be drunken and adulterous, cruel and clever like the Tudors, pious or libidinous like the Stuarts, dim and wilful like the Hanovarians, or prosaically worthy-bourgeois like the Saxe-Coburgs. The succession is a constitutional roulette wheel. Sometimes you win, mostly you don't. Consider the reign of Charles II, one of the most glittering periods of English history. Charles is portrayed as lazy and indulgent, but he was a ruthless, articulate, cultured and sexy man. When asked why he found it necessary to have thirty-nine mistresses, he replied: one for each Article of Faith.

He was responsible for Christopher Wren becoming an architect, for John Bunyan publishing *Pilgrim's Progress*, for the foundation of six of the original thirteen American colonies and the encouragement therein of religious freedom. When he ascended the throne there was £114 in the kitty. He transformed a bankrupt state into the richest and most feared nation in Europe. He was also directly responsible for the patronage of Henry Purcell. Mr Wilson reproves Prince Charles for unseemly intervention in the Gatt negotiations. What matter if he should have said a foolish thing? Why should he yet not find the opportunity to do a wise one? We could do with a Purcell or two, and, most of all, a Wren.

Wilson's final paragraph restores common kindliness and sanity to its lost place in this lunatic debate:

> More than the House of Windsor will fall if the Monarchy is allowed to be hounded out by the bullies and brutes. It will be a symptom of the coarsening of life in Britain today, in which the brashly new inevitably defeats the old, in which the ugly always overcomes the beautiful, and everything of which the British used to be proud is cast down and vilified. Is it too much to hope in modern Britain – filthy, chaotic, idle, rancorous modern Britain – that sweetness and light could ever triumph over barbarism? The Queen is the only individual in British public life who has held out some hope for that.

Even after reading some two hundred pages of such detached intelligence, I was beginning to feel that I had been colonically irrigated with the firm's famous brown soup, and a further flip through the housemaid's dumb twaddling of professional snoopers and barking professors is enough to turn the bowels. Nigel Dempster, as you may know, is an Australian coxcomb who assumes the airs of a floor-walker lately fired from Fortnum's for colonial chippiness and demoted to the counter of a Jermyn Street shirtmaker, from which he jumped into the arms of a Duke's daughter: a bizarre alliance of patrician beauty and fawning braggart.

Together with Peter Evans, he has produced the glossily packaged *Behind Closed Doors*. This one will be the parvenus' pick, and it is by some lengths the most sleazy. Viz Charles: 'He is shy, he is sensitive, he is even sometimes desolately lonely, but he is also a shit,' says a 'polo friend'. An unnamed source claims that, 'the girls' talk was that he wasn't a great lover, not even a very good one.' As for Diana, she can take it or leave it, preferably leave it. How different from the home life of our own dear Queen. Dempster claims that the Duke of Edinburgh found 'Sex without Elizabeth had been wonderful. Sex with Elizabeth had been a revelation.' Anyone who can stomach some six pages of Dempster-speak deserves a straight-cucumber republic.

James Whitaker is the jovial hack they call the big red tomato, and he would clearly rather be a peach. In *Diana v. Charles* he is pro-Di, sort of. His royal opinion-maker's c.v. is impeccable. He was there at the Wales's Majorcan holiday in 1986:

> They read, they sunbathed, they chatted to others, but never once did they address a single word to each other. *I watched through my fieldglasses* [my italics] completely mesmerized ... I have since been told that following this week in the Majorcan sun the Prince and Princess never slept together again.

End of Fairy Tale.

Anthony Holden's *The Tarnished Crown* is a loftier number. Bagehot is Holden's man, and his guns are trained on the Windsor's venality. Holden is *very* pro the sainted Di, who chooses to fly economy in a seat next to the loot.

> The coy, blushing teenager married in front of 700 million people now holds the rest of the world in thrall, and the future of the thousand-year-old British crown in the palm of her elegant hand.

Cor.

> To the British people, their wronged princess is more than ever an object of adoration.

Cor.

Tom Paine is mad professor Stephen Haseler's man (*The End of the House of Windsor*) and the 'royal-state' his target, but there is not much of the zealot's flame in his belly, or prose. This is a sad, mean book. 'The culture of pseudo-mediaeval kingship bears down upon the hapless British subjects in their very daily routine.' Would your tax demand be more bearable if it wasn't marked On Her Majesty's Service? 'The monarchy has added little to the development of Britain as a serious country'. What is a serious country? Don't ask. Or the potty prof. will explain.

Whatever the interpretations of the Windsor Fault, it has brought ignominy and humiliation upon the heart of tolerance, irony and kindliness of the country in which I grew up, a land where the modesty of heroes is now dispatched with the same derision and contempt as the most wickedly ambitious. The seismic prospectors, the malign opinion-makers, have thrown up a generation to whom the word 'honour' is forgotten, meaningless currency. In the face of this aftershock of concerted brutality, I can only cry: 'God Save the Queen,' and confusion to her enemies, for they are mine, too. May God rot the tyrannies of equality, streamlining, updating; the deranged dreams of chimerical classlessness and, most of all, absurd, irrelevant relevance. And God help the Prince of Wales.

Spectator, 5 June 1993

To a T

Sir – In my royal review last week, a tired typist and I allowed a gremlin to claim that the sainted Di flies economy in a seat next to the loot. She does, of course, sit next to the loo, and the loot, we assume, is in her handbag.

John Osborne

Spectator, 12 June 1993

Dear Diary . . .

WELL, IT'S BEEN a funny old week, all right. No, it's been an unmitigated, alarming, yet reassuring bitch of a week. Here I am, in the Scott Fitzgerald black, resounding hours of the early morning, trying to recollect it all with some coherence. The truth of it is that I can't. So many strange and unaccountable things have happened. I can only, as ever, and it would seem with inevitable offence, try not to dissemble. For those not already and understandably wearied of the subject, I have been immersed in the production of a new play. As has been ceaselessly pointed out, the first for sixteen – is it so long? – years. I can see why. A perverse dream of my untutored youth: I think, to whom is it – or indeed this – addressed? Whoever, they would be better off without it. No more plays, no more journalism for me.

Those who have never been in its ugly glare may imagine the limelight seductive. My best recourse would be to put a paper bag over my head. For weeks, I assured my producer that I was an uninsurable liability, but, in the face of something like tears of anguish and reproach, I gave in. All right, I would speak to 'genuinely interested' and 'sympathetic' journalists on the *Telegraph*, the *Standard*, the *Sunday Times*, *Time Out* . . . It seemed less exhausting to agree than to refuse. One of the more squalid aspects of these undertakings is the way the press take you for a fool, their only 'genuine interest' being your anticipated pratfall. And then I made a *really* dumb mistake and allowed myself to be interviewed by the 'Prig's Own Paper', the *Guardian*. This one feigned friendliness too. In her matronly floral frock, she was almost convincing as an unprejudiced witness. Her description of me as a 'thug in a pink tie' still surprised. She asked, 'Have you any friends?' No, I didn't hit her. Mr Show-Biz-Baz of the *Daily Mail* didn't just misspell my name, he called me Orton. My innocent godson was staggered to hear oafish photographers pursuing me down the street yelling, 'Come on, John – give us an angry one.'

All this was predictable in my garish stars long ago. What I didn't expect was the consistent outpouring of simple affection from people whose regard I had no reason to presume upon. From the cab-driver who refused to let me pay my fare, or the concierge who bought me an imaginative first-night present, to hard-pressed actors, directors, producers and stage managers, all of whom might well have felt abused. I am astonished by it all. Another thing, before I write my last printed or performed sentence: I seem to have a reputation for being shabbily anti-gay, anti-feminist and so on, but I have discovered that I have more loving gay and female friends than ever looked out from any loony lighthouse. That's the last from a playwright all but killed with kindness and performance. OK, luvvie?

I HAVE KNOWN for ages that I was palpably 'politically incorrect'. Now I've been told so. But, despite what I read, I really don't have political affiliations, although I suppose I did once believe I must be a socialist. The present Prime Minister may be an easy butt for the sneering classes, but I was relieved at his personal triumph in the election. The prospect of five years snared by a bunch of saloon-bar bullies and middle-class pietists was chilling. Yet the thing that aroused my greatest admiration was John Major's defence of the 1702 Act of Union. I had felt an apprehension of terrible loss. The Scots, whatever they may feel about undoubted injustices, have colonized this country as shrewdly and efficiently as they did the Empire. They have provided parliamentarians, prime ministers and administrators. I regard myself as an honorary Scot.

I even love the bagpipes. I married three ladies, all entitled to the tartan, and I myself have a kilt which I regard as both a battle honour and a badge of historical kinship. It also shows off my legs, my only distinguished feature.

BUT MY GRATITUDE to the good Mr Major took a bit of a pounding in last weekend's Honours List. We all knew that Archer had it coming to him. But Lloyd Webber? In days of yore, you had to be almost dead before they handed it out: old Noël and Rattigan pined for the bauble almost unto their graves. Ivor Novello, to my mother's dismay, never made it at all. Now, you don't have to be terminal, just loaded. Archer and Andrew are both unholy jokers. But they are rich.

I SHALL BE strapped down for yet another session at an outpost of the British Dental Gestapo when the Garrick Club discusses the matter of admitting women. The institution is mainly in the domain of lawyers and journalists, but I can't resist committing my own feelings of sadness and deprivation at the prospect, much as I felt over the impulse to withdraw Scotland from the Union.

Never having been in the army, my only experience of all-male company was at school, when it afforded few enjoyments. Now, once a month, if I'm lucky, I look forward to a long lunch there. Should this barmy ballot be carried, the pleasures of masculine courtliness and hospitality will be gone for ever.

I feel there is a measure of destructive and mean-hearted Cromwellianism here, like the motives behind the ordination of women. There are many glib myths about men's clubs: the public-school food, the predominance of old bores and those who are afraid of women. It simply isn't so. There is an exhilarating arm's-length intimacy afforded by Garrick Street's restriction, a bond that would be inhibited by the gaze of everyday unisex comportment. Besides, most women worth their incomparable salt wouldn't give you tuppence for it; they have their own intimacies, less expensive perhaps, but more exclusive. If the vote doesn't go my way, that mysterious mixture of discretion, reticence and flamboyance will be banished for ever, and I may never again enjoy the heady pleasure of falling down the staircase entangled in the arms of Sir Robin Day.

P.S. ON PEOPLESPEAK: 'No problem'. In the past days I have been assured by British Rail, restaurants and dry-cleaners, among many others, that there was 'no problem'. I hadn't anticipated one but, like the injunction to 'have a nice day', it makes you wonder: trains derailed, tables double-booked and indelible stains. Last week, on doctor's orders, I telephoned a pathology factory to organize a blood test. 'No problem.' How can they possibly know until I've had it? But I do hope they're right.

Spectator, 20 June 1992

[9]
Foreign Fields

My Moscow

Two weeks ago a party of four men and two women left London airport for Moscow, the purpose being to prepare for the production of *Look Back in Anger* at the Moscow Arts Theatre as part of the sixth World Festival of Youth.

The context was so dubious that the invitation to go along for a week before the opening was ultimately irresistible. Going for the ride, or, being taken for it, according to individual temperaments, were Oscar Lewenstein, presenting the play in association with Wolf Mankowitz; his secretary, Miriam Brickman; Tony Richardson, the director; Margaret ('Percy') Harris of Motley; Lindsay Anderson, who had been promised a Russian camera crew to make a documentary film about the whole thing; and myself.

Shortly after we had crossed the border, the train stopped for an hour at a white stone railway station. The evening sun was warm, the flower-beds on the platforms hummed with scent, the railway buildings were clean and glimmering. The white columns in the station hall, and its Ivor Novello staircase, looked freshly scrubbed, and there was not a fag-end or a paper bag in sight. The Russians seemed quiet, casual and dignified, and we changed some currency without any difficulty. This episode was to be remembered later as 'Our Idyl'.

When we arrived at Moscow's Leningrad Station the following day, I was almost the last to leave the train. Oscar, who had already been on the platform, met me in the corridor and pushed a bunch of flowers into my arms. 'Here – you had better have these!' Just behind him was a member of the British delegation to the Festival. He wore a short-sleeved open-necked shirt, with a chest full of badges, and looked as though he had just finished taking a PT period. He said his name was Maurice, and I should be asked to say something on the radio.

Outside, on the platform, were twenty or thirty young people standing shyly around a microphone. Somebody made a speech of welcome in Russian, which was interpreted by a flushed, highly tense girl in a flowered frilly dress which made her look ten years older than anybody else. A Soviet composer of whom I had never heard made a speech addressed to the composer from South Africa who had travelled with us. This was Dr Chisholm, who was to conduct some orchestral concerts and to judge musical competitions. I was beginning to feel uneasy. Dr Chisholm was still getting his welcome. I whispered across to Lindsay, 'What am I going to say?'

'Oh, you know – wanting to contact the Russian people. All that.'

Everyone was applauding Dr Chisholm enthusiastically. I heard my name called out, and stepped up to the microphone, conscious that I was the only person wearing a collar and tie. By this time I was quite certain that nobody knew either who I was or what I was. Feeling better, clutching the microphone and Oscar's flowers, I said a few words that I hoped were enthusiastic and noncommittal.

I stepped back in silence, and another embarrassed interpreter mumbled it back into Russian. Everyone applauded politely, a badge was pinned on to my jacket, and Maurice moved us off to our waiting bus.

We drove off through Moscow, Maurice and the interpreter pointing out the landmarks. My old, highly fallible instinct was beginning to rumble already.

After eight kilometres and about forty-five minutes we got to the Agricultural Exhibition. 'Our hotel's just round the corner!' The word 'hotel' reassured me, but then Maurice leaned forward and pointed out an enormous piece of sculpture in front of the exhibition.

'Now this is *quite* a show-piece!' It represented a brawny man thrusting a hammer in the air and a big-breasted, muscular girl doing the same thing with a sickle. It represented the solidarity of the workers and the peasants, had been shown at the Paris Exhibition of 1937, and reminded me of the china Alsatian dogs they give away at shooting galleries.

I told myself that I was tired and hungry, which was probably the reason for my being the only one of us who was feeling sour and depressed enough to think so.

Our destination, the Tourist Hotel, consisted of about seven large blocks, with stores and post offices on the ground floors, looking like flats or barracks, depending on where you come from. The interior decor resembled a modern swimming bath with Victorian trimmings. We were shown up to Block 18 on the third floor. Tony Richardson and I found ourselves sharing a room – the only one on the whole floor which contained fewer than five beds. Each floor seemed to have about forty rooms. At five beds a room, this added up to 200 people on each floor when we were playing to capacity. There was no doubt that by the end of the week it was going to be a long wait in the washroom – no bath, no running hot water.

The British delegation had been promised accommodation for 1,800, we were told. Now this had been cut down to 1,500. The young man who showed us to our rooms said: 'The Russians are appalling organizers. They've no idea at all.' He was a doctor and came from Croydon. 'They asked me to come a week earlier, settle in before it all started, and enjoy myself. I have never stopped working since I arrived.'

Oscar had asked for some hot water for a shave. This seemed to be difficult, but eventually he was given a kettle of hot water. But Oscar's problems had only just started. We found an interpreter, and explained that there were no plugs in the wash-basins. She turned to a tall Russian called Garry – which is Russian for Harry – and appealed to him. Garry produced some printed vouchers with scissors drawn on them. If we wanted a shave, we could get a voucher for the barber's shop. Oscar pointed out that he wished to shave himself, and the conversation just stopped.

'Ask Garry if he shaves himself.' Garry did, said the interpreter. And would Garry go on shaving himself if he were to go abroad? She put this to him, and after several minutes she replied: 'We consider that a foreigner entering this country should allow himself to be shaved rather than shave himself.'

We went for a meal in a restaurant in another block. As there were thirty-five minute intervals between each course there was plenty of time for discussing the problem of improving our conditions. Maurice assured us that the restaurant service would certainly be better tomorrow – they were putting up a marquee for us across the road. He suggested that we should all go to the Agricultural Exhibition that evening, and he would also arrange for Mr Osborne to meet some Soviet writers. He was obviously delighted when I told him not to bother.

Lindsay wanted to try to contact some film director at the Institute of Cinematography, which was just along the road from the Tourist Hotel. I agreed to go with him while our leaders made arrangements. Miriam and 'Percy' went off to their room. At the Institute we could not find the film director, but we struck up a conversation with one of the students. We asked him whether the Agricultural Exhibition was worth a visit – what was it like?

'It is – 'he grinned. 'It is official.'

We walked around the corridors, waiting for somebody to challenge us, but nobody did. Shortly afterwards we returned to the hotel, and decided to take a shower. These showers were situated several blocks away and were quite the best thing about the whole place.

When we returned to our rooms, a sudden brisk gale blew up the dust over all the courtyard, and whole panes of glass came crashing down from the windows of the main block on to the asphalt below. One or two women screamed, and for five minutes or so people rushed about and glass went on breaking all around us. The next day the windows were put back until it happened again.

Meanwhile our spokesman had been fighting for some concessions to our prestige as cultural representatives of Great Britain, such as our own bus, our own interpreter, a reasonable rouble allowance and some tickets for the Bolshoi. The outcome was not encouraging. 'This is what comes of getting mixed up with a bunch of layabouts from King Street.' I can't remember who said it.

The next morning we went to Stage Two of the Moscow Arts Theatre. This looks like a Bethesda chapel from the outside and a little like our railway station from the inside. The staff were friendly and had made a highly efficient job of the set. After exploring the theatre, I left the others and went for my first walk in Moscow.

It is a little baffling walking in a city where none of the shop signs mean anything at all. The streets were crowded and tiring, and soon everything began to look like a mixture of Streatham High Road and the Brighton Pavilion.

I returned to the theatre, picked up the rest of the party, and we managed to persuade Marian, our interpreter, to take us to a bar. She found it difficult to believe that we really wanted a beer ('I am not a drunkard!') and led us, with obvious distaste, into a workers' dining-hall. This turned out to be something like the old British Restaurant, except that it was hotter and more crowded. There were no tables left and we drank our beer by the toilet in the corridor.

In the evening Bertice arrived. Bertice is a coloured singer, and she had come over with a modern-jazz group. The boys in the band weren't too happy about their accommodation. Neither was Bertice. She had had to sleep on a schoolroom floor with fifteen others in Berlin two nights before. 'Man,' she said, 'I am an artist. I am an artist, and I am egotistical and neurotic, you bet! I have to work myself up to get myself into shape for a performance every night. I don't want to have to come back and find some little chick sleeping in the next bed to me! Anyway, I have a little modesty!'

'That's right!' This was the Scots sax player. 'This stuff is strictly for kids who just come for the kicks. Undergrads and like that.'

'Well, I ain't no Boy Scout – I am an artist.'

'That's right. We're here to do a job of work!'

Jeff the leader, was dubious. 'What are you complaining about? We've got world coverage, haven't we?'

'World coverage! Who do you think's going to give you a job out of this! Do you think you are going to get a job in New York?'

'Anyway' – this was the sax again – 'These kids don't want jazz music. All they want is goofy Dixieland and Rock 'n' Roll.'

Bertice's eyes were wide with indignation. 'You know why we let ourselves in for all this disorganization? Did you see that British delegation? Did you *see* that British delegation! Brother, you really got to scout around to get a whole bunch of weirdies like that all together in one place and at one time!'

Our railway idyll seemed to have happened long, long ago.

I spent a great deal of my week in Moscow in a bus. This is not a very advantageous position for making penetrating observations about the Russian people.

Even if I had been staying at a convenient, reasonable hotel in the centre of Moscow during a normal week, and with integrity falling out of my ears, I doubt that I should have returned with any red stars in my eyes. But to go at this time, while all the sideshows of the youth racket were being set up by every small-time political operator in the business, was to make my resistance to the Soviet self-advertisement machine frankly intractable.

Since I wrote the first part of this article I have been criticized in some pious quarters for having given a deliberately distorted and superficial account of my visit. This may be so. (I remember how cheap everyone considered poor Truman Capote when we were on our train to Moscow; I should have been warned.) To this I can only reply that functions like the World Festival of Youth appeal to nothing in me except all of my decadent, Western, superficial perversity, whether they are in Moscow or anywhere else.

One may be mistaken if one does not consider a city beautiful, but not necessarily ill-tempered. Under the snow, Moscow may look like a wedding cake that is nicer than we thought, but under the sun and surrounded by peace-happy pipers, I found it ugly, boring to look at, a kind of provincial nightmare. One Russian described it to me as a city inhabited by peasants.

One of the most attractive places in Moscow for getting around and talking to people is the Gorki Park. This, like the Festival Gardens, is by the river but it is much bigger – or seems to be – and more ambitious. In place of the slot machines, the dodgems and juke boxes are an astonishing variety of entertainments and open-air theatres.

There is one large stage where I saw a selection of serious-faced amateurs doing their bit as folk dancers, accordionists and ballad singers, watched by a polite (standing) and appreciative audience. Each act marched on modestly without any announcement, performed, and marched off again smartly, scarcely waiting for any applause. It was a relief to be doing without [talent-show host] Carroll Levis. Nearer the centre of the park, there was great enthusiasm for a very good orchestra giving a 'Popular Classics' concert.

Less popular than the orchestra enclosure was a small lecture theatre. Inside this, leaning forward in concentration or, in some cases, asleep, were a dozen or so old people being addressed by a young man in shirtsleeves. He looked like a political orator. I asked our interpreter what he was saying. He was talking about the problem of bringing up children.

I managed to persuade her to translate his words literally. As usual, she did this with some reluctance, as if she were mystified and suspicious that I should want to know exactly what was being said by someone who did not seem to be very important. The lecturer was telling the people that while the economics of bringing up a family continued to be difficult, it was important that parents should be given priorities. For example, if there was a dress to spare it should be given to the mother.

This particular interpreter, Marian, took no trouble to conceal her numerous snobberies. Her parents were both doctors, and it was quite obvious that she did not care for the Gorki Park. There were too many people, she said. We pointed out to her that it was the people who particularly interested us; that this was what we had come to see. Marian endured our whim rather sullenly until the time came for us to go off and admire the next set of oppressively hideous buildings.

When we went into a restaurant garden and sat at a table with beer and sandwiches she became so depressed by the crowds that it became difficult to persuade her to speak at all. However, when we left and began to walk through the park back to our bus she cheered up tremendously, and actually had a mild fit of giggles. She eventually explained that she was amused because she had overheard some of our party being described as *Stilyagi* – the famous Teddy boys of Gorki Street. In fact, *Stilyagi* are probably the nearest thing in existence to Angry Young Men outside the imaginative captivity of Fleet Street.

The atmosphere in the park was relaxed and cheerful, and we liked it so much that we returned to it the following day. On each occasion several young English-speaking Russians came up to us. The pity was that there was never time enough to get much beyond an exchange of platitudinous questions – 'Who do you consider are your most important writers?' The Russian short list of British MIWs always included Jack Lindsay and A. J. Cronin – at the top – and Aldous Huxley and J. B. Priestley ('Unlike Tennessee Williams, he deals with really deep issues').

By Friday morning the corridors of the tourist hotel were full of kilted men rehearsing reels and busloads of new arrivals overloaded with flowers and fatigue. Getting a meal in the marquee was going to be even more difficult than a wash.

It now took considerably more than an hour to get through Moscow. The crowds that had ignored us and our bus all the week, with its 'Great Britain' in large letters on the destination board and festival symbols all over the coachwork, suddenly found us both irresistible, blocking the way at almost regular intervals for miles and beating on the windows.

On this evening, my last in Moscow, I went to the Bolshoi to see *The Sleeping Princess*. I know very little about ballet but my companion told me that the dancers were very fine but the choreography tired stuff.

Two things I enjoyed especially were seeing so many tons of scenery move across the stage at one time and the two girls on either side of the auditorium who seemed to be unofficial claquers. These scarcely bothered to clap at all until the applause had almost died, when they would start with wonderfully projected determination and tough palms and get the whole thing going again.

I watched them carefully for three intervals and at the end of the performance. One of them, whom we named Olga, had a technique as cool and tough as a comedian's and a 'counting the house' smile to go with it. Between them they milked at least an extra dozen calls out of the evening.

Afterwards I found myself in the wrong bus. However, it had 'Great Britain' on the front, so I knew that it would take me back to my hotel. I just managed to get a seat. The man near me was excited by the spontaneity of the audience's reception at the Bolshoi – so different from England. A few moments later he was shouting 'Peace! Friendship!' out of the window.

The entire length of the bus was alive with English heads and hands clutching out into the streets that had seemed so quiet only the night before. Once or twice, as we made our slow progress home, it looked as if the press of the crowd might overturn the bus. But it wasn't the people outside who turned my stomach. They looked nice enough, and it was impossible not to wave back at them.

I lit a cigarette and thought of Olga and her tough young face. Even in the best run circuses everyone quickly begins to look like the freaks. Yes, at times like this you can't see the good for the freaks.

Sunday Times, 4 and 11 August 1957

Market Swindlers

In 1967 the Labour government of Harold Wilson tried to negotiate Britain's entry into the European Economic Community – the Common Market. (The application was vetoed by the French president, Charles de Gaulle, and Britain, then under Edward Heath's Conservative government, did not enter the EEC until 1973, by which time de Gaulle had retired.)

The English conscience has been out for rent or hire for a long time. It is now up for outright purchase. Those who want to sell have called this historic transaction very simply – the Common Market. As drab a name for a monumental swindle has not been coined since a bright German ad-man thought of putting wholesale murder on the market as National Socialism.

Shabby dealing always begets its genteelisms. Going into Europe is the political equivalent of Getting in the Family Way. If we act swiftly and strongly, we may still prevent it. If not, a very ugly and deformed political monster will surely be born in the vestry, and Mr Macmillan, the father of the bride, will be able to mutter what will certainly be the most memorable line of his career: 'Just in Time!'

Has English inertia become finally impenetrable? Our paralysed support of nuclear strategy is understandable as a defect of imagination, or as a profound and abounding urge to self-destruction. But even the dimmest old eyes can outline the spectacle of Britain shuffling like an old tramp begging for a pair of boots at the tradesmen's entrance of Europe.

Such power and influence has not been brought to bear upon a dull and torpid people since the Americans brought corn whisky to the defeated Indians. In the beginning, we could do little more than learn to pick our way through the wearisome, baffling maze of Common Market lies and concealment. The Press has almost unanimously tried to bully the British Public into responding like a bemused housewife on the telly choosing which pile of rubbish has been washed in Mac's Blue Whitener. In the pro-Market Press – which is almost all of it – any breath of misgiving has been abused as foot-dragging, reactionary, fence-sitting – almost as a treasonable act.

Even simple bewilderment about the whole thing leaves one open to being prosecuted by Mr Hugh Cudlipp [then Chairman of Daily Mirror Newspapers Ltd] and the *Daily Mirror* for using insulting words and behaviour or having Lord Beaverbrook's name on your rent book.

Suddenly, we find ourselves already being strapped down like an avaricious little monkey in a capsule about to be hurled into a space called Europe.

But this 'Europe' has never been anything more than an adroit piece of brand-name dropping in a nightmare world of commercial jingle that has turned democracy into a hoax. For it is not a political idea at all. The Six – calling it a number already makes it sound like a Pretty Good Team – adds up to this: a squalid Chamber of Commerce with a large, impressive membership of political mercenaries. Napoleon's gibe about shopkeepers will explode in his tomb when Europe has at last become an explosive alliance of rich money-changers, a bizarre rabble of tradesmen.

Until only last week, the European Idea was a closed intellectual system. The dogma was declared and not to be challenged. The Rome Treaty had become Holy Writ. Self-appointed popes and their inquisitors were in every Party corner and newspaper office. Heretics were denounced – Foot, Beaverbrook, Gaitskell – and quick roasting of them all promised as part of the new continental Sunday.

For the Marketeers are religious men, with a proud intolerance about them that I, for one, thought had almost disappeared from British politics since the decline of Nonconformism. Never was a Church built on such a rock. Not only is there no rock, there is no faith. Only the crawling underside of expediency and dishonour.

A political idea must grow out of man's need, and that need is not simply economic. Otherwise the point of his existence withers away, like the Liberal Party's *nouveau* Marxist state, to a promised land of Common Market milk and honey, a desolate affair of obsessive shopping and guzzling. A nation has to do more than to keep counting its change. It has to count the cost of living without meaning, even if it means less money in the end.

Mr Grimond [the former leader of the Liberal Party], in one of the most appalling political performances in recent history, spoke of the Reformation and made a serviceable joke about haggling over the price of the monasteries. But the Reformation was about Man's relation to God. To some, like Henry the Eighth, it may have been no more than the looting of history, but there have always been men willing to accept a knock-down price for the human spirit.

Last week, to the astonishment of all of us, even Mr Gaitskell decided that it might, after all, be better to eke out your last years in your own house than end up as paying guest in what is probably a brothel. The Marketeers, the *Guardian*, the *Mirror*, the *Herald*, broke ranks at first, as if they were suddenly unsure whether they had been facing the right way and in the correct line of battle all this time. But they rallied.

The illusion of direct European power has become a necessity to a breed of men who are cold for lack of a place in their old Empire Sun. *That* set a long time ago, before the wind ever got round to any changing in a reluctant Tory head. This man admires the concept of the Common Market because it represents Authority to him. He has always admired Authority. He wants it for himself. He wants others to submit to it, and he is prepared to submit to it himself, provided it is strong enough. The Conservative Party thrives on this psychological situation, which is why it has been outward bound on violence for so long, for violence is character-built out of Authority.

Going into Europe is also a cast-off aristocratic idea, with a sophisticated feeling for speaking languages, stemming from the Grand Tour, as well as a cheap mystique of being forward-looking and unsquare.

I always thought I *knew* that upper-class Tories and all those jockeying public-school men were dishonourable, fibbing and disloyal. But what must it have been like to see these qualities stripped raw like a plaster off a wound as the Commonwealth Prime Ministers did?

Like poor Hamlet, they wanted to know too much and they were told quite plainly that they might as well get used to the idea of absenting themselves from felicity for good and all, and buckle down to making the crooked straight and the rough places plain for Mr Heath.

The *Guardian* said that the consequent statement from the Commonwealth Conference was a masterpiece of drafting. Which means that an Oxford First can still make British Lying the envy of the world, especially to those who inherited it from us.

But we are all witnesses to this. If we stand aside, we are as culpable as those men and women who became an army of bystanders while a race of people was being efficiently turned into bars of soap and lampshades.

We cannot pool our sovereignty any more than we can pool our individuality. If the idea of national sovereignty has no meaning then the idea of a free world has no meaning. But it does have meaning; it is not a political abstraction because it is related to the human personality.

We already know how uneasily peace lies in the grasp of mammoth blocs and powers. It must be better to regret our hard times than be ashamed of our prosperity.

Tribune, 12 October 1967

On 5 June 1975 Harold Wilson's Labour government held a referendum on whether Britain should remain a member of the EEC, on renegotiated terms.

What *is* the Common Market? Nobody knows. Nobody has told us.

It is well known that the French hate everybody, the Germans are terrified of them, and nobody likes us particularly, but feel that it might be vaguely advantageous for us to take part in this businessman's razmatazz.

It is, in fact, all a sad little dream proceeding from an hysteria that has been engendered by what is loosely known as 'the media', because otherwise they would have nothing to write about or put on their television screens.

The very words 'anti' and 'pro' are in themselves obviously pejorative. It is like the old joke about the Irishman who does not know what he thinks, but is agin anything.

If you are 'anti', you are by definition unprogressive, not forward-looking, unimaginative and all the other rubbish that is written about the whole thing.

A few years ago, the distant enterprise had at least the cachet of drinking wine and sailing down the Rhine and going to Salzburg instead of Butlins. However, even this snobbish attitude has diminished into meaningless arguments about economics.

As most people must know, economics is not a science, has proved to be wrong throughout its course in history, and the only man who won at this particular roulette wheel was Maynard Keynes, who happened to be around at the right time when there was a war on, or at least on the way.

All the economic arguments are meaningless and impossible to foretell. What one would be entering into is merely the psychiatrist's couch of Europe, and if you want to pay for that, you can well do so.

Finally, the real point is that the British are going through a period of national neurosis. Or at least this seems to be the case. Most people neither know nor care about whether we are in the Common Market, whatever that may be – a Customs Union I believe it is called.

This country invented the greatest language, drama and possibly literature in the world. We create drama and we need drama. There is the meat of it.

But to pretend that a Referendum on 5 June will make any difference to the course of events is quite ludicrous, whichever way you feel about the so-called issues.

Daily Mail, 2 June 1975

Playwrights and South Africa

In a letter to The Times, *the playwright Terence Frisby had argued that, rather than banning performances of their work in South Africa, as a protest against the apartheid regime, it was better for playwrights to allow performances but donate the proceeds to black South Africans. He pointed out that among the authors of an earlier letter in favour of a ban was 'John Osborne, who is a Director of Woodfall, a company which has distributed several films in [South Africa]'.*

Sir – Mr Frisby (10 May) is unaware of the economics of film making. The world distribution of films is not in the control of producers, writers or actors, but distributors. This may be regrettable but it is the situation at present. As for the predictable 'why don't you boycott Russia, Poland, &c.', I should think the cultural influences of the western countries can already be shown to be slowly paying off in these and other Communist, or even Fascist countries, like Spain.

South Africa is a different case. In view of its past associations with this country and our continuing vast financial interests there, our implication in its hideous regime is direct and obvious. Repudiations should be unequivocal, especially at this time when the race issue has begun to cloud the whole future of the west. White South Africans have had long enough to pick up cultural fag ends. To go on dropping them just looks careless.

Yours faithfully.

John Osborne

The Times, 16 May 1968

A Working Man

Sir – I am a regular reader of *The Times*. I even write occasional letters to it, which to my faint surprise, are often published. I am also a worker.

I am not a City financier, nor an habitué of privileged London clubs (I know such places exist and that the food is excellent but no one ever asked me). I have no colonial businesses, and, far from being either provincial or noble, I am an upstart from the London borough of Fulham and the son of a lifelong barmaid and an unemployed commercial artist.

My mother went out to work at the age of twelve, my father at fourteen, myself at fifteen. I am also a writer, and, although at times I have been well paid for it, I have little security for the future and the wheels of the British tax man are almost as crushing as those of the Russian tankmen. I own very little that is properly my own. What there is I have acquired by ordinary toil.

I am exploited ruthlessly by the Iron Curtain countries, who steal my work, performing it and using it without reward for what amounts to a lifetime's labour. I pay my crippling taxes sadly, as I don't wish to die poor and neglected. However, I do know that they are no longer likely to be used to crush subject peoples but that some part of them may go to caring for the sick and aged, and educating the young.

It is not a fair system nor an ideal one and I would like to see much of it radically changed. But it is still largely humane and decent (clichés, but what else?), unlike the United States, where institutions are so flimsy and the capitalist system has degenerated into a new era of squalor, ugliness, brutality and oppression. If I were an American writer I should be looking out for a civilized country to work in. If I were a Russian writer I wouldn't be writing letters to *Isvestia* because I would have disappeared without trace long since. At such a time there is some relief to be a worker, reader of *The Times*, and alive and well and living in London.

Yours faithfully,
John Osborne

The Times, 2 September 1968

The Number of His Name

Sir – How ineffably depressing it is to know that such a thing actually exists officially and functions called 'the International Organization for Standardization' (letter, 19 January). That its address is 1 Rue de Varembe, 1211 Geneva 20. And it has a Secretary-General, 'Olle Sturen. Hasn't he a number?

Yours sincerely,
John Osborne

The Times, 23 January 1973

Smokeless Zone

Sir – For forty years I have smoked various brands of Turkish cigarettes. Untipped, robust and fragrant, they always seemed to me the only cigarette tobacco worth smoking, and one of life's few and reliable pleasures.

I rarely smoked more than a packet a week. But puffing their exquisite fumes in the face of the army of prigs and bullies who dominate national life became an additional delight. Earlier this month, visiting Davidoff's in Jermyn Street for my regular stock-up, I discovered that I am no longer to indulge in this idle, satisfying sport because, so they tell me, a 'European' *diktat* forbids it.

I am perfectly prepared to believe that the issue is more complicated than this: nevertheless, to observe this nation falling over itself in frenzy to submit to such puny tyrannies, which extend to more fundamental principles like the legalities of personal freedom, choice and 'human rights' is dispiriting.

What baffles me about this craven abasement is that these directives are imposed upon us by a collective of countries united by one thing: their recent and superficial experience of democracy. Is raw memory also banished, along with unfiltered fags?

About half of these newly-sprung nation states – Germany, Italy, France, Spain and Portugal – have been administered by regimes that were Nazi, fascist, communist, crypto-fascist for several decades during my own lifetime. These are now charged with the duty and power of inflicting their bloodily acquired standards of justice and respect for 'human rights' on those of my country and generation, who alone and desertedly opposed them all at terrible cost.

So soon, and after such a brief intermission, these successful and happily empowered heirs of Hitler, Mussolini, Himmler, Franco, Honecker, Salazar, Pétain, Laval and the Greek colonels are to be enjoined to deprive me of the liberty and choice, even in the matter of what cigarettes I may be allowed to smoke.

The names of such men, who dictated the destinies of all these states, with the popular support or connivance of their people, are they forgotten so soon? Is no one permitted to ask: from whence comes such another?

As a schoolboy, I narrowly escaped from 'European' bombs on my doorstep. I can forgive this eagerness, but not the compounding of the insult by dashing the tobacco from my lips 40 years on.

Yours faithfully,
John Osborne

The Times, 26 December 1991

Sir – Since you kindly published my letter (26 December), realizing that it was not an idle complaint about choice of cigarettes or smoking itself but a hopeless, figurative tilt at the outrages of 'Europeanism', avidly connived at by those in power and those anticipating it, my front door-mat has been buried beneath expressions of sympathy and shared despair. They have come from dozens of countries, including those in the Continental EC. Some speak a defiant courage, but most match my own apprehension of inexorable defeat.

Still, with many of them, have arrived huge parcels of consoling, yes, Turkish cigarettes, many from Turkey itself, with promises of an enduring supply, which will probably last me out.

Civis Britannicus sum no longer, but I may at least puff delicious, poisonous clouds of vaporous contempt into rings, proclaiming: God rot the powers of Brussels and Westminster – and to hell with Burgundy.

Yours sincerely.

John Osborne

The Times, 13 January 1992

Dear Diary . . .

A FEW WEEKS ago I received, by special delivery, a scroll (I suppose you'd call it), framed and mounted, proclaiming that I had been 'nominated' (along with half a dozen others) for a Laurence Olivier 'Outstanding Achievement' award. I was invited to attend a luncheon with the other nominees.

Since then I have been sent a letter from the BBC on behalf of the sponsors (Swet [the Society of West End Theatres], the *Observer* and American Express) asking me to 'supply us with a copy of a biography regarding your career to enable us to compose a suitable eulogy should you win the Kenneth Tynan/*Observer* award for Outstanding Achievement for which you have been nominated. I look forward to your reply.' It was signed by the assistant floor manager for the awards.

Who can enjoy being a supplicant candidate? The Big Night is this coming Sunday. Anyway, I threw the floor manager's letter into the bin. This may seem churlish, but I see no point in writing my own eulogy for an event I shan't attend in aid of a bauble I haven't a hope of winning. The gristle of fugitive instinct is about all I have left.

THIS PRESENT AWARD reminds me of Ibsen. He was avid for medals, the nineteenth-century equivalent of our novelty-shop statuettes. He sought them out and put himself up for them like a touting film star. He was also in the habit, when inappropriately bemedalled at public celebrations, of becoming disagreeably drunk, cruelly abusive and having to be carried home.

It all came back to me some months ago, when I accepted a gong from the Writers' Guild. It seemed a spontaneous, generous gesture on their part, didn't promote anything in particular, and would almost certainly go unnoticed. A disastrous miscalculation. The evening was not conducted by friendly scribes but commandeered by television bully-boys and moguls, lasted six excruciating hours, during which I snoozed off after a meagre distribution of drinks and, fatally, forgot to take my evening fix of insulin. Like Ibsen, I was carried from the platform, comatose. But sober.

The following day, the Roundhead hoydens of opinion denounced my shame with all the primness the bilious old Norseman might have encountered from the bombazined daughters of the Oslo Band of Hope a century ago. As I was trying to borrow a large sum of money at the time, it seemed less damaging to my chances of escape from penury to allow my conduct to be interpreted as a drunken lapse rather than a diabetic hypo. Old Henrik was fortunate, living in an age of ironclad morality rather than maidenly priggery. I fancy he might have chucked his medals at the lot of them. I didn't get the loan anyway.

ANOTHER HAND-OUT this week from the Daughters of Eve (West) – Boston postmark, typewritten on University of Southern California paper – informing me of their programme for 1993. This one states that Sylvia Plath suffered Fatal Damage and that the Eight Daughters of the Council have decided to 'send a delegate party to the 30th anniversary ritual at the Plath grave in Britain and to bring earth from it for placement in the Daughters' Hearth and bury within the grove the citation of Honorary Daughter. This is now being crafted for Spring readiness.' Their main resolution is: 'The Daughters of Eve continue to research in the US and Britain charges of Fatal Damage against three male persons: Harold Pinter – fatal damage to Vivien Merchant, 1982. John Osborne – fatal damage to Jill Bennett, 1990. Ted Hughes – fatal damage to Sylvia Plath, 1963.' Tippexed over in bright green is the damning accusation: 'They showed no remorse, then or now.' If indicted, it goes on darkly, 'these persons will be tried by the Daughters' Jury. Witnesses will be called from Britain to bear testimony before the Daughters' Jury. In 1993 thirty years will have passed since Sylvia Plath suffered Fatal Damage . . . And all Eve's Daughters shall be free.'

All the latest American lunacies, from tooth-'n'-claw feminism to political correctness, seem to be swiftly absorbed over here, so a transcript of the trial proceedings should make for a fruity evening at the

Royal Court's Theatre Upstairs. With the accused *in absentia*, I would hope. Might the Dotty Daughters contemplate kidnapping? Perhaps I should look up the number of Special Branch. Or plead remorse?

I HAD INTENDED to keep off the subject of the Theatre, partly because I know that it must be tedious to most readers of this journal (or why else would it consistently employ the most flaccid of drama critics?). But I am puzzled by the general antagonism to something few people, these days, choose to experience. The virulence of this antipathy is clear from the glee which has greeted the invention of the species *luvvies*.

Now, I had all but given up resisting the contempt piled upon actors. Few of them are unspotted by ruthlessness and vanity. Some are little better than strolling psychopaths, and actresses, once baptized by fame, often come close to clinical madness. But the appellation 'luvvie' is a calumny, a journalist's jealous perception of something of which they know little and understand less.

Enmity to success is ammunition to every British journalist's gunbelt. It is they who are largely responsible for the hysterical clamour of the Oscars, they who raise the drooling pitch to massed frenzy. The actors are merely the drafted clowns. Players may be excruciatingly silly, burbling about themselves on chat-shows, wearing idiotic Aids ribbons and making embarrassing acceptance speeches. But they often do express their affections openly and sometimes genuinely, which grates on the newspaperman's sullen and frequently suburban heart.

Actors are irredeemably tiresome when they bound onto the political stage, when they rival MPs or writers. They can be shrewd, kind, emotional, calculating, full of frailty and, occasionally, acute intelligence. They can become monsters, but not the very best of them. This is my forty-fifth year in the trade, and I can count the number of 'luvvies' I have known on little more than the fingers of two hands.

THERE WAS A depressing article in the *Telegraph* the other Sunday about the demise of Sunday lunch, a justly treasured punctuation mark in the bourgeois week. I was a bit flummoxed to learn that a cut of beef could cost £60. Not in these parts, however well hung. And although it may be sad but true that women no longer have the inclination or know-how, I suspect it is the rampant microwave which can't cope with a piece of prime. I imagined the whole article to be a jape when I read its claim that Sunday lunch had all but disappeared from Ludlow, a mere 15 miles from my own Aga, until my wife returned from the market there brandishing sun-dried tomatoes. 'At last!' she squealed. What next? Goodbye Yorkshire pud; *ciao* soggy polenta.

Spectator, 17 April 1993

[10]

The Philistines
==

The Epistle to the Philistines

Timothy, an apostle of our Gracious Lady by the Will of God, to the sweet, lovely, loyal people of Great Britain, and to the faithful wherever they may be.

Grace be to you and peace from Our Gracious Lady and all princes and others who have smiled on us from carriages and high places.

I rejoice to bring you tidings of humble men elevated, for it is now said by their fruits ye shall know them and not by their roots.

Inasmuch as the old and once established religion was unsatisfying to the people, it being steeped in some parts in morality and man's relation to the universe, the new gospel has been pronounced and taken root long since.

The people are glad and satisfied for their lives are now rich and full of meaning.

They need not to think of the morrow nor to think at all, for they see clearly as through a glass coach.

Since the power comes not before the glory, through your Simply Divine Rights the power shall be yours and the glory also.

This is the doctrine that shall be spread abroad, for it is revealed of Grace, and shall be known as Justification through the Defender of the Faith and the Ministry of Works.

I tell you: the glory shall be yours and the power also. It shall be yours; the richness, the abundance and the honour.

You shall have rank, privilege, the love even of our Dear Madam Grace and Favour in whose blessed bounty all our well set up hopes shall finally lie.

For Her sake you shall diligently come and go forth, you itinerant painters and wallpaper pickers;

You gown sellers, fashion setters, you ploy makers and play fakers;

You poets and Rolleiflex flickers;

You breathy column sisters and microphone prelates; you dancing rogues and morning-coat vagabonds;

You hushers and high mushers, you guff vendors and you friendless ones also;

All you obsequious, envious ones; you tendentious leader men;

You knights and cringers; you pinched conformers; and indeed all you exquisite things.

You shall be called henceforth the New Set, for many are sybarites but few are chosen;

The Queendom shall be yours and it will come soon; and the day shall come when we are all Queens, each and every one of us.

Therefore rejoice, take heart and be diligent. Thy Queendom Come.

Tribune, 13 May 1960

Watch It Come Down

In August 1964, 'Peterborough', in the Daily Telegraph, *reported, with an accompanying drawing, the 'latest phase in the tragic destruction of Mayfair', with 'practically the whole of the east side of Clarges Street coming down to make more room for office, showroom and residential development'.*

Sir – Peterborough's flow of crocodile tears for the destruction of London by property developers is quite tiresome. Is this constant self-righteousness as self-deluding as it appears? Do try and stop it. It's disgusting to read.

I am appalled every time I pass by Clarges Street. Lady Hamilton's house going. Charles Fox's, and so on. Soon, no doubt, Shepherd Market will disappear, and Curzon Street after it. But that is precisely the price you Tories have always been willing to pay for a society run by moneymakers. Do you expect human values to dominate the aims of businessmen and boards of directors?

I know that Government and local councils are culpable too, and for the same squalid reasons. Greed, paralysed imaginations, and a dotty lust for some vague, shabby modernity will go on destroying. Rich, influential pigs *do* behave in this way, and will go on destroying so that they can put up hideous pens for other hopeful, happy pigs to work in.

But don't complain of it. It's the system *you* promote. You can't have your free-for-all enterprise, your shareholders and chairmen of money-grubbers and decency, taste, comfort and honour as well.

So please, no more nostalgic drawings of condemned beauties. You don't want beauty. You never have, you never will. Not if it costs you anything. You just want the loot. So take it and shut up. That authentic voice of yours becomes more disgusting than ever.

Yours faithfully,

John Osborne

Daily Telegraph, 13 August 1964

This prompted a number of letters asserting that 'most of the beautiful buildings, the destruction of which is so deplorable, were originally put up by and for "rich influential pigs" of another generation.'

Sir – Of course Clarges Street was built by moneymakers. Whigs, I suppose. But at a time when the aristocratic and classical virtues it celebrated had not yet been betrayed by the *Daily Telegraph* (and *Morning Post*) readers of the Industrial Revolution.

They did not go on to build Venice or Bruges. They built holes like Bradford and Wigan. Often they didn't need to actually live in them themselves, but could go on living in Georgian mansions. The sad thing is that a lot of them even lost their taste for this, and were content to live among the squalor they had created.

The inescapable remains: supporters of your sort of newspaper will always sell out even traditional Tory values like loyalty, taste, the enjoyment of beauty and craftsmanship (even though it be necessarily the craftsmanship of others), even tradition itself – for a good old fast, easy buck.

That's all. I simply ask you to own up. You can be quite lovable occasionally.

Yours faithfully

John Osborne

Daily Telegraph, 19 August 1964

Middle-Class Poison

The BBC appears to have become as perilous a place to inhabit as any United States Embassy within a stone's throw of a Students' Union. For observers of national character, it has been an unhappy spectacle to study from behind the safety of one's own barred front door.

As we all know, most of the stones have been hurled up at Mr David Frost and Mr Ned Sherrin, two faces which seem to loom in the dreams of many, and can even be seen by some leering out from every window at the Television Centre. In spite of a great deal of simulated boredom expressed about these two figures, they have set more typewriters rattling in Fleet Street than anyone else who has ever broken and entered our homes from the little box of failed promises.

The middle classes usually have a limited vocabulary of abuse, but for these two young men they have stretched themselves in their search for a dialectic of morality to a range of language that goes all the way from the everyday 'cheap sneers', 'puerile', 'undergraduate', that reliable old standby, and 'bad taste' to Cassandra's thundering 'embarrassing smug adolescent exhibitionism' and on to the visible frontiers of bourgeois protest with 'pedlars of filth and smut and destroyers of all that Britain holds dear'. Like Jeremiah, the pain of these protesters is perpetual, their wound is incurable and refuses to be healed. 'I sat not in the assembly of the mockers nor rejoiced; I sat alone because of Thy hand; for Thou hast filled me with indignation.'

The cry of the English bourgeoisie is desolate indeed when faced with the anarchic implications of freedom. Even Mr Maurice Wiggin [the television critic of the *Sunday Times*], a democrat or nothing, who says he likes a 'bit of bad taste as I like fish and chips and motorbikes', wrote in this newspaper of 'the snide and heartless Sherrin'.

When Orwell said that the English were the gentlest people on earth he meant the people who were actually *on* the end of Wigan Pier. He didn't mean the people who run it. For the voice of English violence is the voice of the threatened profit, of those who believe in the virtue of 'getting on', 'leaving things alone', yet are possessed of the greedy desire to order the lives of all, and especially of those who are young, sexually immoral or who simply speak out of turn. And, most of all, of those who appear to be all three, and are paid large sums of money – the thing the bourgeoisie care most violently about – and become rich and famous for their transgressions. Then the voice of Jeremiah is heard loud and clear in the correspondence columns of the *Daily Telegraph* or in the first-class carriages of trains to Lewes, where, as I have often discovered, more violence smoulders than ever exploded into decent parlours from *TW3* [*That Was the Week That Was*] or *Not So Much a Programme, More a Way of Life*.

The English bourgeois – or bourgeoisie – is violent because his intuition is faulty and his loyalties collusive. His objectives narrowed down to a nagging, painful sore of human undernourishment, he is understandably inaccessible to the relaxations of wit, irony, tones of voice, range of gesture or the delicacy of affection or even love that often huddles beneath the most outrageous lampoon. Malcolm Muggeridge discovered this when he suggested that the Queen should change her hair-do and people threatened to kill him. Many a sermon has been left unfinished in the vicarage study so that a letter peppered with Christian indignation and sexual innuendo can be popped quickly into the post and on its way to astonish some innocent dissenter who has said too much for his own good.

Housewives from Cheltenham and Tunbridge Wells no longer write modest poison-pen letters as our grandmothers did. They have been known to actually enclose the poison itself in their mild stationery, usually with an accompanying instruction: 'This is for you! Why don't you EAT it!' I myself received this particular one. I spilled it while reading the advice, and it left a green stain on my carpet.

Indeed, some parcels which arrive from, say, 'Shocked – of Hastings' or 'Father of Two Girls' can only be decently or safely unwrapped in the open air. Exposed to the same dangers as dustmen, the British postman should demand danger money from all middle-class taxpayers. From Friday to Sunday, even while shocked Fathers of Two Girls have been waiting impatiently to get through to the Duty Officer at the BBC and cry 'filth' down the phone, The Wife has been busily parcelling up some of her own to send him.

But why have these two particular young men aroused even old Lib-Lab lions like Cassandra from their lairs? First, they sin against age because they are both what is still considered, even in these treacherous days, young. Secondly they work in a perversion of creative democracy called a 'medium' in which every viewing Jack likes to think he is as good as his masters. Almost everyone, from dealers in stolen goods and property-developers to schoolgirls and newspapermen, want to get up there and show that they can do just as well if not better.

Third, almost no one *listens* or watches. For instance, no one seems to have grasped that Bernard Levin withdrew both the 'cretin' and 'imbecile' [used in reference to Sir Alec Douglas-Home, the then leader of the Conservative Party] on the programme. Some twenty weeks of the programme passed by before anyone saw the prurient possibilities of attacking it in force and went for the birth-control sketch. It is not surprising that no one understood the point of the Duke of Windsor sketch, which was not an attack on royalty but on the British public's insistence that their totems play out an idea of marriage that is as unreal as a comic opera.

Finally, no one chooses to admit that almost all the best programmes, including what is longingly known as 'entertainment', have been produced by the BBC for ten years. Or that the BBC has often been courageous, serious, and taken its own kind of flighty risks, so unlike the public sham and conspiracy of Independent (mark) Television, with all its golden-hour cake mixes of Sunday Culture for Consumers. ITV is the surplus-goods store of popular culture, a craven parasite on the theatre and journalism, depending on the cupidity of actors, writers and their pimping agents. It is irredeemably third-rate, and one struggles to remember any occasion it has fostered that could pretend to any distinction or seriousness or that was not a cowardly or skimped endeavour.

The creative logic of Commercial Television expressed itself ultimately and most enthrallingly in a programme called *Jim's Inn*, in which all the actors played consumers, just like the viewers, and the ding dong of every day in the life of Father of Two Girls was all about what handy little gadgets to buy The Wife and what Dad could tinker with in the garage. If Mr Grade, or anyone, would allow me a weekly Caliban's viewing of himself in *Sunday's Golden Night at Jim's Inn*, I would give up the BBC's late-night wickedness for ever.

Sunday Times, 11 April 1965

Airstrip One

Sir – Let us go further than the mere advocacy of an extension of Gatwick Airport or proposals for a modest third London Airport. Let England *itself* become an airport, thus leading the world by becoming the first airstrip democracy. The prospect, with its efficiency, economic sweep, the poetic wonder of a skyline black with happy tourists sweeping over endless lanes of productive concrete, reaches the very cloud of decimal unknowing. 'No Man is an Airstrip' is hardly the slogan to shout as we hustle splendidly into the twenty-first or even twenty-second century. For one thing, who would hear it?

Yours faithfully,

John Osborne

The Times, 8 May 1970

Unacceptable Alternative

In November 1979 the Church of England gave its approval to an alternative service of Holy Communion and an Alternative Service Book to the sixteenth-century Book of Common Prayer of Archbishop Thomas Cranmer.

Sir – At last! Cranmer lives yet! May the Turks of the Synod be scattered and all contumaceous priests be silenced forever. 'Let Him be sent for out of hand. This man, I trow, has got the right sow by the ear.' – Henry VIII.

Towering Thomas! A Man for All Series.

Yours faithfully,

John Osborne

The Times, 17 November 1979

Sir – Someone once wrote of the French historian Michelet that he wrote history in a language in which it was impossible to tell the truth. Just so, the language of the Alternative Services is written in a style in which it is impossible *to be religious*. It blasphemes against language itself in its banality and fawning to please. As for its claims to lucidity, these are the appeals of empty men who have lost their nerve and trust in most ordinary understanding. This understanding cannot *explain* 'Through a glass darkly', but can be illuminated by it.

What is distressing is not only the churchgoer's deprivation of a unique, inherited experience, but the cynical, opportunist philistinism of the Turks of Series Three. They have been most cheerfully brutal in their dismissal of the 'preservation of a questionable aesthetic'. There are many existing English languages, those of trade unionists, parliamentarians, lawyers, economists, air hostesses and tax inspectors. Is it to be unchallenged that the language of liturgy should go the way of politics and become that of the grocer? As W. H. Auden said of the latest revision of the Authorized Version, 'Why spit on your luck?'

Yours sincerely,

John Osborne

The Times, 20 June 1980

Treason of the Clerics

The Book of Common Prayer

This new edition of the Book of Common Prayer, compact, delightfully illustrated and printed in like mind to its crystal prose, makes the perfect present for readers of this magazine to distribute among their relatives, young and, yes, even old.

The Prayer Book, the most eminent and glorious jewel of Anglicanism, the last redoubt of unity and the catholic tradition, has been under concerted and systematic attack for more than a generation. 'Why spit on your luck?' asked Auden when invited to give his view on liturgical tinkering with the Church of England's central masterpiece. Since then it has been spat upon with a venom and contempt by the inner forces of rabid radicalism that have made the swift course of its attrition an ugly spectacle.

It is not merely the frenzy of theological vandalism with which the onslaught has been conducted but the manifest vindictive glee accompanying the crunch of the clerical boot in the heart of England's Christendom that have led to present hopelessness and despair. The army of glib populists were fired in their arrogance by the ferocious and commonly held detestation of historical continuity.

The old BCP didn't stand a chance of survival with the publication of the cynically titled Alternative Service Book. The smarmy disingenuousness of its advocates was only too clear in the preface: '[It] is intended to supplement the Book of Common Prayer, not to supersede it.' To supersede it, indeed to demolish it, was the flagrant intention. 'Any liturgy, no matter how timeless its qualities, also belongs to a particular period of culture.' It was this very timelessness of the Old Book that its adversaries were dedicated to destroying. The star of constancy, of use and custom, was up for grabs from an enfeebled and intimidated flock, uncertain of its authority and afraid in the face of diminishing support.

'It can be said with even greater certainty that the gospel of the living Christ is too rich in content, and the spiritual needs of His people are too diverse, for a single form of worship to suffice.' No child in its pram was ever robbed of its cherished prize with so little show of soft-soaping endearment, such callous indifference to its sense of violation, under the pretence of a 'fair swop'.

The sham of the alternative use of the New Book is the most bare-faced swindle of the century. For years the Old Book was either unobtainable or ignored in theological colleges; priests have grown up to whom it is no more than a curiosity like Foxe's *Book of Martyrs*. There are stories of students searching for a copy of the Church of England's official public liturgy and finding only old South African versions – even of ritual book-burnings.

As late as 1981, Dr Runcie, then Archbishop of Canterbury, was still insisting that the Old Book had not been well and truly ditched by all but a few usually, and derisively, described as 'lonely old ladies'. 'The new contemporary rites are only an alternative option to the traditional 1662 Book of Common prayer . . . so there is a choice. The traditional Prayer Book is used and will continue to be used.' Dr Runcie may have spoken in good faith, but few modern statesmen can have given voice to such distortion.

The Prayer Book as a lived, common experience is lost to us, and there it is. All the arguments about the vile infelicities, the hi-de-hi customs-and-excise-speak, the liturgical insensitivities of the new versions, their failure of imagination, poetry and beauty (especially beauty, most reviled by the revisionists), the wrangling and pleadings will be swept away in the avenging storm of female ordination. The aim now is overt: to change utterly the form and faith of the Church of England and cause the wholesale destruction of those who once sheltered and thrived within its national mysteries. The New Era may seem like a triumph of democracy to its exultant adherents, but to others it opens up a new order of chaos, a tyranny of clamour and disordered diversity.

For the immediate present, the Prayer Book 1662, until it is banished from the shelves along with *Robinson Crusoe* and *Little Black Sambo*, remains the most politically incorrect Christmas gift for 1992.

The Oldie, 11 December 1992

Dear Diary . . .

'GOT ANYTHING coming up at all?' the doctor asked as I lay prone. At least he inquired with mild interest, probably (and rightly) wondering about his fee; unlike the lout at dinner recently who turned to me and asked, 'Do you ever *write* anything these days?' By now I should have learned to block such questions, yet I wanted to dent his head with my poor old *œuvre*, some thirty modest volumes, and bound in brick.

Congreve, I remember, sensibly gave up before he was thirty, continuing to be unreservedly honoured until his Abbey burial forty fallow years on. Did Proust or Joyce suffer this dismissive interrogation in the consulting-room or dentist's chair? Is it only writers who are baited in this manner? Are painters asked if they are painting anything, or musicians if they are composing? Are accountants asked how the accounting is going? Newspapers, naturally, dwell on production-line progress: 'Not a full-length play for five/eight/twelve years.'

'Yes,' said I to the doctor, knowing that nothing could interest him about the treadmill of a day-labouring playwright. To console his real anxieties, I added, 'I have an old thing being revived at the National Theatre.' 'Really?' he said, puzzled. 'Do you get *paid* for that?' Of course not. It's a free service, a part-time amusement, an idle hobby to keep me from watching pornographic movies. *That's* why I'm lying here.

I HAVE BEEN intrigued by the success of the current revival of Terence Rattigan's *The Deep Blue Sea*. Rattigan was under the general frown when I first joined the Royal Court Theatre in 1956, and both George Devine and Tony Richardson were appalled when I confessed to being moved by the play. They regarded this as a heresy, a blasphemy against my own emotional and critical credentials. I remember the original West End production vividly. I was accompanied by a friend, an ex-bomber-navigator and DFC, who had been one of Rattigan's lovers. He had also toured in one of those camp Gang Shows, with titles like *Boys in Light Blue*, and possessed proud photographs of himself in a line of high-kicking, tutu-clad heroes, including the famous playwright-director himself, wand in hand, singing, 'I'm just about the oldest fairy in the business.' Peggy Ashcroft's performance as Hester Collyer had been unforgettable, particularly the scene in which she pleaded with Freddie Page, her ex-RAF lover, grounded in adolescence and now in flight from this battlefield of insatiable and unequal desire, to stay one more night. A few years later, when Dame Peggy and I were appearing in one of Brecht's most grimly unimpassioned plays, *The Good Woman* [now *Person*] *of Setzuan*, I asked her if she had enjoyed playing Hester. 'Not much,' she said. 'I got awfully tired of it. You see, she was such a *silly* bitch.'

The fact that the original script concerned two homosexual lovers, which I only learned later, didn't affect my initial response to the play, viewed from my own aching marital despond. Years later, Rattigan wrote to me chiding himself for not having pursued his original intention. He needn't have done so. The Lord Chamberlain would never have countenanced it. That would take another fifteen years of tedious attrition to remedy. This 'respectable' version of *The Deep Blue Sea* became very popular in provincial repertory companies, although I suspect that their middle-class audiences were a little sceptical or alarmed that any of their kind could be seized by such incontinent passion. Even more unforgivable, that a Harrods-homebody should lose control, so unlike the circumspect heroine of *Brief Encounter*. Subsequently, I went to join my first wife in the company at Derby Playhouse where she was playing Hester, and very well too. It was shatteringly ironic to witness the power of a character whom I identified as a tally for myself in the degrading turmoil of our own marriage. That night the auguries seemed horribly clear: she was the very counterfeit presentment of Freddie Page.

A BIBLIOPHILE FRIEND has just sent me a handsome early-nineteenth-century edition of Luther's *Bondage of the Will*, written in answer to the *Diatribe of Erasmus on Free Will*. It is over thirty years since I embarked on a crash course of Luther's works when I was writing a play about him. I wasn't ready for it then, and I have often regretted youthful overreaching, not yet encased in a restricting breastplate of procrastinating caution.

Luther's diatribe against the gentle Erasmus is spellbinding, a brutal, volcanic flow of scalding vituperation:

You take care to be on every occasion slippery and pliant in your own speech. My dear Erasmus, you speak honestly but think wickedly; but if you think it necessary, you speak wickedly and think rightly. How copious an orator! And yet you understand nothing of what you are saying . . . For you crawl upon the ground, and enter upon nothing above what is human.

On it goes, four hundred pages of bare-knuckle prose, vicious body slams and low blows. 'Distasteful,' the modern observer would say, and so often it is, but at such a level of exalted fire-power how it rouses the blood!

It brought me to think about one of the few technological toys which I find pleasurable – the fax. Julie Burchill and Camille Paglia have been conducting a toe-to-toe dialogue by fax, which sadly spluttered out in disorderly hair-pulling. But what a fancy boon, with its unconsidered response of the still-throbbing unsubsided wound, it would have been to Luther and Erasmus. Or to Caesar and Pompey, Elizabeth and Philip of Spain, Wilde and Queensberry, Ruskin and Whistler. What murderous fun the very greatest of damners and haters might have had with their fax: Hazlitt, Tolstoy, Shelley, Byron. Who else? A game for dropping off to, dreams of the impaling master classes.

EVER SINCE I wrote to *The Times* complaining of a crass EEC ban on the import of unfiltered Turkish cigarettes, I have continued to receive parcels of the real thing from kindly people all over the world. Some months ago, in this column, I owned up to a fondness for the sound of the bagpipes. Invited to lunch with an attractive lady historian of these parts, I found myself sitting beside an engaging young solicitor from Chester who turned out to be Neville Chamberlain's grandson. Not only this, but he had brought an impressive set of pipes to play for my pleasure and the surprise of the wild life crouching in these blue remembered hills. More recently, another thoughtful soul appeared at my front door, unkilted and with a German accent, who disarmingly offered me an afternoon of cosy pibrochs by the fireside. It is all very gratifying, if slightly dotty, and surely says something about the pools of goodwill existing in readers of discerning journals. But perhaps I should take care in making known any darker, exotic preferences.

Spectator, 24 April 1993

At Home

My mother's parents were publicans – to be accurate, they managed a succession of pubs in London – until my grandfather 'lost it all'. My mother has worked behind the bar most of her life. She still does because she likes to 'be with other people'. Her own mother, who is now eighty-four, retired a few years ago on a small pension from Woolworths. (If I were to put a detail like that into a play, some bright social observer would be certain to wave me aside: 'One of its strange weaknesses is the apparent wrongness of its sociological facts. For example, one often found oneself wondering if the old woman wasn't merely an intellectual idea sketchily worked out rather than *felt* – that pension, surely we all know . . .') She is a tough, sly old Cockney, with a harsh, often cruel, wit, who knows how to beat the bailiffs and the money-lenders which my grandfather managed to bring on to her. Almost every working day of her life, she has got up at five o'clock to go out to work, to walk down what has always seemed to me to be the most hideous and coldest street in London. Sometimes when I have walked with her, all young bones and shiver, she has grinned at me, her face blue with what I thought was cold. 'I never mind the cold – I like the wind in my face.' She'd put her head down, hold on to her hat and *push*.

The whole family pushed, and whenever they got together for some celebration, there would be plenty to drink however hard things were. That alone is something middle-class people find difficult to understand or forgive. As a small boy I would be given 'a little drop of port', and sit, apprehensively always, while my grandfather told me about *The Bells* and bawled bits of the Bible at me. He was the only man I had met until I was in my later teens who used a cigarette-holder. He was stylish and impressive in the way he could roll out names – Sir Edward Carson, the Prince of Wales, Lord Rosebery, the Lord Chief Justice, the Aga Khan ('Mum always likes me to put a shilling on the black man's horses,' my mother would say). Lord Beaverbrook was a particular favourite because he had seen him once, emerging from his Rolls-Royce. 'One of the finest men in England today!' He seemed to know everything about him. 'When I was with Beaverbrook during that time . . .' He had worked as a canvasser in the north of England for the *Daily Express*. I would sit flushed with port and embarrassment while he told me that he would live to see the day when I would be Prime Minister of England.

During all this, the rest of the family would be yelling news to each other. A lot of it would be about some illness or other. My grandmother would come in and out of the kitchen, usually picking the wrong moments to interrupt my grandfather – I would be the only one listening to him, but then I was the only one who seemed to listen to anybody. They didn't talk to each other so much as to themselves. He would yell some humiliation or if she was sitting near enough kick her imperceptibly but efficiently under the table. Often, if I could escape, I would follow her into the scullery and get a slice of the 'dinner', some winks, and possibly some story about how my grandfather had spent a weekend with some famous music-hall artist at Brighton. She told a story like this with some pride, but I would know that she was scoring off him too. 'Course *he* doesn't know we know about it.' It must have eased the pain in her shin-bone.

By dinner-time – which meant about two o'clock in the afternoon – the emotional temperature would be quite high. There would be baffling shrieks of laughter, yelling, ignoring, bawling, everyone trying to get his piece in. A big celebration would be the worst, like Christmas, when there was invariably a row. Sometimes there would be a really large gathering, and we would all go over to Tottenham, which was the family head-quarters.

Setting out from South London, it was an exciting journey. One never knew what might happen. There would be two or three dozen of us – somebody's brother would have a pint too many at the pub and perhaps hit his wife; carnation buttonholes would be crumpled; there would be tears and lots and lots of noise. The day would end up with someone – usually my father – at the piano and everyone shouting songs at each other. They bawled and laughed and they moaned. There was rivalry in the way they spoke about how hard they worked and there was no question that they did work hard – about the visits to the hospital and the *waiting*. They 'talked about their troubles' in a way that would embarrass any middle-class observer. I've no doubt that they were often boring, but life still had meaning for them. Even if they did get drunk and fight, they were responding; they were not defeated.

My father's family were baffled by them. Their value system was quite different. What impressed me most when I was a small boy about my other grandparents, and all my father's relatives, was the calm that surrounded them. Not only were their voices soft, but they actually *listened* to what you were saying. They came from South Wales and cared for the language they spoke. Not that I am suggesting that this is a ruling pattern among middle-class people, but most of their bawling seems to be done in *public* places, like theatres and restaurants – less at home. Besides, my father and all his family were particularly gentle. There were no fights, few rows, hardly ever tears. Whenever there was an argument, it was nearly always about *income* and mostly characterized by gravity and long stretches of silence.

My grandparents were the poorest members of the family – Grandfather had spent too much time away from his jewellery business, playing cricket. This may seem unlikely, and I shouldn't care to have to 'explain' it in good old competent working-dramatist terms, but it is the literal truth. My grandmother's attitude to cricket was rather similar to that of my other grandmother's attitude to weekends with famous music-hall artists. My father had worn his cousin's cast-off Eton suits, and there hadn't been a cook or maid in the house since the First World War.

They were kind charming people, and I was deeply fond of them. I used to enjoy the time I spent there – which was a great deal – much more than that I spent with my relations in Fulham and Tottenham. They had a sense of fun which was as much a part of their assumption about life as their simple expectation that they should be waited on, that their children should go to public schools, that there should always be 'income'.

One day I was walking with my grandfather, when we were passed by a man who seemed to greet him rather cheerfully. He was answered with a curtness that was surprising for a man as gentle as my grandfather. 'That man's a socialist,' said my grandfather. I knew it couldn't be good from the quiet way he said it. He looked at me, and smiled. 'A man who doesn't believe in raising his hat.' That definition served me for a long time.

from 'They Call it Cricket' in *Declaration*, ed. Tom Maschler (1957)

My Father

My father would have been as old as the century. He was born on 8 May 1900, at Newport, Monmouth. Fifty-six years later my first play to be produced in London opened on his birthday at the Royal Court Theatre. To me it seemed an exact omen.

I do not remember his last birthday except for him sitting up in bed excitedly and explaining how his age corresponded with the century. 'Nineteen hundred and dirty nine, and now I'm dirty nine as well!' In the world of overweening adult patronage in which I seemed to live, my father's voice sounded uniquely direct and truthful. All he ever muted for me was his distress, and sometimes not even that; I have never been a talker but my father was, and I have been a listener ever since.

We saw very little of each other during those first ten years of my life, but when we did it was for long hours or days at a stretch. Much of the time he was away in hospitals or sanatoriums: Brompton, Colindale, Frimley, Menton even. I only remember the first because I was once there myself, and used to have to go there for a 'check-up' every three months.

I would sit on the long wooden benches with my mother for most of a day, my braces chafing my skinny, naked shoulders, get weighed and then examined by a Scots lady doctor who barked and banged every bone I had, gave me a barley sugar and said I needed 'sweeties' for whatever rash or minor nervous complaint I was having at the time.

During the periods my father was able to work or get work as a commercial artist or copywriter he would come up to see me when he got back, but hardly ever before he had been in the bathroom for an unaccountable time washing himself – 'like a pussycat' he said. He was an obsessive hand-washer. This may be fresh Freudian red herring just for throwing back. It may have been mere care for the one part of his body in which he felt he could properly take pride. He would then put on over his trousers and waistcoat what he called his Sherlock Holmes dressing-gown, a heavy black and grey, tweedy affair with a big collar and long heavy tassels that would have looked well with a smoking-cap.

Discovering my father is like reconstructing a dream, a dark series of blots bobbing in oceanic infantile memory. I cannot pretend that my impression of him is accurate, only that the fragments are as true as I can cast them; but then it is my dream.

He was tall, stooping and thin, with elbows like bruised T-squares and beautiful hands, hard and drained white, whiter than any one else's. He manicured them himself with a tiny pair of clippers which he kept in his waistcoat pocket, while his fingertips were bright amber at the edges and burnt oak beneath, which was characteristic, like the way he always tried to change his collar at least twice a day, yet might wear the same pair of unwashed, undarned socks for a week. I am certain he wore the same greasy grime-edged raincoat as long as I knew him, and when my mother once tried to throw away his bowler hat, he bought it back for a couple of bob the following week from the dustman who was wearing it.

His hair, which from his early twenties blended grey to white, was cared for like his fingernails, and with blue eyes recessed in the palest of fair skins gave him an oddly young, frail-vagabondish look. He may have conformed consciously to what was then a popular idea of the aristocratic tramp, Weary Willy, or the ragged philosopher with impeccable manners, the door-to-door ex-officer, the Shavian super tramp underneath the arches.

He spoke very softly indeed so that he was constantly being told to repeat what he had said by bus conductors and waitresses. This may have been because he aroused some instinctive suspicion, for I know his diction was precision sharp, yet he never sounded posh to me like some of his relations did.

The quality of a voice is almost more elusive than anything to retain for long, and I daresay I would not recognize his if I were to hear it now. I do know that certain words like 'toothpaste', 'unusual' and 'particular' had a slight curling Welsh spinster clip about them that I most often recognize now in certain television commentators.

He was christened Thomas Godfrey, called Godfrey by his own family or Goff or Jeff by outsiders and my mother's family, which he seemed to prefer. His Christian name, like his health and his mother's hostility, came as an extra. He would have been grateful to be a Jack or Ted rather than a Godfrey. About 1938 one of his best-loved jokes was an emergent journalistic phenomenon called Godfrey Winn. Watching Mr Winn the other day telling viewers how he always gave himself a Christmas present from his mother, it seemed like one of my father's original inventions.

His own father was the youngest of three sons of a strong-willed young widow who sent him to Hereford Cathedral School and left him a thriving jeweller's shop when she died. My grandfather was a very slow-thinking, gentle old man, a little like my father but a heavier, more cumbersome model in which the spring had gone long ago. I think his whole family had a doomed swagger about it.

Grandad had even developed what he called his 'tramp's walk', which, he claimed, enabled you to walk forty miles a day without discomfort, and seemed to consist of exaggerating the weight on your right foot and putting your shoulder to an imaginary wall. Long, ponderous strides were essential, and your eyes were fixed thoughtfully on your boots. It was a little like the way actors playing characters with wounded left arms make their entrance – Bleeding Sergeants, or Boris Karloff butlers. My father's version was less emphatic, possibly because he was less robust, also because he often used a walking-cane, and with thrilling style too.

I tried the walk for some years myself, but it was much too exhausting to sustain for long, and no one ever noticed the generations linking inexorably as I shambled sideways for miles down suburban streets in anything from sandals to gumboots. No one ever paused and said, 'Ah, that's the Osborne walk, all right!' My grandmother often said it as she watched her husband or son tacking heroically up the street.

Grandfather lost his jeweller's shop when he was still a young man through his own undoubted neglect and incompetence. I know very little of how he managed to survive with his wife and two young children. It is true that it was very difficult for him to get work between the Wars as it was for everyone. Nevertheless, the clear truth is that they lived for the best part of twenty years or more from cadging and wheedling. They became full-time poor relations, and, considering that the rest of the family were often not much better off, they managed astonishingly well.

The inscription over the cross which they carried about with them in their search for someone who might owe them a living and lead them out of suburban Egypt was: We Deserved Better! For although the word they brought with them out of the wilderness was 'self-help' or 'cold bath', they themselves were comfort-loving, indolent and clothed from head to foot in long, woolly winter and summer phlegm.

The thing that roused them most was the perpetual reminder that some blundering shuffler had dealt them the wrong cards from the social pack. Daily and at seasonal gatherings and festivals they talked endlessly about money, about wills, codicils, letters of credit and of administration; of solicitors, sacrifices that had been made at the time and ever since, insurance taken out unwisely and premiums that were not kept up; of jewellery that someone should have had instead; rings and earrings that were pawned and then never redeemed by some stupid mistake of someone's (a special Boxing Day favourite this one); some things that were All That Was Left by the End of It, like fur coats that were too short anyway and you couldn't let down; money that had been thrown away, lived on, lived off, borrowed off and plain embezzled; at least one uncle Having to Go to Canada; bills, school fees, gas bills, rent, rates that were always going up to pay for something for somebody else that we didn't want anyway; library subscriptions, coal bills and, most worrying and burdensome of all, my father's doctors' bills.

My father was ill most of his life. Asthma kept him from school throughout his childhood. My grandmother despised him for his physical weakness and never forgave him or allowed him to forget it or what he had cost in anxiety and hard cash. There was one favourite item she brought up regularly. I remember it very well.

She would usually wait for one of the Sunday morning calls my father would make on her before the pubs opened. He would take me along with him, and very often it was I who would be the cause of the trouble. I would be wearing a new pair of shoes or let something slip about having been to the music hall or the pictures twice. My grandmother would pounce with her hard-backed, stiff brush of a brave smile and I would even feel sorry for her until I saw my father sitting quietly longing for twelve o'clock opening.

The favourite item was this. When my father had been about seventeen he had won some drawing or painting competition in a national news-paper. The first prize was a paid holiday to South Africa. There was much chilly feeling about his wanting to be any kind of artist, his mother having planned a job in an insurance office for him. Shorthand, bookkeeping, accounting were the things for a bright, uneducated boy who couldn't depend on his health. In this she had her way, at least for a while.

However, he was allowed to accept the prize, and she may well have felt a little pride over it, although she would have done her best to conceal it. He went, was taken ill in the Bay of Biscay, put ashore in a storm and sent to hospital in Lisbon for six weeks. Six weeks. It cost £200. Two hundred pounds that had to be *cabled out*, begged, scraped up, borrowed and *cabled out*. Twenty years later he was still being reminded of it in my presence. Two hundred pounds. It sounded like more money than there was in the world and it was the absurd, wasteful, terrible price of art.

When he died, he left an insurance policy worth £400 and grandmother immediately demanded it from my mother as being rightfully hers, as a last crumb of what he owed her over the years. She produced a letter he had written under the clearest emotional duress acknowledging his debts. It included a reference to the £200 that was *cabled out* to Lisbon.

It seems grotesque, inflated and preposterous, but this was the pure juice of family feeling. There is a brilliantly comic and accurate impression of the kind of people they were in Angus Wilson's *Skeletons and Assegais*, except that mine were possibly shabbier and a rung or two lower down here and there.

They *did* say that the miners used to throw food good enough for children to their dogs on pay days and that old Nye Bevan was a wicked jealous man who said spiteful, jealous things that weren't at all clever, just rude; that Lord Tredegar, who was chairman of the local Conservative party, was a very *good-living man* and a friend of brother Tom who had been treasurer himself for many years.

They *did* believe that an Irish maid or cook (yes, they once had both in that far-off well of a lost world. The wonder is how they could keep on plunging the bucket down into it, hoping to rescue something from it) could always be scared into obedience by saying 'priest' at them. That the best cure for chilblains was bathing your feet in a chamber-pot filled with your own urine; that the best English was spoken in Wales; that someone would always have to be a dustman (not *them*) whether some people liked it or not. They said so endlessly.

They were obsessed with public schools, although not all of the men in the family seemed to have been to them or, if they had, they were obscure and ashamed, dowdy ones. However, they always seemed to have a cousin or a nephew or son-in-law who was at Repton, or Shrewsbury or Blundell's or Haileybury or – Big Welsh Headmasters' Conference Deal – Christ College, Brecon. These places alone had perfected the tried and tested way of turning out the very best type of man, who had learned to rough it, take it, not complain, take his medicine, be truthful and not put on airs when all around were not as good as you.

They chewed on this kind of rubbish endlessly, pasturing on the scrub of old ploughed-up clichés until you would think they could stomach it no longer. Sometimes my father would make some protest, but usually he wisely saved himself. If he did persist, my grandmother would stiffen with gratification and redirect some of this load at me.

My grandmother was comfort-loving, but she directed the open nozzle of her puritanism at my father. She thought he should have got a steady job, not drink too much, not stay out all night as he often did, that he should never have married or had children for all kinds of reasons, but principally because it clinched his betrayal of her. This sickly, semi-bohemian sceptic was the joker in the rotten hand she'd been dealt. She actually believed in bohemians, she dreaded bohemianism like she dreaded germs. She would have found some humane way of throwing them out of the pack or burning them if she could, just as she burned my father's blankets when she was told he had TB and gave him old, discarded ones, which she also burned later.

She believed that there were a great many things in life that were not wanted on a sensible person's voyage, and labelled them accordingly – Unnecessary. It was unnecessary to waste money in a restaurant when you could get better at home; going to the pictures was unnecessary, so was the theatre except the pantomime at Christmas, just for the children; buying bought'n or shop cakes or jam was unnecessary when home-made was so much better; so was whisky, except as a hot drink with lemon for a cold, going to public houses, staying up late, divorce; flowers from a florist's shop were unnecessary even if – or especially if – they were bought as a gift for her.

Her distaste and disappointment with life spilled from her on to her son whenever she set eyes on him. Sometimes he must have felt it would drown him. Perhaps the sense of the pain from which it flowed helped to keep his head above it.

When I used to go to see her before she died about three years ago she always avoided any reference to any work I had done or was going to do. She pretended I did nothing at all. She liked me and often gave me money out of her old-age pension when I was hard up. She did it without reproach too, which was even more generous. Perhaps she felt my father had taken all the guilt upon him and with him when he died, and slipping me ten bob without sneering homilies was a way of finally leaving him in peace.

She hardly ever spoke of him for nearly twenty years, and when she did there was always a bitter dismissive note in her voice, even when she seemed about to soften into nostalgia about the clothes he wore as a child or the things he had painted or written instead of going to school or playing games. Often I wanted to attack her violently for having murdered his spirit and helping to kill him. But I never did, and we left each other alone.

My father used to encourage me to sing whenever he could, but he usually had to coax or even bait me gently. Like his mother he could be cruelly adroit at making one feel foolish. Anyway, he could always intimidate me into accompanying him in a song with the most casual menace of mockery in his face. I don't think my singing pleased him much, but my imitations were better and he would select the more tolerable ones (some were very perfunctory indeed) and we would do them together at the piano for some friends, neighbours or family.

He hated bank clerks, accountants and doctors. He loved pubs, pubs all over the place, and I have waited many hours outside the Clarendon, the George, the Spotted Horse, the King's Head and plenty of others, with the glass of lemonade and a packet of cheese biscuits, drinking in the smell of booze and noise from the draughty doorway.

Some places they would let you in if you sat quietly in a corner. But I didn't ever mind waiting outside. I loved being out with him and holding his hand in the street. Perhaps he liked having me with him. For a time I was a rather dandyish, yes, bohemian-looking child dressed in a black beret and a large velvet bow-tie. We must have looked bizarre walking down the street together.

But it was not only to pubs we went. One of the happiest days we ever had was when we left Brompton Hospital unaccountably early one day and spent the rest of the day in the Victoria and Albert and Lyons for tea and rolls and butter. On other occasions there was St Paul's, the Zoo, Westminster Abbey, Hampton Court, The Tower – he was very good on that and used to sing a song of Stanley Holloway's about the Bloody Tower called 'With 'er 'ead Tucked Underneath 'er Arm'.

In 1938, my mother and I saw him off from Victoria on his way to a sanatorium in Menton. We all cried a little, and he gave me a ten-shilling note and said we were to go to the new Warner Cinema to see *The Adventures of Robin Hood* with Errol Flynn. I think it was the first film that I had ever seen in colour, *and* in the West End. I thought about it for weeks afterwards.

My father had written me long postcards for years. He could write more on a postcard than most people can in a letter, my mother said. It was true. One side would have an elaborate drawing on it, done with great care, often in different coloured inks or crayons, and addressed to some fantasy like Captain John Osborne RNVR or Paramount Chief Big Feller Osborne. The text on the other side would be written in beautiful green ink in neat, top-of-a-pin handwriting. He made up words, coined pronunciations, and had his own private words for things like tea or roast meat.

I have one postcard sent to me when I was three from a sanatorium saying: 'Got up seven bells. Him feller doctor say the big *black* Irish booboo in the next bed is to be shot full of gold! Gold! And they're sending me away! Hooray! See you Waterloo with Mum! Tell her will be wearing bathing-costume and bowler hat.'

In September 1939 the three of us went to live in the Isle of Wight. We left in an enormous Daimler ambulance as big as a hearse, with a view from it like a royal carriage. We spent four months together, all of it in his bedroom. I malingered, had extra doses of rashes, and simply stayed away from school as often as I dared. The school inspector was quite patient.

We talked and read new books and books we knew already like Dickens, Maugham, Kipling, W. H. Davies, Rider Haggard, Stevenson, Burns, Arnold Bennett, and then he talked about Shaw, but I don't think we ever read any. He admired Lawrence of Arabia and J. B. Priestley, especially *Angel Pavement*, which he read three times. Turgis and his Arabian Night and Mr Dersingham and their world was something he must have known well.

I gave him four sixpenny Penguin books that last Christmas. I still have them. They were *Ariel*, the Shelley biography; *Death of a Hero*, by Richard Aldington; *A Safety Match*, by Ian Hay, and *Gone to Earth*, by Mary Webb. I do not know why I chose any of them, yet I remember so much else. He never read them.

Sunday Telegraph, 13 January 1963

Dear Diary . . .

FOOD IS ON MY MIND after another prolonged session at the Dental Gestapo, and this enforced regime of slops sets me to mourning the era of Joe Lyons and, in particular, the Corner Houses. With their gypsy orchestras and tango bands they induced heady fantasies of luxury, intrigue and cheap glamour. As a schoolboy, a fugitive from the deadening wastelands beyond Clapham Junction, I would dream myself into the character of worldly observer, drinking in the passing show of some exotic European capital, thronged by cunning, beautiful women, where every other suburban couple stood in for Conrad Veidt and Vivien Leigh.

Each baroque Corner House had its distinctive ambience: the branch at Marble Arch was more Ritz-like than the twentyish Strand. But they all shared an innovation called the Salad Bowl, a huge room displaying mounds of sardines, anchovies, herring, gherkins, coleslaw, hills of cold baked beans, tomatoes, onions, even lettuce. There was the guarantee of fit-to-bust, unmonitored second helpings, a fulfilment only otherwise found in children's comics. And *no*, it wasn't all for fourpence, but 3/6d – half the price of a Sunday newspaper.

Joe Lyons teashops were altogether different. Here the food was fast –

steak-and-kidney puddings and pies, Lancashire hotpot and college pudding – sped from the factory, yet comfortingly appealing in its fake homeliness. You were encouraged to linger in the warmth, and some branches supplied boxes of chessmen, draughts and dominoes. The teashops were havens against despair, loneliness and the cold streets. Then the Nippy waitresses were replaced by self-service, the enterprise was archly rechristened 'Jolyon' and soon was no more.

GLUTTONY, AFTER ENVY, now seems to be the most encouraged of the sometime seven sins. When I take the cab from Euston, men and women streak past, briefcases and bags in one hand, clutching blobs of food to their mouths like babies' comforters.

Eating in the open air should be a delight, a releasing freedom for contemplation, even reverie. At least they might sit down for five minutes and admire the prospect of Nelson's column. We've all had to get used to foreign tourists chomping on the pavement like pit-bulls, but watching young executives and secretaries scoffing on the hoof to the office is a reminder of the nasty habits we have picked up during the years of the Great Tourist Scramble. I suppose this kind of quick refuelling comes naturally to a generation who, as teenagers, preferred to eat standing up out of the saucepan. The establishments which dispense the stuff are mere pit-stops for impatient bellies: 'Fill her up.' It may not be the end of civilization but, like rock concerts and raves, just another refinement of public squalor.

THE ABOLITION of the telegram was another portent of darker things to come. It was such a useful SOS for begging money or dashing off impulsive declarations of passion. It was also an invaluable device in the advancement of plot in stage plays. Terseness was its grammar and, unlike the fax, it presumed no reply. The telephone is a clumsy, unsubtle instrument. I dread its peremptory intrusiveness. It distorts and oversimplifies.

Like many people of my generation, I grew up in phoneless houses. Until I was thirteen, I knew only one boy whose parents possessed one, and that was rarely used and unattended in a draughty corner by the front door.

When I first came to live with my present wife, seventeen years ago, I was aware that she was no heiress. However, I assumed that, as a weathered journalist, she would ease the days with an effortless command of the telephone. She would dial anyone, however awesome, from the Archbishop of Canterbury to Samuel Beckett. I soon discovered that her phobia is almost as severe as my own, often needing a cigarette and a stiff gin before lifting the dreaded receiver. There's no getting away from it, no question of kicking and screaming into the twenty-first century; we are both already bloody and left for dead somewhere in the middle of the twentieth. I still feel bad news is best delayed, good news more welcome on a postcard.

Yesterday the telephone rang at 7.30 in the morning. What demented bearer of ill-tidings could it be? It was the fire-extinguisher maintenance man.

A LESBIAN FRIEND occasionally sends me a Country and Western tape to buck me up. Lesbians are deep into C & W and the singer k.d. lang (as in e.e. cummings), already an icon, has now gone 'global' since she became an 'item' with Martina Navratilova. So. I caught a glimpse of k.d. on the telly in *Rock Steady Special* and she seemed a jolly, bouncy sort of girl. Not that she looked much like a girl, more like Cliff Richard's ballsy brother.

THE OTHER NIGHT I dreamed about Lord Milner, the nineteenth-century imperial administrator, of whom I know very little, a famous actress and someone I haven't seen since I was twelve.

I won't go on. I am a dream bore. Like all one-time performers, I dream I am in a play of which I know nothing. I seek desperately for a copy of a script in order to improvise a character in a plot withheld. Like *Rosencrantz and Guildenstern*, only this is an endurance of terror rather than reflective joking. I wonder if men dream more than women? Is it mostly those with troubled spirits or fervid imaginations that never truly sleep? Think of the references to dreams in Shakespeare, in *Hamlet* alone. Is the Ghost a dream? What dreams to come, perchance to dream, a little dream. Do solicitors dream? Tax inspectors? Do they have their own regular, professional dreams? I have been reading Graham Greene's selection of his dreams, *A World of My Own*. As he says, it is a world shared with no one else, to which there are no witnesses. Dreams are not lies, no one can deny their truth. A dream is the one thing in this life, terrifying or blissful, premonition or adventure, that is entirely your own. And you don't even have to pay VAT on it.

In the foreword to the book, Graham Greene's friend, Yvonne Cloetta,